China in Xi Jinping Era

Moderrn China Series

China in Xi Jinping Era

Shu Xiaohui
Li Yangkuo
Tian Guang

North American Business Press

China in Xi Jinping Era

ISBN: 978-1-948915-26-7

NORTH
AMERICAN BUSINESS
P R E S S

North American Business Press
Atlanta, Georgia
Miami, Florida
New York, New York,
Toronto, Canada

FIRST PRINTING, 2022

About Modern China Series

As one of the oldest civilized regions globally, China has emerged as a "new world" because it embraces its essence and heritage and links them to viable economic strategies. In the last 25 years, China has made tremendous strides. The country and its people have every right to take pride in these accomplishments. Many Chinese leaders and intellectuals anticipate continuing growth with these successes. Furthermore, China's plans and strategies are often based upon this premise.

There is tremendous interest in the U.S. on the Chinese economy and business environment. China has emerged as a global superpower, and scholars and business people in the U.S. are keenly interested in learning how this will affect them and do business with China. In response to growing interest from international and Asian scholars, North American Business Press is pleased to announce our Modern China Series (MCS) books. It is the first book series about modern China in the U.S., garnering tremendous interest in the U.S. and worldwide. With our first book reaching stores in September 2011, this initiative develops relationships between NABP and Chinese scholars. They desire to promote their academic and applied business writings to the rest of the world.

We have had an overwhelming demand for the Modern China Series from both authors who would like to publish in the series and people who would like to read the books. There are currently ten books published in the series, and we have a couple of dozen books that we are considering for the series. The books have been viewed by thousands of people from the U.S. and the rest of the world.

We have published books on several areas revolving around the Chinese business environment. We have a few that focus on the best practices in marketing in China; some are compared to "best practices" in doing business in China, and a few on the outlook of the Chinese economy. The market for the Modern China Series is enormous. There are tens of thousands of scholars that are keenly interested in the continued growth of the Chinese economy and the implications that it will have on the business world. Even more significant are the millions of business people interested in the impact that China will continue to have on the global economy. It is difficult to pin down the exact demand for the series, but it Is enormous.

We have big plans for growing the Modern China Series. It can be one of the most significant economic/business series ever produced. We are very selective with the books we will add to the collection, but we encourage scholars who think they have unique and exciting perspectives on China to submit their book manuscripts. From the readers' perspective, we are committed to producing high-quality books regularly so that readers should expect a steady stream of insightful books to be coming out for many years to come.

This initiative is headed by Dr. Robert Tian, a renowned researcher and academic, who spearheads our efforts in partnering with foreign authors and administering the day-to-day operations of this series. Dr. Tian, a Vice-President with North American Business Press and Editor of this series, spends much of his time in Beijing, Shanghai, and other Chinese cities, focusing on developing and managing our interests with authors and universities. Below is the list of the books we have published:

Enterprise Strategy: New Horizon authored by Zhang Xiuyu
Governance of Private Enterprises in Modern China authored by Zhong Qin
The Art of War and Enterprise Strategy Management authored by Fu Shouzhi
Marketing Issues in Modern China edited by Robert Guang Tian et al.
The Footprints of the Academician authored by Fu Zhouzhi
Marketing and Economics in Modern China (I) edited by Xiaoguang Qi et al.

Marketing and Economics in Modern China (II) edited by Wang Tianjin et al.

An Islamic Heritage in China authored by Ma Zhanming

China Environmental Anthropology authored by Wang Tianjin, Tian Guang, and Ma Jianfu

Can China Rule the New World authored by Tian Guang and Chen Gang

Critiques on Pan-marketization authored by Li Cunlin, Liu Hongfei, and Tian Guang

Economic and Business Anthropology in China edited by Xiaoguang Qi and Tian Guang

SME Managers Turnover in Modern China authored by Ji Yun

Political Connection and Financial Fraud in China authored by Peng Jinqian

China-Mongolia Economic Corridor authored by Eerdun Taoketao, Zhang Zhe, Wang Gang, and Wei Lisi

Anthropology of Chinese Foodways authored by Tian Guang and Chen Gang

Urbanization of Rural China authored by Li Taohong

The Science of Success in China authored by authored Zhang Xiuyu

Child Rearing in Rural China authored by Jiang Youchun and Yang Yunyi

ABW Management Theory and Practice authored by Zhang Xiuyu

Belt and Road vs. China and World authored by Tian Guang and Chen Gang

Modernization of China by Tian Guang, Luo Kanglong and Chen Qian

China in Xi Jinping Era by Shu Xiaohui, Li Yangkuo and Tian Guang

Table of Contents

Preface

Looking back on China's development, from the Mao Zedong era to the Xi Jinping era, several generations of Chinese have sought the path to achieve the great rejuvenation of the Chinese nation. China has become the second-largest economy and made a great leap from standing up to getting rich. In the new era, the sixth Plenary Session of the 19th CPC Central Committee adopted the Resolution of the CPC Central Committee on the Major Achievements and Historical Experience of the Party's Centennial Effort. This document put forward the urgent requirement for the full implementation of Xi Jinping Thoughts on Socialism with Chinese Attributes for a New Period. Xi Jinping Thoughts on Socialism with Chinese Attributes for a New Era is the scientific theory that guides the Party and the country to forge ahead in the new era and is an essential guide to achieving the Chinese nation's great rejuvenation. In-depth study and understanding of Xi Jinping Thoughts on Socialism with Chinese Attributes for a new era is of great significance in promoting the Party and State's undertakings and providing Chinese wisdom and Chinese solutions for other countries worldwide.

Since 2012, Xi Jinping has insisted on combining the basic principles of Marxism with the concrete reality of China in his historical journey of leading the Chinese people to build a modern socialist country and achieve the great rejuvenation of the Chinese nation. By profoundly summarizing and fully applying Mao Zedong Thoughts, Deng Xiaoping Theory, the Important Thoughts of the Three Represents and the Scientific Outlook on Development, Xi Jinping has formed his Thoughts on Socialism with Chinese Attributes in the new era. This volume summarizes Xi Jinping's Thoughts on Socialism with Chinese attributes in the new era. It also demonstrates the practical experience of China in the new era. The book aims to arm the mind better, guide practice, promote work with Xi Jinping's Thoughts on Socialism with

Chinese attributes in the new era and provide new development opportunities for the world with China's progress.

The authors of the first chapter are Dr. Tian Guang, a professor of business administration at Huaihua University, and Mr. Li Yangkuo, an economics lecturer at Hunan Huaihua College. They outline the historical development of China from the first generation of the CPC leadership with Mao Zedong as the core to the new leadership with Xi Jinping as the core. This chapter briefly introduces the ideas developed by Mao Zedong during the construction and development of China. It discusses the main theoretical ideas of General Secretary Xi Jinping from the Chinese perspective of putting the people at the center, leading the Chinese people to achieve the great rejuvenation of the Chinese nation, and promoting the building of a community of human destiny.

Chapter 2 is written by Dr. Shu Xiaohui, a professor of economics at Huaihua University, and Mr. Li Yangkuo. It focuses on Xi Jinping's practical activities in leading the Chinese people in their journey to achieve the great rejuvenation of the Chinese nation and his formation of Xi Jinping Thoughts on Socialism with Chinese Attributes for a new era. As a theoretical achievement of Marxism's Chinesization, Xi Jinping's Socialist Thoughts on Chinese Attributes is rich in connotation, covering all aspects of politics, economy, ecology and diplomacy.

Dr. Tian Guang and Mr. Li Yangkuo authored Chapter 3. It is an in-depth summary of domestic and foreign economic development in the new era, summarizing Xi Jinping's views on China's economic development. They provide a systematic overview of Chinese scholars' research on Xi Jinping's economic Thoughts on socialism with Chinese attributes. In the new period, Xi Jinping made a significant strategic judgment that China has entered a new economic normal, pointing out the attributes, opportunities and challenges faced by the new normal of China's economy. Xi Jinping's economic Thoughts of socialism with Chinese attributes is a socialist economic theory with Chinese attributes.

Chapter 4, written by Professor Wang Tianjin, an economics professor at the Minzu University of China, illustrates China's urbanization process's environmental problems and solutions utilizing empirical analysis. In response to a series of problems encountered in the urbanization process, China has proposed a strategy for constructing main functional areas and the orderly transfer of industries to the west. Regarding the construction of major functional zones, China has divided the national land space into optimized development zones, key development zones, restricted development zones and prohibited development zones. It is crucial to fully play each zone's comprehensive functions and unify the deployment to promote healthy economic and social development. The results show that the construction of the main functional area is in line with the reality of China and an act with Chinese attributes.

Chapter 5 is authored by Kong Fanchao and Zhang Hongkai from the School of Statistics, Shandong University of Finance and Economics, and Meng Xiangyan from the School of Insurance, Shandong University of Finance and Economics. It introduces the leading role of urban agglomerations in China's coordinated regional development in modernization. This chapter constructs a difference-in-difference analysis (DID) model to test the impact of NUA implementation policies on economic development and environmental pollution in China, using 280 Chinese cities as the study sample from 2005-2018.

Yanyu Wang and Shi Wei of Fujian Yango University are the authors of Chapter 6. They discuss a new model of industrial integration in Yongan Village, Fujian Province and propose an industrial integration development program to help rural revitalization. The study found that the village suffers from scattered industries, awful experience, lack of talent and inadequate policy implementation. Based on the analysis of the industrial integration development of the "1+3+2" development model, it proposed a path of industrial integration development from the perspective of empirical economy.

The authors of Chapter 7 are Gao Jian, Tian Yamei and Yang Li at Shantou University. In the new era, China is implementing large-scale higher education reform and is committed to building a modernized higher education system with Chinese attributes. They analyze the process of reforming the internal governance structure of universities based on data from the first "double first-class" universities in China. The results indicate that there are some problems with the governance of higher education in China and that institutional barriers need to be broken down through institutional strengthening.

Chapter 8 is written by Pu Lili, Chen Xingpeng and Lu Chengpeng at Lanzhou University, Jiang Li at Qinghai Normal University, and Ma Binbin at Northwest Normal University. The authors developed regression and mediating effects models to analyze recreational and impulse consumption in rural tourism. The study shows that the entertainment of rural tourism stimulates consumers' impulsive consumption behavior. Enhancing tourism consumption capacity requires fully exploiting the unique rural tourism resources.

Yanyu Wang and Xiao Huang from Fujian Yango University authored Chapter 9. This chapter briefly analyzes Chinese WeChat users and their behavioral attributes from an interpretive perspective, revealing four behavioral attributes of WeChat users. WeChat is now fully functional and has become the fastest-growing social networking software in China. Scholars have studied various aspects of the social influence of WeChat, the relationship between WeChat and communication, and the connection between WeChat and traditional media. It also demonstrates that the new social connections created by WeChat will bring new issues to China's social order, institutions, and laws and, at the same time, will bring opportunities and challenges to corporate marketing.

Our work focuses on China's development experience in the new era. This book is rich in content and novel in perspective, as the authors analyze and describe different aspects of Xi Jinping's development strategy for China in the new era. Despite the efforts made during the writing process, the content contained in this book cannot provide a comprehensive picture of China's development under Xi Jinping's leadership due to various reasons. We are showcasing the ongoing efforts and brilliant achievements of the Chinese Communists in leading the Chinese people to realize the dream of the great rejuvenation of the Chinese nation under Xi Jinping's Thoughts on Socialism with Chinese attributes in the new era.

Acknowledgment

Many Chinese scholars have supported the successful completion of this work; they have inspired us in many ways. Many domestic and international literature and research results have been consulted in the writing process, and we would like to express our sincere gratitude to the related authors and researchers. Meanwhile, the project has received strong support from the leadership of Huaihua University, and we would like to express our sincere gratitude to the university.

We sincerely thank all the Chinese scholars who inspired our ambitions to make this book. We thank Dr. Gao Jian, Dr. Jiang Youchun， Dr. Jiang Lifang, Dr. Li Rong, Dr. Liu Yu, Dr. Ma Jianfu, Dr. Ma Zhanming, Dr. Wu Hexian, Dr. Xu Zonglin, Dr. Zhao Peihua, Dr. Zheng Muqiang, and Professors Le Guobing, Li Dekuan, Wang Tianjin, Zhang Shaoping, and Ms. Zhong Ni for their insightful comments on and constructive suggestions to the initial manuscript, without their encouragements and supports this book may not be able to get published in time. Our student Wei Xiaoqing helped us in collecting data and formating the manuscript. We thank her for her contribution to the book. We want to thank the editorial team of North America Business Press for their encouragement and dedicated work. The Academic and Scholastic Publishing Foundations of Huaihua University supported this book's publication.

Acknowledgment

[illegible]

[illegible]

Foreword

Ali Kutan

According to the World Bank, since the beginning of economic reforms in 1978, the Chinese economy has grown about 10 percent annually. There has been a significant decline in poverty as more than 800 million citizens have escaped poverty. Such an extraordinary growth performance has been achieved through a combination of low-wage workers, exports, and resource-intensive manufacturing. As a result, China has become an upper-middle-income country and the second-largest economy globally. China is now a significant player in the world economy.

The close co-operation between China and the World Bank has played a substantial role in reducing poverty in the poor economies worldwide. When China joined the World Bank in 1980, it was a borrower; now, it is a significant donor. However, high growth achieved has also caused economic, social, and environmental concerns, including a recent slowdown in economic growth as the export-driven growth strategy reached its limit, income inequality, rapidly aging population and air and water pollution. The development of COVID-19 and its variants has also raised concerns for economic growth. Hence, policymakers have needed to design a new economic growth strategy based on increasing domestic consumer spending, improving the regulatory system, and introducing further market reforms to make the economy move to a new, high-quality economic growth stage.

This book volume is an excellent and timely addition to the literature on the Chinese political economy. It includes several chapters covering General Secretary Xi Jinping' s thoughts on a socialist market economy with Chinese attributes for a new period of high-quality economic growth and many significant economic, social and environmental issues facing China today. The book edited is by Dr.

Robert Tian and his co-authors, Shu Xiaohui and Li Yangkuo. Dr. Tian is a well-known scholar, a Vice-President with North American Business Press (NABP) and Editor of several books published on China by the NABP. Dr. Tian has been critical in helping young Chinese scholars to improve their academic skills and publish in international journals. He develops conferences, workshops, and other events to strengthen China's scholarly research output published internationally. He is constantly in touch with young Chinese academic faculty to improve their research output in reputable international journals. He is an excellent asset for Chinese academics.

The volume has nine chapters. Chapter 1 discusses the views of Chairman Mao Zedong, first chairman of the People's Republic of China, and the ideas of Xi Jinping from a national perspective. Chapter 2 focuses on the formation of Xi Jinping's views on socialism from a Chinese perspective. Chapter 3 includes Xi Jinping's views on economic development, covering both domestic and foreign developmental issues. The following five chapters focus on critical issues facing China today. Chapter 4 discusses environmental problems brought by the urbanization process and offers solutions. Chapter 5 describes the establishment of the National Urban Agglomeration program and its effect on economic development and environmental pollution. Chapter 6 covers the issues of integration of Industries and rural economic development. Chapter 7 is about higher education reforms and introduces China's "double first-class" universities. Chapter 8 is on the development of tourism in rural areas, focusing on consumption behavior in rural tourism. Finally, Chapter 9 is about WeChat users and their behavioral characteristics.

This volume is an excellent handbook for international students specializing in Chinese affairs. It is also recommended for students majoring in international economics and business and political economy. Moreover, it is a valuable reference for those doing business in China and prospective companies in the future. It provides readers with an understanding of China's economic policies and social and environmental issues. The chapters offer important lessons for policymakers in other developing countries as well. Practical case studies and empirical evidence provided in several chapters allow for applications and a rich platform for researchers specializing in Chinese economics and emerging markets. Overall, this volume is an essential resource for international and domestic audiences.

Feb. 4, 2022
Southern Illinois University Edwardsville, USA

Xi Jinping New Era and the Great Accomplishments of Socialism with Chinese Attributes

Jiang Youchun

The Sixth Plenary Session of the 19th CPC Central Committee was held on November 11, 2021. In the history of the Communist Party of China (CPC), this is a significant landmark and groundbreaking historical significance meeting. The plenum adopted a resolution of the CPC Central Committee on the Party's substantial achievements and century-old historical experience. The solution is a comprehensive review of history and summing up experience and is one of the most outstanding achievements to date. The historic resolution on the CPC adopted at this Plenary session confirmed Comrade Xi Jinping's core position in the CPC Central Committee and the guiding role of Xi Jinping Thought in building socialism with Chinese Attributes in the new era. This conference is a milestone because the theory of the driving force for progress was discovered from the Party's historical development logic. It pointed out the political direction and charted the political line to realize the second goal and promoted the unity of the whole Party, unified thinking and action, and established the leadership core.

Xi Jinping, as the people's leader of China with a tremendous ancient Oriental civilization, his name represents a new meaning in the world political stage and the hearts of the Chinese people. He is a positive symbol full of positive energy. He is active on the world political stage. More importantly, he directed the Chinese people under the leadership of the Communist Party of China to get rid of thousands of years of poverty and backwardness into a happy, well-off society in an all-around way. He laid the material and spiritual foundation for the complete construction of a modern, powerful country. Under his leadership, China enjoyed political integrity, prosperity, happiness and social stability. When the world economy is weak, COVID-19 is raging, and the international situation is full of uncertainties, China is showing a rare picture of prosperity, making historic breakthroughs in political, economic, cultural, social, ecological and ecological other fields.

We call China in this era a new Era of Socialism with Chinese Attributes. We call the CPC's thought on governance in this era Xi Jinping Thought on Socialism with Chinese Attributes for a New Era. This collection of essays, compiled by my colleagues Dr. Shu Xiaohui and other Chinese scholars, explored the new achievements and experiences of Xi Jinping's socialism with Chinese Attributes in the new era and summarized the Oriental wisdom of Xi Jinping's governance of the country. They tell stories of China to western readers and help the world of the west understand contemporary China. I believe that this is also the wish of western academic colleagues, and I think that this collection can fully meet this wish. As a Chinese reader of this anthology, I would like to discuss my own experience.

Xi Jinping Thought on Socialism with Chinese Attributes for a New Era

Socialism with Chinese Attributes has entered a new era. It is a unique historical juncture set by the Communist Party of China based on the latest international and domestic situations and developments. Time is the mother of thought, and practice is the source of theory. The era breeds new ideas, and the practice of political and economic development provides the inexhaustible motive force for theoretical innovation. I argue that Xi Jinping Thought on Socialism with Chinese Attributes for a New Generation is the core thought and crystallization of the collective wisdom of the CPC leadership. It explores the strategic layout of the new historical conditions of China's political and economic development. Xi Jinping carries forward the fine tradition of the Party and makes strategic arrangements in the face of the leading social contradictions in China's transition period.

The most notable contribution of Xi Jinping Thought is that it leads the mainstream ideology of Chinese society. The content is rich, broad and profound, covering philosophical thought, political economy and scientific socialism, China's reform, development and stability, domestic and foreign affairs, national defense and other fields. It is a complete theoretical system to discuss the ruling idea of the ruling party in a systematic, logical scientific and academic approach. To understand this critical thought, we need to grasp it from the time background, experimental conditions, historical logic, visionary innovation and other multi-dimensions.

First of all, the international and domestic background of the times requires the CPC to make the correct strategic response. Due to the unprecedented changes brought about by the global economy, geopolitics and clash of civilizations, the Western world once saw anti-globalization and conservative forces. However, economic globalization, application, and cultural diversity remain the prevailing trend in a multi-polar world. The world is still faced with weak economic recovery, frequent local conflicts and worsening global problems.

At the same time, after decades of reform and opening up, the principal contradiction in Chinese society has changed from the contradiction between the people's ever-growing material and cultural needs and backward social productive forces to the contradiction between the people's yearning for a better life and unbalanced and inadequate development. To achieve this, we need to adhere to a people-centered development philosophy and adjust the country's political, economic, social, cultural, ecological, diplomatic, military and other institutional arrangements based on the people's sense of happiness and gain. We should solve China's development problems and offer Chinese wisdom and solutions to the development of the world. It shows that the CPC leadership with Xi Jinping as the core is people-oriented and caring for the world.

Secondly, Xi Jinping Thought on Socialism with Chinese Attributes for a New Era is a theoretical innovation based on the practical experience of China's reform and opening up and the historical development logic of the Communist Party of China. The resolution of the CPC Central Committee on the party's significant achievements and historical experience in the past 100 years adopted at the Sixth Plenary Session of the 19th CPC Central Committee is a great historical document. It clearly stated that Comrade Xi Jinping is the principal founder of this new generation of socialism with Chinese Attributes thought. This thought and Mao Zedong Thought, Deng Xiaoping theory shared the same status in the history of the Communist Party of China. It is a pioneering Marxism in contemporary China, the essence of Chinese culture and the spirit of the times. It has laid a solid theoretical foundation for the great rejuvenation of the Chinese nation. It is the action guide for the Communist Party of China to lead the Chinese people and the Chinese government forward.

To truly understand China's propositions on the world political and economic stage, it is necessary to fully understand Xi Jinping's thoughts on socialism with Chinese Attributes in the new era. In addition, it also provides a golden key for the western world to understand the ancient culture of the East and promote better communication between China and the West in the political, economic, cultural and other aspects.

Several Core Achievements of the Xi Jinping Era

In my view, the core achievements of the Xi Jinping Era began with his "Chinese Dream," which reflects his great ambition and lofty sentiments as the leader of the Chinese people. This dream is to realize the great rejuvenation of the Chinese nation. It has been the goal of the Communist Party of China since its founding in 1921 and to reinvigorate the Chinese people's pride and consciousness as an ancient civilization. Every Chinese enjoys the dividend of development and feels the happiness of the new era, which is the reconstruction of moral order. An old Chinese saying goes: Plenty of granaries know propriety; plenty of food and clothing know honor and disgrace. It can be seen that the material basis of the people's life plays a decisive role in the moral and cultural order of a country and a nation. Since he took over the leadership of the Chinese Communist Party, Xi Jinping has set out to eradicate poverty, a problem that has plagued ordinary Chinese for thousands of years.

Poverty has long plagued humankind and affected the development history of all countries and regions. Poverty eradication is a common challenge faced by people of all countries worldwide. China is the largest developing country globally and has the largest poverty-stricken population. Nevertheless, the Chinese government has always been fighting against poverty. From the 1970s, it focused on solving food and clothing problems for the poor to the beginning of building a well-off society in an all-around way after the reform and opening up. China has formed a series of political, economic, social welfare and other institutional arrangements to eliminate poverty. From the beginning of his term as China's leader, Xi Jinping visited poverty-stricken areas many times and guided poverty alleviation work. After summarizing practical experience, He proposed the targeted poverty alleviation strategy, gradually forming the idea of targeted poverty alleviation and initiating the world's most unprecedented poverty eradication campaign.

Xi Jinping first put forward the concept of targeted poverty alleviation during his visit to Shibadong Village in Xiangxi, Hunan Province, China, in 2013, stressing that "poverty alleviation should be based on facts and measures taken following local conditions. We should take targeted measures to alleviate poverty, avoid Shouting slogans and setting ambitious goals." Subsequently, the CPC Central Committee and The State Council began implementing the "five at a time" project to achieve "six precision." The so-called "five groups" project refers to implementing poverty eradication policies in light of local conditions, such as the development of production, relocation of people from barren areas, ecological compensation, education, and social security benefits. According to the village, the so-called "six precision" is the target of support, project arrangement, use of funds, measures to households, according to the village, poverty alleviation effect, and other precision.

By February 2021, after more than eight years of hard work, nearly 99 million rural people had gotten rid of poverty measured by the current national standards. Eight hundred thirty-two counties had their poverty titles removed. One hundred twenty-eight thousand villages had all been moved out from the poverty list. As a result, the overall regional poverty problem had been solved, the arduous task of eliminating absolute poverty had been completed. It is another human miracle shining in history had been created.

Poverty is a persistent disease of human society; Anti-poverty has always been a significant issue governing the country. The elimination of poverty is conducive to the stability of the social structure and the harmony and peace of the people and conducive to personal development. It is a permanent monument in the history of human civilization that such an arduous struggle against poverty was successfully won in the era of Xi Jinping. It also provides a rich experience for other countries and regions to reference.

Building a new development pattern with a new development philosophy and promoting high-quality economic development has laid a solid foundation for the great rejuvenation of the Chinese nation. The latest development concept is innovative, coordinated, green, open and shared development. Creative development focuses on solving the problem of the driving force of development; Coordinated development focuses on addressing imbalances in development; Green development focuses on harmony between man and nature. Open development focuses on solving the problem of inter-linkage between domestic and external growth. Shared development focuses on addressing social equity and justice.

The proposal of this concept reflects Xi Jinping's deliberate and scientific reflection on the western industrial civilization. He has been trying to find a way to absorb the successful experience of the modernization process of the world's developed countries and avoid the "depression" of modernization caused by excessive industrialization, to put forward the road of modernization with Chinese Attributes. The new development concept shows that Xi clearly understands China's rapid industrialization and low-level and high-consumption science and technology since reform and opening-up, and a correct judgment of the sluggish global economic recovery. Under the new development philosophy, the Chinese economy must achieve higher quality, more efficient, fairer, and more sustainable development.

In Xi Jinping's view, economic development cannot meet the needs of the present generation by consuming future generations' resources. It cannot be limited to high speed to achieve high-quality economic development. To this end, he implemented a series of radical reforms in the economic system. For example, supply-side structural reform has been carried out to shut down many energy-intensive enterprises and industries. We will implement the Belt and Road Initiative to achieve international and domestic resource and technology allocation integration. We will address the "three major imbalances" in China's economic structure: the structural imbalance between supply and demand in the real economy, the imbalance between the financial sector and the real economy, and the imbalance between the real estate sector and the real economy.

Adhere to the principle of cooperation between the market and the government, and improve the socialist market economic system. We should adhere to the decisive role of the market in the allocation of resources and pay attention to giving full play to the advantages of the socialist system and the positive part of the party and the government. We should learn to use the "visible hands" of the government's macro-control to prevent the failure of the "invisible hands" of the market. We will accelerate the implementation of the "innovation-driven" strategy, build a comprehensive modern economic system, promote scientific and technological innovation, move from "Made in China" to "made in China," and transform China from a manufacturing powerhouse into a manufacturing powerhouse.

"Made in China 2025" is the first ten-year program of action to implement the strategy of manufacturing power. We will promote more profound integration of the Internet, big data, and artificial intelligence with the real economy and encourage resources and factors of production to converge, policies and measures to favor the real economy. More employment will be offered in the existing economy. This series of economic development measures and strategic arrangements is a scientific choice made by Xi Jinping and his leadership team based on a profound review of the successful experiences and failures of global economic and technological development. It is an institutional arrangement that suits China's unique historical and cultural soil and benefits the Chinese people profoundly. China has completed building a "moderately prosperous society" in all respects and embarked on a new journey to become a "great modern country." His thoughts and actions always revolve around the "Chinese dream" of the great rejuvenation of the Chinese nation, which shows his national consciousness, people's feelings and cultural aspirations as a visionary and determined leader of great power.

Caring for rural areas and farmers has always been the focus of Xi Jinping's "people-centered" development philosophy. Without understanding this, it is impossible to understand the significant achievement of the Xi Jinping era. The countryside is the subsistence land of nearly 600 million rural people in China and the fundamental guarantee of food supply and ecological security. The rural-urban relationship is thus a pivotal clue to understanding contemporary China. In 2021, the Central Rural Work Conference issued the first document, making "comprehensively promoting rural revitalization" the focus of future rural work. It is an essential strategic adjustment from "targeted poverty alleviation" to "rural revitalization" since the first proposed rural revitalization strategy in the 19th CPC National Congress report. If the nation is to be revitalized, the countryside will be rejuvenated.

Restoring the countryside has been one of the original aspirations and missions of the Communist Party of China since the revolutionary era. After founding the people's Republic of China, the Communist Party of China has carried out a series of experiments and explorations to change poverty and backwardness in rural areas. In particular, implementing the "contract responsibility system based on output" since the reform and opening up, various agricultural business models, beautiful rural construction, new rural construction and other systems has finally lifted China out of poverty in 2020.

During this period, the correct handling of the urban-rural dual system directly determines the quality of rural economic development. In 2002, China put forward the plan of "balancing urban and rural development and promoting the integration of urban and rural development." Although the focus of economic construction is directed to rural areas, it still focuses on urban development. Or urban construction can be applied to rural development, such as the construction of small urbanization, which still shows the achievements of urban construction. Xi Jinping first clearly put forward the "rural revitalization strategy" after entering the new era. He took "establishing and improving the system, mechanism and policy system of integrated urban-rural development" as an essential strategy to accelerate the modernization of agriculture and rural areas and realize rural revitalization.

Urban and rural integrated development focuses on reforming the allocation of urban and rural economic factors. It regards rural areas as an organic whole of equal importance with cities, realizes the free flow of resources between urban and rural areas, and thus changes the long-standing one-way flow of various development resources to cities. Xi Jinping has clarified that a system and mechanism for integrated urban and rural development should be established by 2020. The system and mechanism for integrated urban and rural development should be improved by 2035, and the countryside should be fully revitalized by 2050.

In May 2019, the CPC Central Committee and the State Council issued opinions on establishing and improving the institutional mechanism and policy system for the coordinated development of urban and rural areas. This document emphasizes improving the property rights system and the market-oriented allocation of factors, resolutely eliminating the disadvantages of systems and mechanisms, promoting the free flow, equal exchange of production factors between urban and rural areas and the rational allocation of public resources. At present, these policy documents are aimed at promoting rural-urban integration in the context of the era that rural revitalization strategies should consider.

The one-way flow of development factors from rural to urban has been transformed into a two-way flow between urban and rural areas. At the same time, based on building a new urban-rural relationship, the realization path and method of national rejuvenation are put forward. Its core is to integrate market, capital, talents, management. Based on the consideration of this series of historical and practical conditions, Xi Jinping proposed to build a "five in one" Rural Revitalization pattern of "industrial prosperity, ecological livability, rural civilization, effective governance and rich life," and achieve the construction goal of "strong agriculture, rural beauty and rich farmers" through "industrial revitalization, talent revitalization, ecological revitalization, cultural revitalization and organizational revitalization." It can be predicted that Xi Jinping's rural revitalization strategy, just like his targeted poverty alleviation strategy, will surely add an unprecedented achievement to the history of human civilization.

Conclusion

The Xi Jinping New Era means a new era in which the Communist Party of China leads the Chinese people in their independent socialist modernization drive and means that China, an ancient civilization, has regained its dynamics and vitalities. Most of the authors of this book are young and middle-aged Chinese scholars who are active and energetic. They directly feel the happiness brought by the outstanding achievements of the Xi Jinping Era through the vivid practice of scholarly work and scientific research. Therefore, they are greatly enthusiasm for China's latest achievements to their Western counterparts. I think the western readers will surely learn some inspiring Chinese wisdom from reading this book.

March 9, 2022
Jishou, Hunan Province, China

Chapter 1
From Mao Zedong to Xi Jinping

China is a large socialist developing country, and the CPC is the core leadership force chosen by the Chinese people to lead it. Mao Zedong was the creator of the Communist Party of China and the People's Republic of China. He led the Chinese people to complete the cause of liberation, carried out socialist construction and began to march toward modernization, forming the Mao Zedong Thought. The Chinese scholars agreed that Xi Jinping inherited Mao Zedong Thought and brought China into a new era. He put forward the strategic vision of realizing the Chinese Dream, the great rejuvenation of the Chinese nation. In the new international environment and under the new historical conditions, Xi Jinping has formed a series of highly relevant and continuous theoretical thoughts. His theoretical thoughts have become the guiding ideology for China to become prosperous and strong and make more excellent global contributions. This chapter Outlines the historical process of China from Mao Zedong to Xi Jinping and discusses Xi Jinping's main theoretical ideas from the Chinese scholars' perspective.

Introduction

China is the largest socialist developing country globally, and the Chinese people select the Communist Party of China (CPC) as the core leadership force of the country. The most prominent socialist country under the leadership of the Communist Party is the unique characteristic of China. Anyone studying contemporary China must recognize and respect China's unique characteristics. It is easy to understand that the leadership of the Communist Party of China is, therefore, naturally the country's leadership. Xi Jinping, the first General Secretary of the Communist Party of China Central Committee, born in New China, climbed onto the Tiananmen Rostrum to attend a ceremony marking the

70th anniversary of the founding of the People's Republic of China on Oct. 01, 2019.

Mao Zedong proclaimed the founding of the People's Republic of China in 1949. Now, Xi Jinping is steering the great ship "China" into a new era and continues to break the waves and sail far. Over the past 70 years, China, a socialist country ruled by the Communist Party of China, has gone through an extraordinary journey. The Chinese people have turned themselves into masters of the country, removed the hat of "sick man of Asia" and "poor and white," and become the world's second-largest economy. China has made a historic leap from standing up, becoming rich to strong.

This chapter briefly describes Mao Zedong's thoughts on China's construction and development. Then, from the perspective of Chinese scholars, it discusses the theoretical and ideological essentials and practical activities of Xi Jinping since 2012 in the historical process of leading the Chinese people to build a solid socialist country and realize the great rejuvenation of the Chinese nation.

Remove Poverty and Realize Modernization

Mao Zedong felt deeply the humiliation of modern China being divided and bullied by foreign powers in his youth and agreed with Gu Yanwu that "every man is responsible for the rise and fall of the world." He believed that the Chinese people should strive to enrich the country and strengthen the army. Reform to save the country with the big original as the call, "the world can do, the country is not rich and happy people?" To this end, he joined the army after the 1911 Revolution and served as a soldier in the New Army for four months. In July 1921, he participated in the founding of the Communist Party of China and had since made arduous efforts to realize the great rejuvenation of the Chinese nation. On the eve of the outbreak of the War of Resistance against Japanese Aggression, he became the core leader of the first generation of the Communist Party of China (Shi, 2013).

Mao Zedong appealed against the Japanese imperialists' arrogant ambition to launch a full-scale war of aggression against China. He stressed that the Chinese nation has the spirit to fight with its enemies to the end of blood, is determined to recover the lost territory based on self-reliance, and can stand on its own feet in the nation's forest. This appeal he made is on behalf of the Central Committee of the Communist Party of China. He stressed that the Chinese would fight for the independence and liberation of the Greater China nation to the last drop of blood! After the Anti-Japanese War broke out, he led the Chinese people's army to become the mainstay of the victory of the war. Later in the Liberation War, he led the Chinese People's Liberation Army to overthrow the reactionary rule of the Kuomintang government (Li, 2020).

Mao Zedong was not the first revolutionist with the thought of national rejuvenation. However, he was the first leader who proposed the strategic idea of national rejuvenation. When the People's Republic of China was founded, he solemnly declared: "From now on, the Chinese people, one-quarter of the total number of mankind, have stood up." The Chinese nation will join the big family of peace-loving and freedom-loving nations and create its civilization and happiness with courage and diligence. A new era opened up in the history of China. Thus, after 22 years of arduous armed struggle, the People's Republic of China was established, the Chinese nation was "greatly transformed," and the first step of the "Chinese Dream" was realized (Fei and Chen, 2019).

After the recovery of the national economy, Mao Zedong proposed to build an economically and culturally backward country into a great industrialized socialist country with a high degree of modern education through ten "five-year" plans. The convening of the National Congress of the CPC marked that socialist transformation was completed, and our country entered a period of large-scale socialist construction. The tasks of the Communist Party of China are set out in the Eight New Party Constitution: to build China into a great, prosperous and advanced socialist country by giving it a solid and modern industry, agriculture, transportation and national defense. It is the initial expression of the "four modernizations" and mainly reflects the requirements of socialist material civilization construction and will lay a solid material foundation for building a solid socialist modern industrial country.

In 1957, Mao Zedong published "On Correctly Handling Contradictions Among the People" and "Speech at the National Conference of the Communist Party of China on Propaganda work." In the previous report, he clarified: We are now going to wage war on nature, develop our economy, develop our culture, strengthen our new institutions, and build our new nation. In the latter speech, he gave new thought to the meaning of modernization, proposing to "build a socialist country with modern industry, modern agriculture and modern science and culture." The construction of modern science and culture proposed here embodies the requirements of socialist spiritual civilization. When reading the Soviet Textbook on Political Economy at the end of 1959 and the beginning of 1960, he further enriched this thought, saying, "In building socialism, the modernization of industry, agriculture and science and culture was originally required, but now national defense must be added to it." Thus, he formulated the thought of the four modernizations relatively ultimately (Song and Zhai, 2020).

As for the realization of the "four modernizations," Mao Zedong in 1954 put forward the idea of building China into a powerful socialist industrialized country in about 50 years. During the Eighth National Congress of the Communist Party of China in 1956, he said that it would take 50 to 100 years for China to become a strong and prosperous country. In his speech to the conference of 7,000 People in January 1962, he pointed out that given China's large population, weak economic foundation and backward economy, it would take more than a hundred years for China to develop its productive forces significantly. Then China could catch up with and surpass the most advanced capitalist countries. It is, in fact, the goal of national rejuvenation (Yang, 2013).

In his report on the work of the Government delivered to the First Session of the Third National People's Congress, Zhou Enlai proposed a "two-step" strategy. The first step was establishing a relatively complete industrial and national economic system with three five-year plans. The second step is to strive for the complete modernization of agriculture, industry, national defense and science and technology by the end of the 20th century. China's economy will take the lead in the world. This plan is the grand blueprint of realizing socialist modernization that the Party and the government put forward formally at the earliest (Chen, 2011). At the first session of the Fourth National People's Congress in 1975, Zhou Enlai reiterated this grand blueprint and became the most vital voice to inspire the people in the difficult years of the Cultural Revolution. The "Chinese Dream" of the first generation of leaders with Mao Zedong as the core has not been fully realized, but it has accumulated historical lessons for the successors to find the right direction.

From the Era of Mao Zedong to the Era of Xi Jinping, Deng Xiaoping, and Jiang Zemin, Hu Jintao experienced the leadership of the transition period. They had established Deng Xiaoping Theory, the critical thinking of the "Three Represents," and the scientific outlook on development. Deng Xiaoping's theory is a theoretical viewpoint based on the inheritance of Marxism and Mao Zedong Thought. It combined with the contemporary characteristics of Chinese practice, raising the understanding of socialism to a new scientific level and forming a new scientific system of the theory of building socialism with Chinese Attributes. The Three Important Thought of the Three Represents proposed by Comrade Jiang Zemin summarizes all the theoretical and practical activities of the CPC and the state, including the fundamental direction, fundamental guidelines and fundamental basis of all work, and is the action guide for the CPC and the state to make great strides in the new century. Hu Jintao put forward the scientific concept of development, whose first critical meaning is development. The core is people-oriented, and the essential requirement is comprehensive coordination and sustainability. The fundamental method is to coordinate and take into account. And on this basis, he proposed the idea of national defense and military construction, which reveals the fundamental laws of national defense and military construction in the new century and new stage, and is a scientific guide to promote the national defense and military construction under the new historical conditions (Cao, 2007).

Usher Socialism with Chinese Attributes into New Era

On Nov. 15, 2012, Xi Jinping, newly elected general secretary of the Communist Party of China (CPC) Central Committee, met with more than 500 Chinese and foreign journalists at noon after the first plenary session of the 18th CPC Central Committee. In his book Great Power Ambitions, Martin Jacques, a British scholar, said that Xi's appointment as general secretary of the Communist Party of China marked the beginning of an era. At the time, the effects of the 2008 global financial crisis were still spreading. After decades of development, China became the second-largest economy in 2010 and entered a critical period of realizing socialist modernization. The rise of some emerging countries accelerated. The global landscape is undergoing profound changes. Speaking to reporters, Xi outlined the mission of the new central leadership as "three responsibilities." These responsibilities are our responsibility to the nation, the people, and the Party. "The people's aspiration for a better life is our goal," he said. Fourteen days later, Xi proposed the "Chinese Dream" to "realize the great rejuvenation of the Chinese nation." He ate food and clothes for the next few years, night after night. Shortly after he was elected as the General Secretary, Xi Jinping systematically reviewed the origin and evolution of socialism over the past 500 years. He summarized for senior Party officials the successes and losses of China's choice of the pluralist system. Further, he declared that we must stick to the path of socialism with Chinese Attributes (Han and Xie, 2020).

After taking office as the General Secretary of CPC, he visited the holy lands of the Chinese revolution many times. In Xibanpo, he said, this is the place where rules are made; In Jinggang Shan, he said his journey was thousands of miles long, and he did not forget his original aspiration. 'This is the spiritual home of Chinese Communists,' he said at the site of the First Congress of the Communist Party of China. In Xiangshan, he said to "rush for the exam," sober and firm answer the new era (Yan, 2019). At the 19th National Congress of the Communist Party of China in 2017, Xi Jinping Thought on Socialism with Chinese Attributes for a New Era was formally established. The idea attracted worldwide attention. "Xi Jinping: The Governance of China" is a global bestseller. Some state leaders even took the initiative to discuss the book's contents with Xi during their visits to China. The new guidelines place greater emphasis on overall party leadership. Xi Jinping is determined to lead the Communist Party of China, with nearly 90 million members, in self-revolution. Xi Jinping has launched a campaign to govern the Party with strict discipline comprehensively, promoted the introduction of the Eight-point Code of Conduct, and presided over the formulation of the Code of Conduct for Intraparty Political Life under New Circumstances and the Regulations of the Communist Party of China on Intra-Party Supervision. He directed four thematic education activities to "purify" the party. He metaphorically said, "We have to brush our teeth and wash our face, clean our house, wash dishes and clothes every day. We also have to do these things to build the Party" (Li, 2017).

He has led an unprecedented anti-corruption campaign with no blind spots. In the five years from the 18th CPC National Congress to the 19th CPC National Congress, 440 party officials at or above the provincial military level and other officials under the central government were investigated and punished. By the end of 2018, the CPC Central Commission for Discipline Inspection and the State Commission for Supervision had placed more than 70 officials under investigation. Until September this year, provincial and ministerial officials were sacked, and the fight against corruption was always on the way. The website of foreign Affairs, a bimonthly US magazine, said Xi leads the world's largest and most successful Marxist-Leninist organization and is determined to ensure that it remains so. The Sixth Plenary Session of the 18th CPC Central Committee in 2016 confirmed Xi's position as the core of the CPC Central Committee and the whole Party. In March 2019, Xi Jinping met with the Italian Speaker of the House of Representatives, Giuseplo Fico. Fico asked Xi, "How did you feel when elected president of China?" "Such a big country has heavy responsibilities and arduous work," Xi answered: I will live up to the people without myself. I am willing to live in a "no ego" state and contribute to China's development (Meng et al., 2018).

"We are closer, more confident and capable than ever before to realizing the goal of national rejuvenation," Xi said. According to the blueprint drawn up at the 19th CPC National Congress, after completing the building of a moderately prosperous society in all respects by 2020, China aims to realize socialist modernization by 2035 and build itself into a great modern socialist country by the middle of this century. Chinese leaders aim to deliver a satisfactory answer to the people with a strong sense of mission. In the seventh year of Xi Jinping's leadership, China's economy has exceeded 90 trillion yuan, firmly ranking second. China is also the world's largest industrial country, the largest trader of goods, the largest holder of foreign exchange reserves, second-largest recipient of foreign investment and second-largest consumer of goods.

According to data from China's National Bureau of Statistics and the World Bank, China's economy grew at an average annual rate of about 7 percent from 2013 to 2018. The world economy grew at an average annual rate of about 2.9 percent during the same period. China has the complete industrial chain globally, with over 220 industrial products topping the world. It has one of the most extended high-speed rail networks to send probes to the moon's far side. The number of Chinese companies in 2019 Global 500 has increased to 129, topping the list first. These achievements result from the Chinese people's hard work and the deepening of reform and opening-up. Deng Xiaoping's 1978 reform and opening-up were seen as a "social revolution" (Wang, 2008).

Xi Jinping is determined to see this "revolution" through to the end. In 2012, on his first visit to Beijing after becoming general secretary of the Communist Party of China (CPC), He said in Shenzhen that "reform and opening-up is a crucial move that determines the destiny of contemporary China" and that "stagnation and backsliding will lead nowhere." The reforms led by Xi are characteristic of a new era: a greater focus on breaking through the barriers of entrenched interests. The reform pays more attention to top-level design and emphasizes "systematic, integrated and coordinated development." At the Third Plenary Session of the 18th CPC Central Committee in 2013, a seven-year timetable for comprehensively deepening reform was set out, and a large-scale reform plan was introduced. Xi Jinping has set "improving and developing the system of socialism with Chinese Attributes and modernizing China's system and capacity for governance" as the general goal of comprehensively deepening reform.

Over the years, Xi has presided over dozens of meetings of the Central Leading Group and committee for Comprehensively Deepening Reform. The most recent meeting, held in September, deliberated and approved more than a dozen reform plans and opinions, from supporting the reform of private enterprises to promoting labor and talent mobility, from lightening the burden of teachers to combating plastic pollution. It embodies the top-level design and is very detailed, reflecting the spirit of driving nails. Some of Xi's mottos may help outsiders understand why "China Speed" and "China project" have been produced so frequently in the new era that they are amazed. Here are some of his mottos: "Do what you do and take the lead," "Empty talk will ruin the country, but solid work will rejuvenate the country," and "If you grasp an iron, you leave a mark; if you step on a stone, you leave a mark."

In the seven years from 2012 to 2019, Xi made more than 60 visits to China, conducting in-depth investigations and research at the grassroots level to guide economic and social development and reform and opening-up. There are factories, villages, communities, ports, schools, and barracks. Sometimes he would go as high as thousands of meters above sea level; sometimes, to get to a village, he would get off the plane, transfer by train, and take a bus. Sometimes, when it rained during the expedition, he would roll up his trousers and hold up an umbrella to communicate with others. In 2019, he inspected work in Henan and proposed a strategy for ecological protection and high-quality development of the Yellow River Basin. He launched the

Yangtze River Economic Belt development strategy a few years ago. China's two "mother rivers" are bursting with new vitality in the new era. Xi has designed more market-oriented reforms and encouraged private firms to take their stakes. "Private entrepreneurs are our people," he said when he presided over an unprecedented forum on private enterprises. One of Xi's words most was "innovation" for seven years. "Core technology, key technology, begging is not changed." He used to say.

In 2019, Xi Jinping visited Dunhuang and gave new instructions on the protection and development of culture. Cultural confidence, he often says, is "more fundamental, broader, deeper confidence." Xi has led the reform of party and state institutions to create more efficient and modern government institutions. In the past few years, the number of items approved by the Chinese government was cut by a third. With online approval and a one-stop office in many places, enterprises no longer need to spend months going to many places to get their stamps stamped. Xi Jinping has advocated the rule of law in an all-around way. He stressed the importance of "100-1=0," meaning that the negative impact of one wrong case is enough to destroy the excellent image accumulated by 99 impartial judges. The reform of the judicial system is being explored in terms of exercising judicial power independently and impartially by the law, improving the operation mechanism of judicial power, and improving the judicial protection system for human rights. In terms of ecological environment, he put forward the famous "theory of green mountains and clear waters." Xi Jinping personally delivered the instrument of ratification of the Paris Agreement on climate change to the UN Secretary-General. The achievements of "green China" have been recognized and praised globally. There has been a marked reduction in pollution in many cities. Xi Jinping plans to promote the coordinated development of the Beijing-Tianjin-Hebei region and build the Xiongan New Area. The Shanghai Pilot Free Trade Zone, established in 2013, has been successfully expanded to 18 such zones, including the entire island of Hainan. Xi also announced greater openness in industries ranging from banking to automobiles.

Since entering the new era, China's investment environment has improved. According to the World Bank's Doing Business 2019 Report, China has jumped from 78th to 46th in terms of ease of doing business. China is a growing market -- data suggest it is on the verge of becoming the world's largest consumer market. According to data released by China's Ministry of Commerce in August, more than 24,000 foreign-invested enterprises were established in China in the first seven months of this year, with the actual use of foreign capital exceeding 530 billion yuan, up 7.3 percent year on year. Xi attended the world's first import-themed expo in Shanghai and mentioned "openness" 52 times in his 35-minute speech. The turnover at the exhibition is very encouraging. More businesses from around the world have signed up for the second CIIE. In 2018, Xi Jinping revisited Shenzhen. "We are here to show the world that China will never stop its reform and opening-up," he said. In the next 40 years, China will surely make new achievements that will impress the world" (Yang and Xin, 2018).

Every Thing is for People's Gain, Happiness and Security

In 2019, about 16,500 businesses were newly registered in China, and about 40,000 new jobs were found in urban areas. Over the past seven years, more than 80 million new urban jobs have been created in China, which is equivalent to the population of Germany. "Employment is the most important aspect of people's livelihood," Xi said. The development of the new economy, such as e-commerce, has created more jobs than ever before. Xi Jinping has encouraged and promoted this. Once, in a Beijing hutong, he suddenly appeared in front of a group of delivery boys and expressed sympathy for their hard work. China now has the world's largest express delivery industry, with more than 3 million couriers. Xi addressed in his 2018 New Year's speech: "I know the people are most concerned about education, employment, income, social security, medical care, elderly care, housing and the environment."

The principal contradiction facing Chinese society has evolved between unbalanced and inadequate development and the people's ever-growing needs for a better life. As general secretary, Xi Jinping, every year on the Spring Festival will come with ordinary people: braved the cold of minus 30 degrees Celsius border town see hard worker, also for the folks on his own to the procurement of necessities and played Ziba and the masses, to the door of the old neighborhood affixed happy word, concerned about the poor farmers have enough food to eat, the doctor has to safeguard, children can go to school. This vital judgment made by Xi Jinping in the report to the 19th CPC National Congress reflects his scientific and accurate judgment and grasp of the national conditions and public opinions (Xu and Zhang, 2018).

During the education-themed "Stay true to our original aspiration and keep our mission firmly in mind," Xi repeatedly said that the purpose of the CPC is to serve the people wholeheartedly. It also reflects Xi's personal experience and will (Qu, 2019). Under the age of 16, he went to poor rural areas in Shaanxi province to join the queue, settle down and work for seven years. He wanted most of the villagers to have a hearty meal of meat. He said he came from a place of poverty. He understood the sufferings of the people. For a while, Chinese house prices were rising faster. Xi warned that houses are for living in, not speculation. He added that a city couldn't have high-rises on one side and squalor shantytowns. In 2018, the per capita floor space of urban housing in China reached 39 square meters, up 3.7 times from 8.3 square meters in 1949. About 200 million poor people can live in housing (Chen, 2020).

Xi Jinping thinks very carefully about the people. He often inspected the toilet of ordinary people's homes in the grassroots investigation and was entrusted with garbage classification. During a recent visit to a village in Henan province, he proposed modernizing and facilitating living facilities so that villagers "can take hot showers." He also advised on the high incidence of myopia among students. A few decades ago, China's social security system was blank. By 2019, China had achieved full coverage of basic medical and old-age insurance for over 900 million people, forming the world's most extensive social safety net. In 2013, Xi proposed "targeted poverty alleviation." He set a goal of eradicating absolute rural poverty by current standards by 2020. It is ten years ahead of the UN's goal of eradicating absolute poverty worldwide. More than 82 million people have been lifted out of poverty in seven years. Xi indicated that the problem of absolute poverty, which has existed in the Chinese nation for thousands of years, will be solved historically in the hands of our generation.

Kishore Mahbubani, a professor at the National University of Singapore, said that the most outstanding achievement of China is the remarkable improvement in the standard of living of the Chinese people. Even in the glory days of Chinese civilization, a vast underclass of people still lived in poverty. In Today's China, even low-income people enjoy suitable accommodation, education, health care and employment. Xi has made good on his words: "Love the people like your parents." At the first session of the 13th National People's Congress in March 2018, Xi Was re-elected as President, winning the unanimous support of nearly 3,000 NPC deputies.

Build a Community with a Shared Future for Humanity

In 2014, the number of Chinese outbound tourists exceeded 100 million for the first time. China's outbound direct investment exceeded 120 billion US dollars, with two-way direct investment approaching balance for the first time. Thousands of Chinese workers study and live all over the world. "China is moving closer to center stage" has become a common expression in the news. Handling the relationship between China and the world in the new era is a significant task facing Chinese leaders. Nearly 20 years ago, when He was governor of Fujian Province, Xi promoted the implementation of Fujian's assistance to Papua New Guinea's East Highlands province for the demonstration project of fungus grass and upland rice cultivation technology. Fungus grass projects with functions such as desertification control, livestock breeding, power generation and new material development have spread to more than 100 countries, bringing hope to developing countries in Africa, Asia and the South Pacific (Liu, 2019).

During his visit to Papua New Guinea in November 2018, President Xi Jinping witnessed the signing of a package of agreements on China's assistance to Papua New Guinea, including fungus and upland rice technology. This incident reflects Xi Jinping's aspiration and thinking about building international relations. In his view, countries should respect each other; pursue fairness, justice and win-win cooperation. In March 2013, during his first overseas trip as Chinese President, Xi Jinping expounded on the concept of "a community with a shared future" and "a new type of international relations" at the Moscow Institute of International Relations (Liu, 2021). Xi Jinping comprehensively expounded on the primary connotation of a community with a shared future for humanity two years later in his first speech at the UN. He elaborated on building a world free from fear, universal security, free from poverty and shared prosperity, free from isolation, openness and inclusiveness, clean and beautiful (Chen, 2019).

Xi Jinping proposed the Belt and Road Initiative is a platform for building a community with a shared future for humankind. The grand idea was to link continents and oceans with trade and investment. Different from the "doubts" of some Westerners, its purpose is to "integrate more countries and regions into economic globalization and jointly blaze a path of mutual benefit." By the end of July this year, China had signed 194 cooperation documents on belt and Road Cooperation with 136 countries and 30 international organizations. According to a World Bank study released in June, the full implementation of the Belt and Road Initiative could lift 32 million people out of moderate poverty, increase global trade by 6.2 percent, trade-in economies along the routes by 9.7 percent and global income 2.9 percent. "Stadium diplomacy" has become a shining "name card" of the new era. From the circa summit, APEC meetings in Beijing, Shanghai, Hangzhou, the G20 summit, the BRICS leaders meeting in Xiamen to the SCO summit in Qingdao and the boat Asia BBS, since the "area" of international cooperation of the two peaks BBS, the Beijing summit of the BBS on China-Africa cooperation dialogue among civilizations to the park in Beijing and Asia congress, China has become a hub for discussions on global governance and development (Su, 2019).

While presiding over these events, Xi told stories of how China's development has given other countries a "free ride." He explained the true meaning of a community with a shared future for humanity. He promoted innovation and improved the global governance system under extensive consultation, joint contribution and shared benefits. In recent years, Chinese nationals have served as heads of the UN Food and Agriculture Organization and other international organizations, contributing more Chinese wisdom to global governance on relevant issues. The RMB has been included in the IMF's Special Drawing Rights basket. The Asian Infrastructure Investment Bank and the Silk Road Fund were also created.

China has become a vital force in resolving global and regional hotspot issues. They range from climate change to counter-terrorism, from nuclear proliferation to the wealth gap, from fair trade to war peacekeeping. In 2019, China became the second-largest contributor to UN membership dues after the United States. It is also one of the major contributors to UN peacekeeping operations and the most significant troop contributor among the Security Council's permanent members. The 10-year us $1 billion China-UN Peace and Development Fund, established by China, was officially put into operation in 2016. For years, China has contributed more than 30 percent of global growth. China has steadily solved the food and clothing problem for over one billion people and contributed to over 70% of global poverty reduction. The World Bank calls it "one of the greatest events in human history." China's development experience and model have broadened the path for developing countries to achieve modernization (Zheng, 2021). As in Xi Jinping's words: The Communist Party of China has always taken it as its mission to make new and more significant contributions to humanity (Zhang and Kong, 2018).

Through the Rough Seas to the Big Dreams

The word "struggle" appeared nearly 60 times when Xi gave the "first lesson of the term" to young and middle-aged officials at the Party School of the CPC Central Committee (National Academy of Governance) in September 2019. "The great rejuvenation of the Chinese nation is by no means an easy task," he said. "To realize our great dream, we must fight hard." Xi's sense of struggle can be traced back to when he jumped the queue at Liangjiahe. The hardships of that time had trained him into an unyielding, courageous man. On the way forward, Xi said, the risks and tests we face will only become more complex, and "we may even encounter unimaginable tempests" (Yang, 2019). He sees the fight against corruption as a life-or-death battle. The war has gone from "corruption and anti-corruption are at a stalemate" to "overwhelming momentum is forming," to "overwhelming momentum has formed," to "overwhelming victory." He boldly and wisely led the whole Party and the Chinese people to respond to the economic downturn challenges. He put forward the "new normal of economic development," "New development concept," and "supply-side structural reform" to promote high-quality economic development. He launched three critical battles against significant risks, targeted poverty alleviation and pollution prevention and control (Lan, 2021).

When economic and trade frictions broke out between China and the United States, under Xi Jinping's direction, China responded with the principle and attitude of "not willing to fight, not afraid of fighting, and having to fight when necessary." (Guan, 2019). He met with US President Donald Trump in Buenos Aires and Osaka to push for an essential step in resolving trade frictions between the two countries. On the Hong Kong issue, Xi said that if Hong Kong falls into the vortex of "pan-politicization" and artificially creates confrontation and confrontation, it will not help the situation but will seriously hinder economic and social development. When meeting with the new Chief Executive of the Macao SAR, he pointed out that facts proved that the principle of "one country, two systems" is feasible, achievable, and popular. Xi actively promoted the reunification of the motherland. He proposed to explore the “two systems” plan for Taiwan and enriched the practice of peaceful reunification. “We do not promise to renounce the use of force and reserve the option of taking all necessary measures. We are targeting the interference of external forces and the minimal number of ‘Taiwan independence’ separatists and their separatist activities, not our Compatriots in Taiwan,” he said (Wu, 2019).

Xi Jinping has taken bold steps to reform national defense and the armed forces, firmly establishing combat effectiveness as the only fundamental criterion. Protecting China’s overseas interests has become one of the military’s new-era missions. Mr. Xi has directed evacuations during unrest in West Asia and North Africa. The resulting film is a record box office hit in China. “He is more determined to protect his interests." “Foreign Affairs magazine wrote in a recent article.” We face the struggles not short-term, but long-term,” Xi said. “At least, they should accompany the whole process of realizing the second Centenary Goal.” (Xu, 2019). Xi Jinping and his ruling team are keenly aware of the complexity and volatility of the outside world and keenly aware that China is still the largest developing country. In May 2019, Xi Jinping visited Yudu County in Jiangxi province, where the Red Army gathered for the Long March and called on people to follow the new Long March. In the 1930s, the Chinese Workers’ and Peasants’ Red Army fought the long March of 25,000 li against the harsh nature, heavy enemy forces and the wrong line of the Party. They made great sacrifices and finally won the victory of the revolution. In the eyes of Chinese Communists, all the hard work is to achieve their glorious and sacred goal.

Conclusion

From Mao Zedong to Xi Jinping is a historical development process of Chinese society from weak to strong. Mao Zedong and Xi Jinping hoped to realize the Chinese dream of great national renewal. It has been the common pursuit of a generation of Chinese Communists for nearly a century. Although they may have slightly different standards, goals and priorities for the "Chinese Dream," it is essential and common to make the country prosperous, revitalize the nation, and bring happiness to the people to realize socialist modernization and build a community with a shared future for humankind. Leaders of different eras have slightly different "Chinese dreams" because they have both broad and strict interpretations of the great rejuvenation of the Chinese nation.

Mao Zedong's goal was to catch up with and surpass the most advanced capitalist countries globally, developed countries. In his vision, it may take half a century to catch up with and surpass the developed countries in the world from the full realization of modernization. He set the goal of achieving the great rejuvenation of the Chinese nation because, in his view, China is a big country, accounting for a quarter of the world's population. Still, its contribution to humanity is not commensurate with its population. It embarrasses us and will change in the future. He believes That China should make a more significant contribution to humankind.

The theoretical system of Xi Jinping Thought on Socialism with Chinese Attributes is a continuation and development of Mao Zedong Thought and a high summary of the ideology and values of contemporary China. Its core content is to realize the great Renaissance of the Chinese nation and fulfill the Chinese dream. Stand in the height of the human history development, construction of deep thinking what kind of world, such as how to build the world's essential topics about human fate, actively advocate and promote the construction of human destiny community, the depth of the building close relations between China and the world. He elaborated on the idea of building a community with a shared future for humankind and expounded on China's willingness and confidence to follow the path of peaceful development.

This thought has responded to the concerns and expectations of the international community and demonstrates China's responsibility as a significant country. Xi Jinping Thought on Socialism with Chinese Attributes for a New Era takes the world and humankind as coordinates and stage. It is based on China and strives to modernize China's system and capacity for governance. It also looks to the world and actively provides Chinese wisdom and solutions for global governance, demonstrating profound global vision, general human feelings and superb strategic thinking.

Chapter 2
Xi Jinping Thought on Socialism with Chinese Attributes

Socialism with Chinese Attributes has entered a new era with China's new historical development orientation. Confronted with the new situation at home and abroad, Xi Jinping has initiated some new concepts, ideas and strategies to lead the Chinese people to advance towards the great rejuvenation of the Chinese nation. Xi Jinping Thought on Socialism with Chinese Attributes for a New Era summarizes the historical experience and the engine for China's future development. His idea of the Chinese Dream depicts a dream of prosperity, national renewal, and happiness, injecting a new connotation and spirit of the times into the adherence to and development of socialism with Chinese Attributes. In the new journey of the new era, Xi Jinping proposed to facilitate the building of a community with a shared future for humankind, establishing a deep and close relationship between China and the world. This study elaborates on the theoretical ideas and practical activities of Xi Jinping, leading the Chinese people to develop a great socialist culture in China and achieve the great rejuvenation of the Chinese nation.

Introduction

China is the largest developing socialist country, and the Communist Party of China (CPC) is the core leadership chosen by all Chinese people. All the achievements the Chinese people have made in the past century were under the leadership of the CPC. At noon on November 15, Xi Jinping met with more than 500 journalists from domestic and abroad, as General Secretary elected after the First Plenary Session of the 18th CPC Central Committee. According to Martin Jacques, author of When China Rules the World: The End of the

Western World and the Birth of a New Global Order, Xi Jinping's presidency as General Secretary of the CPC Central Committee marked the beginning of a new era (Jacques et al., 2016). At the time, the effects of the 2008 global financial crisis were still being felt. After decades of development, China became the second-largest economy in 2010 and was critical to achieving socialist modernization. The world landscape was undergoing a profound evolution. Some emerging countries have accelerated their ascension. Xi outlined the mission of the new central leadership group as "three responsibilities": responsibility to the nation, responsibility to the people, and response to the Party. He stated that the people's aspiration for a better life is CPC's goal of struggle. Subsequently, Xi proposed "the Chinese Dream" to "realize the great rejuvenation of the Chinese nation." He spent his days and nights achieving the dream during the next seven years. Soon after he was elected General Secretary, Xi systematically reviewed the origins and evolution of socialism over the past five centuries. He summarized and shared the successes and failures of the political systems adopted by China with senior CPC cadres since modern times. It further demonstrates the significance of the path of socialism with Chinese Attributes (Han et al., 2020).

Since taking office as General Secretary, Xi Jinping has visited many revolutionary sites. He stressed that the rules of the Communist Party of China were formulated there at Xibaipo and that the Chinese government should never forget its original intention at all times on Jinggang Mountains. When visiting the site of the first National Congress of the Communist Party of China, Xi Jinping regarded it as the spiritual home of the Chinese Communists. When visiting Xiangshan Mountain, he said that the Chinese government should answer the new era with sobriety and determination as if taking a test. In 2017, Xi Jinping Thought on Socialism with Chinese Attributes for a New Era was formally established at the First Plenary Session of the 19th CPC Central Committee, when Xi was re-elected General Secretary of the CPC Central Committee. This concept has received worldwide attention. Xi Jinping was determined to lead the Chinese

Communist Party, self-revolution with nearly 90 million members. He initiated the campaign to exercise complete and strict governance over the Party, accelerated the introduction of the Eight Rules, and presided over the formulation of The Norms Regarding Intra-Party Political Life in New Situation, and Regarding Regulations Intra-Party Supervision. Also, he directed four thematic education campaigns to "purify" the Party.

Xi Jinping has led an unprecedented "anti-corruption campaign" that has left no room for error. Between the 18th and 19th CPC National Congress, 440 party cadres above the provincial and ministerial levels were investigated and punished in the five years. Since the conclusion of the 19th CPC National Congress, the Central Commission for Discipline Inspection of the Communist Party of China and the National Supervisory Commission has investigated more than 100 cadres on file with the Department of Organization of the Communist Party of China and many provincial and ministerial-level officials were convicted. The Foreign Affairs website remarked that Xi Jinping leads the world's largest and most successful Marxist-Leninist organization and is determined to ensure that it sustains that status. The Sixth Plenary Session of the 18th CPC Central Committee in 2016 established Xi Jinping as the core of the CPC Central Committee and the core position of the Party. In March 2019, Xi Jinping met with Roberto Fico, the Italian Chamber of Deputies president. Fico asked Xi Jinping, "How did you feel when elected President of China?" Xi said: "It is a weighty responsibility to manage such a big country, and the work is very challenging. I will fully commit to the people and never fail them. I am willing to accomplish a state of 'no-self' and dedicate myself to the development of China."

Reform and Socialist Modernization

Xi Jinping pointed out that the Chinese government is closer to, more confident in and capable of achieving the great rejuvenation of the Chinese nation than at any other time in history. According to the blueprint of the 19th CPC National Congress, a moderately prosperous society will be achieved throughout China. Based on this, socialist modernization will be achieved by 2035 with 15 more years of hard work. Subsequently, with hard work for another 15 years, China will grow into a great modern socialist country by the middle of the 21st century. The leadership of China, with a strong sense of mission, is determined to deliver an answer that will satisfy the people. In the seventh year of Xi Jinping's leadership, China's economy exceeded 90 trillion yuan, ranking second. China is also the world's largest industrial country, the largest trader in goods, the largest foreign exchange reserve holder, the second-largest recipient of foreign direct investment, and the second-largest consumer of goods.

According to the National Bureau of Statistics of China and the World Bank, China's economy will grow by 8.5% in 2021, while the global economy will grow by 5.6% in the same period. China has the world's most complete industrial chain, with the world's most significant production of more than 220 types of industrial products. It has the most extended high-speed rail network by mileage and has launched a probe to the moon's back. In 2021, there are 143 Chinese companies on the list of the world's top 500 companies, and for the first time, China topped the list. These achievements are the fruits of the hard work of the Chinese people and the result of the comprehensive and in-depth promotion of reform and opening up. The reform and opening up initiated by Deng Xiaoping in 1978 are regarded as a "social revolution," while Xi Jinping is determined to take this "revolution" to the end. After being elected general secretary in 2012, he visited Shenzhen, addressing that reform and opening-up is a game-changing move in making China what it is today. Stop or reverse reforms and opening up would only lead to a blind alley (Wang, 2008).

Under Xi Jinping's leadership, the reform indicates a new era focusing on cracking the barriers of solidified interests. The reform is more oriented to top-level design, emphasizing systemic, holistic and synergistic development. In 2013, a seven-year timetable for comprehensively deepening the reform was set by the Third Plenary Session of the 18th CPC Central Committee, and a large-scale reform program was unveiled. Xi Jinping defined the overall objectives of comprehensively deepening reform as developing and improving the system of socialism with Chinese Attributes and modernizing China's system and capacity for governance. Xi Jinping stressed that the Chinese government should be results-oriented and pioneering, that empty talk is harmful to the nation, while practical jobs can help it thrive. The Chinese government must start with specific things and ensure their implementation. These remarks may help outsiders understand why the marvelous "China speed" and "China projects" are frequently produced in the new era.

Since 2012, Xi Jinping has visited various parts of China, going deep into the grassroots to investigate and guide economic and social development and reform and opening up, visiting factories, villages, communities, ports, schools, and schools barracks. Sometimes, he had to reach high mountains several thousand meters above sea level. Sometimes, to get to a village, he got off the plane, changed to a train, and took a bus. He sometimes pulled up his trouser legs and held up an umbrella to communicate with the people when it was raining during the visit. A few years ago, he launched the strategy for developing the Yangtze River Economic Belt. In 2019, he visited Henan Province and proposed a strategy for ecological protection and high-quality development of the Yellow River Basin. The two river basins of China present new energy in the new era. Xi Jinping designed a more market-oriented reform program for state-owned enterprises and encouraged private companies to take their stakes. He remarked that private businesses and entrepreneurs are also inseparable country members at the symposium on private enterprises. One of the most frequently mentioned concepts by Xi Jinping is "innovation". Xi believes that begging alms will not get the core and critical technology.

In 2019, Xi Jinping visited Dunhuang and gave new instructions on preserving and developing culture. He frequently stated that cultural confidence is a more fundamental, broader and deeper confidence. He has led the reform of Party and state institutions, working to create more efficient and modern government agencies. The Chinese government has cut administrative approvals by a third in the past few years. Online approvals and "one-stop" services have been implemented in many places, so enterprises do not need to get their documents sealed for months. Xi Jinping advocates comprehensive law-based governance. He stressed the importance of understanding that the negative impact of a misjudged case can destroy the positive image accumulated by 99 fair decisions. The reform of the justice system is being carried out by exercising judicial and procuratorial powers independently and impartially according to the law, improving the mechanism for the operation of judicial power, and perfecting the judicial protection of human rights. In terms of ecological environment, he launched the famous concept of temperate waters and lush mountains. Xi Jinping personally delivered the instrument of ratification of the Paris Agreement on climate change to the UN Secretary-General. The effectiveness of "Green China" has been recognized and praised worldwide. Many cities have seen significant reductions in pollution. Xi proposed to promote the synergistic development of the Beijing-Tianjin-Hebei region and create the Xiong'an New Area. The China (Shanghai) Pilot Free Trade Zone, established in 2013, has been a success, and now the number of pilot free trade zones has grown to 18, with the entire area of Hainan Island to be built as a pilot free trade zone. Xi also announced the further opening of industries ranging from banking to automobiles.

Since the advent of the new era, China's investment environment has been continuously improving. According to the World Bank's report Doing Business 2019: Training for Reform, China jumped from 78th to 46th place in the Doing Business rankings. The Chinese market is growing in size. Data show that it is closing in on becoming the world's largest consumer market. China's Ministry of Commerce in August 2018 announced that more than 24,000 new foreign-invested enterprises were established in China in the first seven months of that year. The actual foreign investment exceeded RMB 530 billion, up 7.3% yearly. Xi Jinping attended the world's first import-themed expo in Shanghai, where he referred to "openness" 52 times in his 35-minute speech. The turnover of the Expo was encouraging. More businesses from different countries signed up for the second China International Import Expo. In 2018, Xi Jinping revisited Shenzhen when it celebrated its 40th anniversary of reform and opening-up to tell the world that China will not stop its reform and opening-up. He addressed that China will undoubtedly deliver a bigger miracle that draws worldwide attention (Yang et al., 2018).

As China moves into a new era and people's living standards continue to rise, people's demand for law-based governance grows. The CPC must continue to improve law-based governance to meet the growing needs of the people for a better life. Xi stated the need to actively advance legislation in national security, science and technology innovation, public health, biosecurity, ecological civilization, risk prevention, and foreign-related law-based governance. The Chinese government should improve the legal system urgently needed for national governance and the legal system necessary to meet people's growing demand for a better life (Zhang, 2021).

In recent years, Xi Jinping has positioned, laid out and practiced the law-based governance from a global and strategic perspective of adhering to and developing socialism with Chinese Attributes. He creatively introduced new concepts, ideas, and strategies on comprehensive law-based governance, resulting in Xi Jinping's Thought on the Rule of Law. Xi emphasized that since the people make up the broadest and most profound foundation for comprehensively advancing law-based governance, the Chinese government must ensure that their interests and wishes are reflected, their rights are protected, and their well-being enhanced. The Chinese government should strengthen legislation in key areas, including public health and ecological civilization, all of which are of vital interest to the people (Yang, 2021).

Xi attaches great importance to the critical role of law in governing the country, permanently adheres to the people as the center, and clarifies the prominent position of the people in law-based governance. Given that China is a socialist country where the people are the masters, the Chinese government must always prioritize the interests of the people and safeguard the principal status of the people, which is the primary embodiment of the people-centered nature of Xi Jinping Thought on the Rule of Law (He, 2021). People's procuratorates and public security organs at all levels adhere to Xi Jinping Thought on Socialism with Chinese Attributes for a New Era as a guide, fully implement Xi Jinping Thought on the Rule of Law, and adhere to the principle of division of labor, cooperation and mutual restraint. Moreover, they should continue to deepen the investigation supervision and cooperation mechanism, punish all kinds of crimes under the law, and provide a solid law-based guarantee to maintain social stability, promote social fairness and justice, and protect people's happiness.

The practical actions of public security officers practiced Xi Jinping Thought on the Rule of Law. In January 2021, Xi Jinping gave essential instructions on celebrating the 100th anniversary of the founding of the Communist Party of China by building a safer China, enhancing law-based governance in China, securing people's happiness, and enhancing national security and social stability (Zhu et al., 2021). It has sparked a warm reaction in all sectors of society, especially in the political and legal system. Xi underlined that 2021 is the start of the "14th Five-Year Plan", and political and legal organs should conscientiously implement the instructions of the Fifth Plenary Session of the 19th CPC Central Committee and the central work conference the rule of law. They should also pay more attention to the rule of law and effectively promote high-quality political and legal work development.

Xi Jinping pointed out that the public security forces are the most sacrificed during peacetime, with outstanding contributions. The Chinese government should extend particular care to this special team, with political care, work support and welfare, and fully implement measures to treat the police preferably at all times. According to statistics, since the founding of the People's s Republic of China, more than 16,000 police officers have lost their lives in the line of duty, of whom more than 3,700 were awarded as martyrs. Three thousand seven hundred seventy-three police officers died on duty in the past ten years, and more than 50,000 police officers were injured. He stated, "Over the years, I was deeply touched when learning about the heartfelt needs of the public security officers and heartbroken when I heard the public security officers sacrificed their lives in the frontline. Xi Jinping's loving care has greatly inspired the people's police forces to better the critical mission entrusted by the Communist Party of China and the people. The efforts of the public security officers demonstrate the people-oriented thought on the rule of law, and Xi Jinping's condolences on these officers manifest his emphasis on the comprehensive rule of law. It accurately depicts Xi Jinping's thoughts on the Rule of Law.

Serve the People and People's Happiness

Every day in 2019, 16,500 new enterprises were registered in China, and about 40,000 people were newly employed in urban areas. Over the past seven years, more than 80 million new jobs have been created in China's cities and towns, which is equivalent to the population of Germany. Xi Jinping said, "Employment is the most important livelihood." The emerging economy formats, such as e-commerce, have resulted in outstanding jobs. Xi Jinping has been highly encouraging and encouraging in this regard. He once came across a group of couriers in a Beijing hutong and expressed his condolences for their hard work. China now has the world's largest courier industry, with more than 3 million couriers. In his New Year's greeting for 2018, Xi indicates that he was aware of the people's biggest concerns, such as education, employment, income, social security, healthcare, old-age security, housing and the environment. Since becoming General Secretary, Xi Jinping has been with the people every year at the Chinese New Year. He visited the struggling workers in the border town in the cold of -30°C, delivered New Year's goods to the villagers at his own expense, made Ciba with the people, and stuck the Chinese character "福" on the doors of the residents' houses. He expressed concern about whether poor farmers have enough food to eat, have medical care coverage, and whether their children can go to school. The principal contradiction of Chinese society has been transformed into the contradiction between the people's growing need for a better life and unbalanced and insufficient development (Xu & Zhang, 2018). The significant assertion made by Xi Jinping in the report of the 19th CPC National Congress embodies his scientific and accurate judgment and grasp of the national conditions and people's opinions.

Xi Jinping repeatedly stated that the purpose of the CCP is to serve the people wholeheartedly (Qu, 2019). It also reflects Xi Jinping's personal experience and will. He went to the poor countryside in Shaanxi Province before he was 16 years old to settle in the communes and lived in labor for seven years. He wanted most for his fellow villagers to have a full meat meal. He said he came from a poverty-stricken village, and he well understood the people's hardships. For a while, housing prices in China were soaring. Xi Jinping warned that houses are for the living, not for speculation. He added that cities could not be filled with high-rise buildings and dirty shantytowns on the other side. In 2018, China's urban areas' per capita housing floor area reached 39 square meters, up 3.7 times from 8.3 square meters in 1949. Housing security efforts have enabled about 200 million people in need to live in peace.

Xi Jinping has taken people's affairs very seriously. During his visits to the grassroots, he repeatedly inspected the toilets of ordinary people's houses and instructed them to sort garbage properly. During a visit to a village in Henan Province, he proposed modernizing and facilitating living facilities to take a hot bath. He also gave instructions on the high incidence of myopia among students. China's social security system was a complete blank a few decades ago. By 2019, China has achieved full basic medical insurance and pension insurance coverage for more than 900 million people, forming the world's largest social security network. In 2013, Xi Jinping proposed the concept of "targeted poverty alleviation" to thoroughly eliminate absolute rural poverty under the current standards by 2020. He set the goal of eliminating absolute poverty in rural areas by 2020 under current standards, ten years ahead of the time set by the United Nations to eradicate absolute poverty globally. More than 82 million people have been lifted out of poverty in seven years. Xi Jinping said, "the Chinese government will have brought to an end, once and for all, the extreme poverty that has shackled the Chinese nation for millennia in this generation (Chen, 2020)."

According to Kishore Mahbubani, a professor at the National University of Singapore, the most remarkable achievement of China is the substantial improvement in the living standards of Chinese people (Xu, 2018). Even at its best time in Chinese civilization, many lower classes still lived in poverty. Even those with low incomes enjoy access to better food, accommodation, education, health care, and employment in today's China. Xi Jinping is living up to his promise: "Love the people as I love my parents." At the first session of the 13th National People's Congress of China in March 2018, Xi Jinping was re-elected president, winning the unanimous support of nearly 3,000 NPC members.

At the 19th CPC National Congress, the strategic arrangement was proposed to secure a decisive victory in building a moderately prosperous society and achieving China's second centenary goal in two stages. Based on this, Xi Jinping explicitly outlined the objectives and tasks of implementing the rural revitalization strategy. Rural revitalization strategy insists on prioritizing the development of agriculture and rural areas. Its objectives are to establish and improve the institutional mechanism and policy system for integrated development of urban and rural areas and accelerate the modernization of agriculture and rural areas by the general requirements of prosperous industry, pleasant ecology, civilized countryside, effective governance and wealthy living. The Chinese government should start from seven aspects to implement the rural revitalization strategy.

First, the Chinese government should reshape the relationship between urban and rural areas and take the integrated development of urban and rural areas. Secondly, the Chinese government should consolidate and improve the basic rural management system and take the path of shared prosperity. Thirdly, the Chinese government should deepen the structural reform on the supply side of agriculture and take the road of flourishing agriculture with quality. Fourthly, the Chinese government should adhere to the harmonious coexistence of man and nature and take the road of green development in the countryside. Fifthly, the Chinese government should inherit, develop and enhance the farming civilization, and take the road of rural cultural prosperity. Sixthly, the Chinese government should innovate the rural governance system and take the road of good governance in the countryside. Seventhly, the Chinese government should do its best for targeted poverty elimination and take the road of poverty reduction with Chinese Attributes.

From March 29 to April 1, 2020, Xi Jinping stressed during his visit to Zhejiang province that building China into a modernized socialist country in all aspects requires both urban modernization and agricultural and rural modernization. The Chinese government should make more significant efforts to promote rural revitalization throughout the countryside. It is also vital to advance and strengthen the rural economy, the rural rule of law, rural culture, rural governance, rural ecology and party construction, and enable villagers to live a better life. On September 18, 2020, Xi Jinping stressed during an inspection tour in Hunan province to adhere to the prioritization of agriculture and rural areas and drive the implementation of the rural revitalization strategy. He added that the departments concerned should guarantee food security, steadily raise grain output, implement the responsibility system for arable land protection, cultivate more high-standard farmland, and curb illegal arable land appropriation.

Moreover, the government should deepen the structural reform on the supply side of agriculture, cultivate and grow advantageous industries according to local conditions, and promote the integrated development of primary, secondary and tertiary industries in rural areas. The government should deepen agricultural and rural reforms to activate the endogenous power of rural revitalization. Also, it is necessary to implement the principle of insisting on responsibility, support, policies and supervision even after poverty is eliminated. It should also establish a sound long-term mechanism to avoid falling back into poverty and conduct an in-depth study to promote the compelling connection between comprehensive poverty elimination and rural revitalization (Hu, 2021). Since the introduction of the rural revitalization strategy, Xi Jinping has visited and inspected various parts of China, thoroughly investigating the situation of poor villages and continuously exploring and practicing, putting forward the vital idea of targeted poverty alleviation. He commanded the CPC and the whole country to win the battle against poverty, laying a solid foundation for further rural revitalization and setting a new milestone in Chinese history.

Removing the label of extreme poverty is not the end but the beginning of a new life and a new journey. In the grand gathering held in Beijing to mark the country's accomplishments in poverty alleviation and honor its model poverty fighters, Xi Jinping emphasized that the Chinese have no reason to be complacent and rest on their laurels. They must move forward, make further efforts and continue the struggle, and inspire the cadres and masses to make new achievements in building a modern socialist country in all aspects and realizing China's second centenary goal. Also, at the grand gathering, Xi Jinping pointed out that rural revitalization is a significant task to rejuvenate the Chinese nation (Zhang, 2021).

According to the new requirements arising from the new development concept and patterns in the new era, the Communist Party of China should prioritize the three issues of agriculture, the countryside and farmers. It should adhere to the prioritization of agriculture and rural areas, follow the road of socialist rural revitalization with Chinese Attributes, and continue its efforts to narrow the gap between urban and rural areas. In this way, the low-income population and the less developed regions can share the fruits of development and not fall behind in the modernization process but catch up (Li, 2021). In 2021, Xi Jinping repeatedly researched and spoke about rural revitalization, emphasizing the comprehensive implementation of the rural revitalization strategy. There will be no national rejuvenation without a thriving countryside—Xi Jinping's affirmation of the importance of the rural revitalization strategy.

Community with a Shared Future for Mankind

In 2014, the number of Chinese outbound travelers exceeded 100 million for the first time, and China's foreign direct investment exceeded $120 billion, bringing two-way direct investment closer to balance for the first time. Thousands of Chinese people are working, studying, and living worldwide. It has become a standard statement that China is moving closer to its center stage. The relationship between China and the world in the new era is a significant issue facing Chinese leaders (Liu, 2019). Nearly 20 years ago, when Xi Jinping was the governor of Fujian Province, he promoted a demonstration project of mycorrhiza and upland rice cultivation technology in the Eastern Highlands Province of Papua New Guinea. Mycorrhizal projects with sand control, livestock rising, power generation, and new material development have spread to more than 100 countries, making it possible for developing countries in Africa, Asia, and the South Pacific to alleviate poverty.

In November 2018, during his visit to Papua New Guinea, Xi Jinping witnessed the official signing of a package of agreements on China's assistance to PNG for mycorrhiza and upland rice technology. This event reflects Xi's desire and thinking about the international relations he wants to build. There should be mutual respect, fairness and justice, and win-win cooperation between countries as he sees it. In March 2013, during his first trip to Moscow after assuming the presidency, Xi Jinping elaborated on the concept of a community with a shared future for humankind and new types of international relations at the Moscow Institute of International Relations (Liu, 2021). Two years later, Xi Jinping delivered his first speech from the UN rostrum, comprehensively illustrating the primary meaning of a community with a shared future for humankind. Later, he further elaborated on building a world free from fear and universally safe, free from poverty and universally prosperous, free from closed doors and open and inclusive, clean and beautiful in all its landscapes (Chen, 2019)." The Belt and Road Initiative, proposed by Xi Jinping, is a platform for facilitating a community with a shared future for humankind. This ambitious idea connects continents and oceans with trade and investment.

Contrary to the "misgivings" of some Westerners, its aim is simply to "integrate more countries and regions into economic globalization, and to work together to create a mutually beneficial and win-win path." By the end of July this year, China has signed 194 cooperation documents with 136 countries and 30 international organizations to construct the Belt and Road. According to a study released by the World Bank in June, the full implementation of The Belt and Road Initiative could lift 32 million people out of moderate poverty, increase global trade by 6.2%, increase trade of economies along the route by 9.7%, and increase global income by 2.9%. "Diplomacy as host" has become a shining "business card" in the new era. China has hosted various events, from APEC in Beijing, the Fourth Summit of the Conference on Interaction and Confidence-Building Measures in Shanghai China, the G20 Summit in Hangzhou, the BRICS Leaders' Meeting in Xiamen, the SCO Summit in Qingdao and the Boao Forum for Asia, the two Belt and Road Summits on International Cooperation, the Beijing Summit of the Forum on China-Africa Cooperation, the International Horticultural Exhibition and the Conference on Dialogue of Asian Civilizations. It marked China's emergence as a hub for discussing global governance and development. In presiding over these events, Xi Jinping told, in a personal way, the story of how China's development has allowed countries to "take a free ride" in a personal and engaging way. He explained the true meaning of a shared future for humankind. He proposed to accelerate the innovation and perfection of the global governance system based on extended consultation, joint contribution, and shared benefits (Su, 2019).

China has become a vital force in addressing global and regional hotspots ranging from climate change, anti-terrorism, nuclear proliferation, the gap between rich and poor, fair trade and peacekeeping in war. Many Chinese have served as the principal heads of international organizations such as the Food and Agriculture Organization of the United Nations, contributing more Chinese wisdom to promote global governance on related issues. The Chinese currency, Renminbi, was eligible for joining the International Monetary Fund's Special Drawing Rights (SDR) currency basket. The Asian Infrastructure Investment Bank and the Silk Road Fund were also created.

In 2019, China became the second-largest contributor to the United Nations after the United States. It is also one of the major contributors to UN peacekeeping operations and the most significant contributor of troops among the Security Council's permanent members. China's China-UN Peace and Development Fund, established for ten years with one billion USD, was officially launched in 2016. China has contributed more than 30 percent to world economic growth. It has also steadily resolved the subsistence problems of more than one billion people and contributed more than 70 percent to global poverty reduction, which the World Bank has called "one of the most extraordinary events in human history. China's development experience and model have expanded avenues of modernization for developing countries (Zheng, 2021). Xi Jinping said that the Communist Party of China has always made its mission to make new and more outstanding contributions to humankind (Zhang & Kong, 2018). Contributing to humanity is the vision of the Communists.

Fight for a Great Dream and Power of China

The Chinese word douzheng (struggle) appeared nearly 60 times in his speech at the Party School of the Central Committee of the Communist Party of China (National Academy of Governance) in September 2019, when Xi Jinping delivered the speech at the opening ceremony of a training program for younger officials. He stresses that the rejuvenation of the Chinese nation will not be easily achieved, so the Chinese government should struggle to achieve the great dream. Xi Jinping's sense of struggle can be traced back to when he went to the countryside in Liangjiahe and became a production team member. The hardships of that time have sharpened him into an unyielding and courageous person. Xi Jinping said that the Chinese government's risks and tests would get more complicated, to the extent that it may encounter unimaginable storms (Yan, 2019).

Xi Jinping viewed the fight against corruption as a life-and-death duel. This fight started with corruption and anti-corruption opposing in a stalemate. Then an overwhelming anti-corruption situation began to take shape and was then developed, and finally, a victory was achieved. He led the whole Party and the whole nation to cope with the economic downturn challenges turn with his sobriety and wisdom. He launched three significant campaigns to guard against and defuse major risks, eradicate poverty in a targeted manner, and prevent and control pollution. And he proposed strategies such as the "new normal of economic development," "new development concept," and "supply-side structural reform" to promote high-quality economic development (Lan, 2021).

At the time of the China-US economic and trade frictions, China does not want a trade war, but it is not afraid of one and will fight one if necessary under the deployment of Xi Jinping (Guan, 2019). He met with President Trump in Buenos Aires and Osaka to take a significant step forward in resolving economic and trade frictions between the two countries. On the issue of Hong Kong, Xi pointed out that if Hong Kong were to fall into the whirlpool of "pan-politicization," artificial confrontation and rivalry would be created. It would serve no useful purpose and seriously hamper economic growth and social development. When he met with the new Chief Executive of the Macao SAR, he pointed out that the "one country, two systems" policy has proved feasible, workable, and supports the people. He requested an appropriate policy of "two systems" for Taiwan to advance the peaceful resolution of the Taiwan question for the complete reunification of China. The Chinese government makes no promise to renounce force and reserve the option of taking all necessary means. This does not target compatriots in Taiwan, but the interference of external forces and the minimal number of "Taiwan independence" separatists and their activities (Wu, 2019).

Xi Jinping has taken a bold step to reform the national defense and military, firmly establishing combat effectiveness as the only fundamental standard. It has become one of the military's missions to protect China's interests abroad in the new era. Amid unrest in West Asia and North Africa, Xi Jinping directed the evacuation of overseas Chinese. The movie based on it set a record at the Chinese box office. In a recent article, Foreign Affairs magazine wrote, "He is among the more assertive when defending interests." According to Xi, the various struggles the Chinese government face are not short-term but long-term and must accompany us for at least the entire process of achieving the second-century goal. He led the ruling team with a deep insight into the complexities and changes of the outside world and a clear understanding that China is still the world's largest developing country. In May 2019, Xi Jinping came to Yudu County in Jiangxi Province, the starting point of the Central Red Army's Long March, and called on people to walk solidly on the new Long March. In the 1930s, the Chinese Workers' and Peasants' Red Army fought a 25,000-mile march against harsh nature, heavy enemy siege and the Party's erroneous line, and eventually achieved revolutionary victory at great sacrifice. In the eyes of the Chinese Communists, all the hard work was done to achieve their glorious and sacred purpose.

At the end of 2019, a sudden epidemic swept the world. China's central government quickly decreed the city's lockdown, effectively curbing its spread and winning the initiative. In this battle, the people's power was united. Xi Jinping pointed out that the Chinese people empowered the government to overcome the epidemic. In the darkest moments of the epidemic, countless ordinary people stepped forward, and the love from the ordinary people lit up the land. In the face of the COVID-19 pandemic, Xi Jinping repeatedly emphasized the need to be determined to fight and win the battle against the epidemic by mobilizing all resources; and blocking the spread of the virus (Wang et al., 2020). It answers the questions of who and how to fight against the

COVID-19 pandemic and what to do, fully reflecting Xi Jinping's high positioning, accurate grasp, and strong determination to prevent and control the epidemic and his superior strategic wisdom (Wang, 2020).

In the prevention and control of the epidemic, Xi Jinping took the overall picture and carried out timely and effective social mobilization, unleashing the governance effectiveness of China's socialist system. The Chinese have made a significant contribution to the world's public health, fully demonstrating the institutional advantages of socialism with Chinese Attributes and Chinese wisdom in building a community with a shared future for humankind (Wang, 2021). It is essential to be mentally prepared and ready to work for a prolonged period to deal with changes in the external environment. Xi Jinping pointed out that China should strengthen strategic, systematic and forward-looking research and planning, cultivate new opportunities in crises, open up new situations in changes, and adjust its strategies of struggle in time according to the changes in the situation. In a sense, it will be a protracted battle (Ruan, 2021).

In July 2021, some provinces and regions in China were flooded in emergencies. Xi Jinping gave essential instructions on flood control and disaster relief work. Xi stressed that authorities must always put people's safety and property first and take the lead in fighting the floods. He ordered authorities to organize flood prevention and disaster relief forces promptly, adequately accommodate those affected, strictly prevent secondary disasters, and minimize casualties and property losses. Party committees and governments at all levels earnestly implemented the spirit of Xi Jinping's important instructions. In the spirit of extreme responsibility for the people, they assumed the political responsibility to promote the development of an area, ensure its security, and fully exercise the principal responsibility for flood control and disaster relief. They adopted more vigorous measures to strengthen organizational leadership and responsibility for the implementation and effectively undertake the work of flood control and disaster relief, resolutely to do their duty of guarding the land. The CPC members and cadres moved towards the flood, the people's soldiers came to the rescue. The firefighters made every effort, the people in the affected areas joined together, the volunteers stood firm on the front line, and countless people expressed their concern. In the face of the grim flood control situation, the entire country quickly gathered a potent force for flood control and disaster relief.

Ecological Civilization and Beautiful China

Since the 18th CPC National Congress, the CPC Central Committee has incorporated the construction of ecological civilization into the overall layout of socialism with Chinese Attributes. In advancing the construction of ecological civilization, it has developed the Xi Jinping Thought on Ecological Civilization. This thought has facilitated understanding the laws of nature and human social development (Li, 2021). On October 18, 2017, Xi Jinping emphasized in the 19th CPC National Congress report that man and nature are a community of life. Humans must respect nature, conform to nature, and protect nature. The construction of ecological civilization is credited to the current generation and benefits thousands of years. The Chinese government should firmly establish the socialist concept of ecological civilization, promote the formation of a new pattern of modernization for the harmonious development of man and nature, and make this generation's efforts to protect the ecological environment!

On September 18, 2019, Xi Jinping presided over a symposium on the Yellow River basin's ecological protection and high-quality development in Henan Province and delivered his keynote speech. He explicitly proposed that the protection of the Yellow River is critical to the great rejuvenation and sustainable development of the Chinese nation (Zhang, 2021). Subsequently, Xi hosted the symposium on promoting the development of the Yangtze River Economic Belt in Chongqing, the symposium on further promoting the development of the Yangtze River Economic Belt in Wuhan and the symposium on comprehensively promoting the development of the Yangtze River Economic Belt in Nanjing. These symposiums were designated to promote the 11 provinces and cities along the Yangtze River to make concerted efforts to control pollution and repair ecosystems. He stressed the need to take care of global protection, not engage in large-scale development, and take a new path of ecological priority and green development. The water quality of the Yangtze River is getting better and better.

Xi draws a long-term picture in his mind, and he has continued to promote ecological development. He has also been committed to deploying the development of the Yangtze River Belt with general protection without large-scale development works, promoting ecological protection and high-quality development in the Yellow River Basin, removing illegal villas and repairing ecological damage in the northern Qinling Mountains in Shaanxi Province, and accelerating the construction of nature reserve systems centered on national parks. During his visit to Beijing and Hebei from January 18 to 19, 2021, he pointed out that China will continuously promote sustainable development and fully implement the UN 2030 Agenda for Sustainable Development. The Chinese government will accelerate the construction of ecological civilization, adjust and optimize the industrial and energy structures, and promote a green and low-carbon production and lifestyle. China will strive to reach peak CO2 emissions by 2030 and achieve carbon neutrality by 2060.

On January 25, 2021, at the World Economic Forum Virtual Event of the Davos Agenda, Xi Jinping emphasized that China should uphold the concept that lucid waters and lush mountains are invaluable assets and prioritize ecosystem conservation for an environmentally friendly development model (Han, 2020). During his visit to Qinghai from June 7 to 9, 2021, Xi Jinping proposed that China should respect, respond to, and protect nature and build a green home together in the face of the fragile ecological environment. In the face of the severe challenges climate change poses to human survival and development, the Chinese government should take up the responsibility and work together to find a way to harmoniously coexist with nature (Wang et al., 2021).

At the same time, the concept of "a community with a shared future for mankind" proposed by President Xi Jinping has become increasingly influential in the international community. The concept of "a community with a shared future for mankind" aims to give proper consideration to the legitimate concerns of other countries while pursuing national interests and promoting the common development of all countries in the pursuit of national development. Humanity has only one Earth, and all countries share one world, and we need to promote the awareness of a community with a shared future for humankind. Humans should respect each other, non-human life, and inanimate objects (Liao et al., 2021).

Conclusion

In leading the Chinese people to realize the Chinese Dream, Xi Jinping, with profound insight, keen judgment and strategic determination as a Marxist statesman and theorist, has proposed some groundbreaking new ideas, thoughts and strategies. Xi Jinping Thought on Socialism with Chinese Attributes for a New Era, which originates from and guides practice, contains rich connotations and encompasses all aspects of the economy, politics, ecological civilization, national defense and military construction.

The core of Xi Jinping's theory of socialism with Chinese Attributes is to adhere to the people's desire for a better life as the goal of struggle, to make a better life for the people as the starting and ending point of all work, and to always speak for the people, to stand up for the people. It fully embodies the concept of governing for the people, the mission of working for the happiness of the Chinese people and the rejuvenation of the Chinese nation, and the value of pursuing the people first.

Xi Jinping's approach to governance has a strong contemporary flavor and practical relevance. He has insight into the times, grasps the trend of the times, leads the trend of the times from the forefront of human development, actively explores the significant issues related to the future and destiny of humankind, and contributes Chinese wisdom and Chinese solutions to the global challenges facing the world today and to the common problems facing humankind. The entry of socialism with Chinese Attributes into the new era is the fruit of the epochal changes that have taken place under Xi Jinping's outstanding leadership and the result of the long and ongoing struggle of the Chinese people.

Chapter 3
Xi Jinping's Socialist Economic Thoughts

Chinese theorists have been actively interpreting and theorizing Xi Jinping's Socialist Economic Thoughts in its formation and evolution in recent years. They unanimously agree that as an economic thinker, Xi Jinping has comprehensively comprehended the world's development trends and profoundly summarized the experiences and lessons of economic and social development in China and abroad. Moreover, Xi proposed some new concepts, ideas and strategies for the country's governance systematically and comprehensively, starting from the significant issues and practices of economic development of socialism with Chinese Attributes in the new era. Ultimately, Xi Jinping introduced his thoughts on China's economic development, offering a far-sighted vision of China's economic reform and development practice in the new era. Moreover, historic achievements have been facilitated in economic and social development. This study provides a systematic and comprehensive overview of Xi Jinping's economic thinking among the Chinese theorists. It will introduce Xi Jinping's Socialist Economic Thoughts to foreign theorists to provide guidance and reference to other developing countries' economic and social development.

Introduction

In recent years, scholars in the academia of economic theories in China have extensively discussed the economic thoughts of Xi Jinping, the leader of China. They unanimously agree that as an economic thinker, Xi Jinping has comprehensively comprehended the world's development trends and profoundly summarized the experiences and lessons of economic and social development in China and abroad. Moreover, Xi proposed some new concepts, ideas and strategies for the country's governance systematically and comprehensively, starting from the significant issues and practices of economic development of socialism with Chinese Attributes in the new era. Ultimately, Xi Jinping introduced his thoughts on China's economic development, offering a far-sighted vision of China's economic reform and development practice in the new era. Moreover, historic achievements have been facilitated in economic and social development. Since the COVID-19 pandemic, Xi Jinping has coordinated the implementation of the strategies for the great rejuvenation of the Chinese nation and taken measures in response to the substantial changes unseen in a century in the world. With superb leadership capabilities, steadfast political conviction and perseverance, Xi has led China to secure the stable, sustainable and healthy development of its economy and society, further enriching and developing Xi Jinping's Socialist Economic Thoughts in practice (Bai, 2021).

Chinese theorists have been actively engaged in interpreting and theorizing on Xi Jinping's Socialist Economic Thoughts in its formation and development. They have made remarkable progress in both breadth and depth of research. By reviewing these research results, we can understand the core meaning and essence of Xi Jinping's Socialist Economic Thoughts and identify its spiritual significance and value pursuit to know more about the inner logic of China's rapid economic development in recent years. In 2017, on behalf of the Communist Party of China, Xi Jinping made a critical judgment that China has ushered in a new era of socialism with Chinese Attributes (Ren & Xiao, 2021). Chinese experts and scholars have interpreted the call of a new era for new economic thinking from different perspectives. The new era calls for new theories, guiding new practices. Socialism with Chinese Attributes into a new era constitutes the prerequisite for Xi Jinping's Socialist Economic Thoughts and its most extraordinary development.

First, from the perspective of the change of the principal contradiction of Chinese society: In the new era, the principal contradiction of Chinese society has been transformed into the gap between unbalanced and inadequate development and the people's growing expectation for a better life. The development between regions, cities, rural areas and industries is still unbalanced, and the quality, efficiency and driving force of development need to be changed and improved. A group of new contradictions, problems and challenges arising in economic development desperately needs new ideas as answers and solutions.

Second, from the perspective of the changing stage of economic development: The new era means that China's economy has shifted from the stage of high-speed growth to the stage of high-quality development. In the high-quality development stage, the focus is more on better meeting the growing needs of the people for a better life. New issues are emerging in the new stage, and new theories are needed to lead the way.

Third, from the perspective of a heavy burden of building China into a leading modernized country: In the new era, the Chinese nation has made a great leap from standing up, getting wealthy to strengthening itself, and it has become a realistic goal to build China into a leading modernized country. It should be supported by a new economic development model and guided by a new development philosophy.

Fourth, from a problem-oriented perspective: The international community is becoming complicated, severe and ever-changing, and today's world is undergoing substantial changes unseen in a century. Given the significant global problems and challenges in world governance, China is expected to play a more significant role and contribute its wisdom and strength. While China has made outstanding economic and social development achievements, it has also encountered new problems and challenges. Scholars believe that Xi Jinping's Socialist Economic Thoughts is, in a sense, the solution to the problems of the times and a new interpretation and answer to the eternal theme of "development" in the new era (Zou & Han, 2021). This study systematically and comprehensively introduces Chinese scholars' theoretical research on Xi Jinping's Socialist Economic Thoughts to the international theoretical community.

Main Content of Xi Jinping's Socialist Economic Thoughts

Before Xi Jinping's Socialist Economic Thoughts on Socialism with Chinese Attributes for a New Era was officially introduced, scholars used "Xi Jinping's Important Discourse on Economic Work" and "Xi Jinping's Economic Strategic Thought" more frequently. After Xi Jinping presented the concept of "new normal" during his visit to Henan in 2017, some scholars have taken the "new economic normal" as an essential aspect of research (Wu, 2018).

In October 2015, the Fifth Plenary Session of the 18th Communist Party of China Central Committee adopted The Proposal of the Communist Party of China Central Committee for Formulating the 13th Five-Year Blueprint for China's Economic and Social Development, introducing the concept of innovative, coordinated, green, open and shared development. At the speech delivered at the second complete assembly of the Fifth Plenary Session of the 18th Communist Party of China, Xi Jinping pointed out that philosophies yield actions and that the development is a strategic, programmatic and leading idea, manifesting the thinking, direction and focus of the development. Xi Jinping has scientifically explained the logical relationship between the five development concepts: innovative development focuses on solving the problem of development drivers; coordinated development focuses on solving the problem of unbalanced development; green development focuses on solving the problem of harmony between human beings and nature; open development focuses on solving the problem of internal and external linkage of development; and shared development focuses on solving the problem of social equity and justice. In several vital speeches afterward, Xi Jinping emphasized that the new development philosophy is a profound change concerning the overall situation of China's development (Deng, 2021).

The Economic Work Conference of the Central Committee of the Communist Party of China held in December 2017 pointed out that China's economic development has been successfully managed by adhering to the general situation, planning the overall situation and undertaking pragmatic work. Furthermore, Xi Jinping's Socialist

Economic Thoughts on Socialism with Chinese Attributes for a New Era has been formed in practice with the new development philosophy as its primary content. China's top leadership first introduced the concept of Xi Jinping's Socialist Economic Thoughts. It is also specific to one area in Xi Jinping's Thought on Socialism with Chinese Attributes for a New Era, fully demonstrating the importance of Xi Jinping's Socialist Economic Thoughts. It was noted that Xi Jinping's Socialist Economic Thoughts takes the new development philosophy as the main content and emphasizes seven insistences. It should adhere to the centralized and unified leadership of the Communist Party of China on economic work to ensure that China's economy develops on the right track. Adhering to the people-centered development ideology, the Chinese government will coordinate the Five-Sphere Integrated Plan and the Four-Pronged Comprehensive Strategy. The Five-sphere Integrated Plan refers to China's overall plan for building socialism with Chinese Attributes. This plan is designed to promote coordinated progress in the economic, political, cultural, social and eco-environmental fields. The Four-pronged Comprehensive Strategy refers to China's strategic plan for building socialism with Chinese Attributes. It is designed to make comprehensive moves to complete a moderately prosperous society in all respects, further reform, advance the rule of law, and strengthen Party self-governance.

China should adapt to the new normal of economic development, identify the developmental laws based on the overall situation, and allow the market to play a decisive role in allocating resources. The role of the government should be brought to better play, and the institutional obstacles to economic development should be thoroughly removed.

A new strategy for economic development should be deployed in a problem-oriented manner, with far-reaching implications for transforming China's economic and social development. It should adhere to the proper working strategies and methods, prioritize stability while pursuing progress, maintain strategic resolve, think about worst-case scenarios, and move forward (Qiao & Zhang, 2021).

Moreover, it should consistently adapt to the changes in the main contradictions in China's economic development, improve macro-control, make the right choices, and make the supply-side structural reform the main task of economic work.

Chinese economic theorists summarize Xi Jinping's Socialist Economic Thoughts in two aspects. One is "1+7", where the number "1" refers to the new development philosophy, and "7" refers to the seven insistences. The other is directly summarized as the seven insistences. Most scholars hold the former view, and many discussions fall within this range, although from different perspectives. In addition to the new development philosophy and the seven insistences, many scholars have reviewed the theoretical judgments and strategic plans related to the general situation of China's economic development. They argue that the following assertions are also essential components of Xi Jinping's Socialist Economic Thoughts (He & Ye, 2021).

First, it involves the theory of the primary stage of socialism. The basic economic system of socialism with public ownership is the mainstay, and multiple ownership economies develop together. The distribution system according to labor is dominated, supplemented by multiple distribution methods. The socialist market economy system is adopted. It is an essential pillar of the socialist system with Chinese Attributes and the foundation of the socialist market economy system.

Second, it insists on integrating development and security. It upholds a holistic approach to national security to strengthen the national security system and capacity building. Also, it reinforces national economic security and incorporates security development into all areas and processes of national development, thus preventing and resolving various risks and challenges affecting China's modernization.

Third, it promotes high-quality development, which is economical and social development in the new era. High-quality development is a general requirement for all aspects of economic and social development. The new development philosophy should be reflected in many aspects, such as supply, demand, input and output, distribution, and macroeconomic cycle, to meet the people's growing needs for a better life.

Fourth, it builds a modern economic system, which is the strategic goal of China's development. China should build a coordinated industrial system dominated by innovations and an urban-rural regional development system that highlights its advantages and coordinates. Besides, it should establish a diversified and balanced, safe and efficient system for all-round opening up, a unified and open, competitive and orderly market system. An income distribution system that manifests efficiency and promotes fairness, a resource-saving and environment-friendly green development system, and an economic system that entirely plays the role of the market and better plays the role of the government should be established. These systems are a unified whole, and they should be developed and advanced as one.

Fifth, it promotes the supply-side structural reform, which is the main task of economic work for the current and a long-term period in the future. The general requirement of promoting supply-side structural reform is consolidating, strengthening, upgrading, and ensuring unimpeded flows, focusing on the five priority tasks: cutting overcapacity, destocking, deleveraging, reducing costs and identifying growth areas. The fundamental purpose is to resolve the structural imbalances in China's economic development, improve supply quality, and make the supply capacity meet the people's growing needs for a high-quality life.

Sixth, it accelerates the construction of a new development pattern with the domestic circulation in China as the main body and the domestic and international circulation promoting each other. The new development pattern clearly defines the path of China's economic modernization. It emphasizes that the Chinese government should take full advantage of China's domestic mega-market and link it with the global market utilizing the potential of domestic demand, as the domestic demand boosts China's economic development.

Seventh, it promotes social equity and justice and gradually realizes shared prosperity for everyone, which is the essential requirement of socialism and a fundamental goal of socialist modernization. The Chinese government should focus on the shared prosperity of the people in high-quality economic development, expand the middle-income groups, and further regulate the high-income groups. Also, it should enable equal access of all people to essential public services, enrich their spiritual lives, and improve the income and living standards of farmers and rural areas (Li & Wang, 2019).

Other scholars have specifically studied Xi Jinping's significant statements on development philosophy and strategic planning in some critical issues and specific areas, such as finance and taxation, real economy, digital economy, ecological economy, rural revitalization, regional coordination, global economic governance, the Belt and Road Initiative, and a community with a shared future for humankind. These are also essential components of Xi Jinping's Socialist Economic Thoughts system (Ji et al., 2021).

Theoretical Origin and Practical Foundation

Scholars in China have combined Xi Jinping's Socialist Economic Thoughts' theoretical, historical, and practical logic from different perspectives to grasp its core meaning better. The academic community widely recognizes the generalization of "1+7". The new development philosophy occupies a leading position in Xi Jinping's Socialist Economic Thoughts, and the "seven insistences" serve as specific requirements and strategic measures. The two are combined to constitute a complete ideological system with strict logic and rich content. It is generally believed that the logical starting point of Xi Jinping's Socialist Economic Thoughts is that a new era of socialism with Chinese Attributes has dawned. Some scholars believe that "people-centeredness" is the foundation and the guideline for the systematic construction and innovative development of Xi Jinping's Socialist Economic Thoughts. Other scholars argue that the logical starting point is the change of the leading social contradiction (Zhang & Dai, 2019).

Some scholars summarize the theoretical framework of Xi Jinping's Socialist Economic Thoughts with one judgment, one goal, five concepts, one primary line, one method and fundamental guarantee. One judgment is that China's economy has shifted from high-speed growth to the stage of high-quality development. One goal is to build a modern economic system. Five concepts refer to the new development philosophy, and one mainline refers to the supply-side structural reform as the mainline of economic work. One method refers to the general principle of prioritizing stability while pursuing progress. The fundamental guarantee refers to the centralized and unified leadership of the Communist Party of China on economic work (Sun, 2020).

Some scholars have elaborated the rich connotation, structure and logical system of Xi Jinping's Socialist Economic Thoughts from five dimensions: essentialism, value theory, epistemology, practice theory and methodology. Adherence to the leadership of the Communist Party of China is the essential characteristic of a socialist economy with Chinese Attributes. People-centeredness manifests the value orientation of Xi Jinping's Socialist Economic Thoughts and answers the question of whom the socialist economy with Chinese Attributes should be developed for in the new era. The new normal is the key to recognizing and understanding Xi Jinping's Socialist Economic Thoughts. It insists on making the market play a decisive role in the allocation of resources, giving better play to the role of the government, with supply-side structural reform as the main task of economic work and a new strategy for economic development to be deployed in a problem-oriented manner. These concepts have clarified the practical requirements and priorities in building a socialist economy with Chinese Attributes in the new era and give a systematic answer to how to achieve development. An essential methodological principle of Xi Jinping's Socialist Economic Thoughts is to pursue progress while ensuring stability and thinking about worst-case scenarios (Wu, 2018).

To comprehend Xi Jinping's Socialist Economic Thoughts, some scholars consider it necessary to adhere to a holistic and systematic approach and analyze Xi's economic thoughts and ideas in different periods since the 18th National Congress of the Communist Party of China. Chinese scholars have theoretically traced Xi Jinping's Socialist Economic Thoughts from the following aspects.

First, the theoretical foundation of Xi Jinping's Socialist Economic Thoughts is the Marxist political economy. Xi Jinping initially studied, researched and applied Marxist political economy, adhered to the major principles of socialist political economy with Chinese Attributes, and then continuously improved the theoretical system of socialist political economy with Chinese Attributes. In this process, he has integrated the basic principles of Marxist political economy with the reality in China and modernized Marxist political economy, ultimately developing Xi Jinping's Socialist Economic Thoughts. The fundamental value orientation of "people-centered" and "development for the people" lies in the theoretical basis of adhering to the Marxist labor theory of value.

Second, Xi Jinping's Socialist Economic Thoughts inherits and develops the economic development ideas in Mao Zedong Thought and the theoretical system of socialism with Chinese Attributes. Xi made it clear that a series of primary economic and social development relationships should be correctly handled, adhering to the theory of the primary stage of socialism, the liberation and development of productive social forces, and peace and development as the theme of the times. In addition, the value orientation of maximizing people's interests should be adhered to, the goal of building a moderately prosperous society and achieving modernization, the basic socialist economic system and the establishment and improvement of the socialist market economy system should have adhered. China should insist on strengthening the leadership of the Communist Party of China in economic work, based on the principles of taking a whole-of-nation approach, overall consideration and pursuing progress while ensuring stability.

Third, Xi Jinping's Socialist Economic Thoughts draws on the excellent traditional Chinese culture. China believes that "man is an integral part of nature." When the Great Way prevails, the world belongs to all the people." An unchanging principle of state governance ensures that all systems and government decrees should aim to deliver benefits to the people." These ideas of governance and development, which have been handed down in China for thousands of years, are often quoted in Xi Jinping's speeches and applied creatively to his governance practices.

Fourth, Xi Jinping's Socialist Economic Thoughts draws on the beneficial elements of Western economics and profoundly summarizes the lessons from the development of the modern capitalist economy. In the 28th study session of the Political Bureau of the Communist Party of China Central Committee in 2015, Xi Jinping pointed out that adhering to the Marxist political economy's fundamental principles and methodology does not exclude the reasonable elements of foreign economic theories. We should pay attention to the aspects of Western economics that reflect the general laws of socialized production and market economy. Meanwhile, we should discard the dross, select the essential, eliminate the false and retain the true in Western economic theories, thus making them applicable to China (Zhang, 2021). Scholars in China have argued that the practical origins of Xi Jinping's Socialist Economic Thoughts can be traced in three ways.

First, the significant initiatives and successful experiences of socialist development since the founding of the People's Republic of China is the practical source of the theory of socialism with Chinese Attributes, especially since the reform and opening up. Xi Jinping's Socialist Economic Thoughts inherits and extends these excellent achievements.

Second, the excellent practice and brilliant achievements of developing socialist economy with Chinese Attributes since the 18th National Congress of the Communist Party of China: Since the 18th National Congress of the Communist Party of China (Communist Party of China), the world's economic recovery has been sluggish, local conflicts and turmoil have recurred, and global problems have intensified. In response, China's top leadership, with Xi Jinping at its core, has proposed a series of new philosophies, new ideas, and strategies, introduced a series of significant policies, launched a series of significant initiatives, and pushed forward a series of significant ones tasks. In the end, many long-standing problems tried to be solved are resolved. Also, many significant tasks tried to be done in the past are accomplished. Hence, the Communist Party of China and the state underwent historical changes. It is the primary practical basis of Xi Jinping's Socialist Economic Thoughts.

Third, Xi Jinping's unique personal experience and rich experience in political affairs: Xi was relocated to the countryside in northern Shaanxi Province as an urban middle school graduate in the late 1960s. He got on well with the local peasants and the yellow earth, thus becoming determined to serve the people wholeheartedly and laying the foundation for his people-centered economic thought. Xi's leadership and explorations in local economic work in Hebei and Fujian provinces contributed to the birth of Xi Jinping's Socialist Economic Thoughts. During his work in Fujian, Xi Jinping made seven trips to Jinjiang and put forward six persistent ideas, including always insisting on developing productive social forces as the fundamental direction of reform and development and always insisting on market-oriented economic development. During his administration in Zhejiang and Shanghai, his above practical wisdom was further deepened. Then, he proposed the strategy of making full use of eight advantages and implementing eight significant measures. He introduced the concept that lucid waters and lush mountains are invaluable assets (an excellent ecological environment is the fairest public product, and the most accessible welfare for the people, during his tenure in Zhejiang Province. Xi Jinping's grassroots experience enabled him to accumulate rich experience in economic affairs. He was directly exposed to agriculture, rural areas, rural people, livelihood, poverty alleviation, coordinated development, opening up to the outside world, ecological environment, and innovative development. Such experience and perceptions constitute the realistic foundation for his economic thought (Ji et al., 2021).

According to Chinese scholars, Xi Jinping's Socialist Economic Thoughts has distinctive qualities. It has the theoretical character of advancing with the times, the core meaning of deepening reform comprehensively, and the value of pursuing the great rejuvenation of the Chinese nation and the remarkable improvement of people's living standards. Moreover, it clearly understands China's economic and social development goals and paths and firmly follows a modernization path consistent with China's national conditions. More specifically, they believe that the theoretical characteristics of Xi Jinping's Socialist Economic Thoughts can be explored from the following perspectives:

First, it is political. The political nature is the fundamental quality of Xi Jinping's Socialist Economic Thoughts, centrally embodied in adhering to the direction of socialism and adhering to the centralized and unified leadership of the Communist Party of China in economic work. The political system is taken as an essential factor. The relationship between politics and economy and the effect on the economy are emphasized, making Xi Jinping's Socialist Economic Thoughts a "political economy" with distinctive Chinese Attributes, Chinese style and Chinese temperament.

Second, it is the people's position. Adherence to the people-centered approach is the foothold of Xi Jinping's Socialist Economic Thoughts. It is a theoretical principle that embodies the fundamental purpose and position of the Communist Party of China. It is implemented in all aspects of economic development throughout the promotion of the Five-sphere Integrated Plan and the Four-pronged Comprehensive Strategy.

Third, it is scientific. Xi Jinping's Socialist Economic Thoughts inherits and evolves Marxist political economy and socialist economic theory with Chinese Attributes. Combined with a systematic analysis of new changes in China's economic and social development in the new era, Xi's thought has contributed to China's high-quality economic and social development. It implies deep academic rationality, with rich connotations and rigorous logic.

Fourth, it is practical. Xi Jinping's Socialist Economic Thoughts has a deep practical foundation, originating from practice as an answer to the practical issues of the new era and evolving in practice. This thought is full of practical wisdom, planning the practical path of building a modernized economic system and achieving the Two Centenary Goals, and is the fundamental guideline for the Communist Party of China to lead economic work.

Fifth, it is a global approach. Xi Jinping's Socialist Economic Thoughts reflects the typical value pursuits of humankind. It insists on promoting people's welfare and overall human development as the starting and ending points of economic development, reflecting humankind's common aspiration for a better life. Xi is committed to peaceful development, emphasizes mutual benefit and sharing, actively participates in global economic governance, and builds a community with a shared future for humankind, reflecting the familiar voice of humankind for peaceful development, equal development, and typical development (Chen, 2018).

The new era yields new ideas, and new ideas guide new practices. Xi Jinping's Socialist Economic Thoughts provides a fundamental compass and action guide for good economic work. Some scholars have suggested several vital perspectives for understanding the guiding significance of Xi Jinping's Socialist Economic Thoughts on economic work practice. First, the Communist Party of China should lead the economic work through a centralized and unified institutional mechanism. Second, an economic policy system guided by the new development philosophy should be established. Third, an economic development thinking with supply-side structural reform as the mainline should be shaped. Fourth, a methodology of economic work should be developed for progress while ensuring stability, emphasizing scientific thinking such as problem orientation and worst-case scenario thinking (Chen, 2021).

In December 2017, priorities should be given at the Central Economic Work Conference for high-quality development in eight areas. Specifically, the Chinese government should further supply-side structural reform, stimulate the vitality of market entities, and carry out a rural vitalization strategy. It should also carry out a regional coordinated development strategy, push forward a new pattern of all-around opening-up, and improve social security and people's wellbeing. Meanwhile, it should put a housing system that ensures supply through multiple sources, provides support through multiple channels, encourages housing purchases and rentals, and promotes ecological progress. Some scholars have attributed these initiatives to the practical path to achieving the strategic goal of building a modernized economic system (Liu, 2019).

Chinese scholars generally agree that the historic achievements and changes in China's economic development since the 18th National Congress of the Communist Party of China have been made possible by Xi Jinping's Socialist Economic Thoughts' scientific guidance and the successful practice of this critical thought. Xi Jinping's Socialist Economic Thoughts provides new scientific answers to the crucial questions of China's development in a new era and how the country should achieve it. The new development philosophy and the "seven insistences" provide a scientific and practical guide to achieving more efficient, equitable, sustainable, and safer higher quality developments. Scholars argue that the overall victory of the brutal battle against poverty and the outstanding achievement of building a moderately prosperous society have centrally demonstrated Xi Jinping's Socialist Economic Thoughts (Liu, 2020).

China's 2020 high-level economic work conference emphasized the regularity of understanding the economic work under severe challenges. The Communist Party of China Central Committee's authority is the fundamental reliance of the whole party and the people of all nationalities in times of crisis to rise to the occasion. Putting the people first is the fundamental premise of making the right choice, while the institutional advantage is the fundamental guarantee of forming a majestic force to overcome the difficulties. In addition, scientific decision-making and creative response are fundamental methods of turning crises into opportunities. Scientific and technological self-sufficiency and self-improvement are fundamental support to facilitate overall development. According to some scholars, the Central Economic Work Conference's summary of the reasons for China's significant achievements in epidemic prevention and control and economic and social development under the problematic situation reveals the significant practical guidance of Xi Jinping's Socialist Economic Thoughts on economic work (Hu, 2021).

Theoretical Innovations

Scholars in China believe that Xi Jinping's Socialist Economic Thoughts is a theoretical crystallization of Marxist political economy combined with the concrete reality of China's economic development and is an innovative achievement of socialist political economy with Chinese Attributes. It has broken through the traditional barriers of Western economics, expanded the way of developing countries to modernization, and contributed Chinese wisdom and Chinese solutions to resolving human problems.

Evolving and Innovating Marxist Political Economy

Firstly, it has tackled several challenging issues in the political economy. The people-centered ideology develops Marx's labor theory of value. It breaks some people's doubts about whether the labor theory of value can support the value orientation of socialist market economy reform with Chinese Attributes. Xi Jinping's Socialist Economic Thoughts insists on making the market play a decisive role in allocating resources and giving better play to the role of the government. Xi Jinping's Socialist Economic Thoughts has solved the theoretical problem of whether public ownership and market economy can be unified. The idea of supply-side structural reform further deepens the theory of Marxist political economy on productive forces and relations of production. It is a new theory to promote the advanced development of productive forces.

Secondly, it enriches the new connotation of Marxist methodology. Adhering to the problem orientation deepens the dialectical relationship between practice and cognition. Upholding the underlying principle of pursuing progress while ensuring stability reflects the dialectical unity of movement and stasis, quantitative and qualitative change, and is a vivid application and innovative development of material dialectics. Maintaining strategic resolve is a creative application of contradiction analysis. Insisting on worst-case scenario thinking highlights the control of the materiality of things, which is a significant innovation of the philosophical way of thinking.

Thirdly, introducing the category of "socialist political economy with Chinese Attributes" is a profound change in the theory of political economy. The Decision of the Central Committee of the Communist Party of Chi On the Reform of the Economic Structure was adopted at the Third Plenary Session of the Twelfth Central Committee of the Communist Party of China. At that point, Deng Xiaoping emphasized that the Decision was the first draft of the political economy that combines the basic principles of Marxism and the practice of Chinese socialism. At the Central Economic Work Conference held in December 2015, the Chinese government was required to follow the major principles of a socialist political economy with Chinese Attributes to liberalize and develop productive social forces based on the socialist market economic reform. Furthermore, the market should play a decisive role in allocating resources. The introduction of the category of socialist political economy with Chinese Attributes systematically summarizes and sublimates the theories of socialist economic construction with Chinese Attributes since the reform and opening up and opens up a new realm of Marxist political economy in contemporary China (Ye, 2020).

Breaking the Barriers of Western Economics

Xi Jinping's Socialist Economic Thoughts draws on valuable elements of Western economics and achieves breakthroughs and surpasses it in several ways. Firstly, it breaks through the analytical paradigm of the dichotomy of government and market in modern Western mainstream economics.

Secondly, it adheres to the primary people-centered position, which seeks to achieve the unity of equity and efficiency in economic growth, thus realizing the overall development of human beings. It goes beyond the hypothesis that profit maximization is the premise of the theoretical development of mainstream Western economics and avoids the resulting contradictions and the various crises that constantly evolve in Western economies.

Thirdly, it emphasizes the independent pursuit of a modernization development path that conforms to China's national conditions, which enriches and develops the connotation of the modernization development path and breaks through the theoretical assumption and orientation that modernization equals westernization, implied in the context of mainstream Western economics.

Fourthly, the supply-side structural reform is substantially different from the Western supply-side school's proposition and marks innovation and a significant transcendence of the latter—the Western supply-side school deals with economic stagnation, with massive tax cuts as the primary means. In contrast, China's supply-side structural reform focuses on liberating and developing productive social forces, promoting supply-side restructuring, improving supply quality, and increasing total factor productive forces. China's supply-side structural reform aims to improve the supply capacity to meet the growing, upgrading and personalized material, cultural and ecological needs of the general public.

Fifthly, it transcends Western economics' economic growth and development theory and formulates the concept of economic development and development path with Chinese Attributes. Beyond the Western theory of comparative advantage in international trade and factor endowment theory, it insists on ensuring the autonomy of the country and the principle of mutual benefit and win-win in opening up to the outside world, thus breaking and transcending the "development trap" of falling into economic growth stagnation, dependence on the international division of labor, and debt crisis (He & Ye, 2021).

Restructuring the Theory of International Economic Relations

The deepening economic globalization has brought the interests and destinies of all countries in the world closer together, making it more and more imperative for all countries to negotiate on matters in the world and for all countries to cooperate to address global challenges. Under such a new situation, Xi Jinping proposed building a community with a shared future for humankind. Xi called for the Chinese government to show concerns about other countries while securing China's interests, promoting joint development of all countries while developing China's economy. Xi added that a new type of equal and balanced global development partnership should be established to safeguard the common interests of humankind and jointly build a better global home.

It has been pointed out that a community with a shared future for humankind is a pioneering concept, which has comprehensively upgraded the original concepts of global power, shared interests, sustainable development and global governance. Moreover, it scientifically determines the primary starting point of international economic relations in socialist modernization and indicates the path to address global problems and promote global governance (Wei, 2018).

Some scholars also point out that constructing a community with a shared future for humankind can resolve such problems as counter-globalization, populism and trade protectionism in the current globalization process and better guide the new globalization to a fairer and more harmonious development path. It is a significant new theoretical contribution made by China in the light of the new global economic situation, which has promoted the restructuring of the theory of international economic relations (Zhou & Feng, 2019).

Socialist Economic Theory with Chinese Attributes

Due to China's new positioning and changing main social contradictions, it can judge the reality of economic development and determine that China's economy has entered a new stage of development. Given this, the orientation of macroeconomic policies in China can be clarified. People-centered thinking runs through the economic development of the new era. It takes targeted poverty elimination and prosperity in all aspects as the most important forms of contemporary practice. It provides a scientific answer to "for whom to develop economies" and becomes the economic work's starting point and primary position.

The new development philosophy is the new development concept of cracking the real problems facing China's economic development in the new era of socialism with Chinese Attributes, enhancing development momentum, building up development advantages and leading economic development. It is a breakthrough in the combination of socialism and market economy to insist on strengthening the centralized and unified leadership of the Communist Party of China on economic work, making the market play a decisive role in the allocation of resources and giving better play to the role of the government (Gao, 2021).

In November 2015, Xi Jinping stressed that the Chinese government should reveal new features and laws based on China's national conditions and development practices. Furthermore, it should refine and summarize the rule-based achievements of China's economic development practice, upgrade the practical experience into systematic economic doctrine, and continuously develop a new realm of Marxist political economy in contemporary China. In July 2016, Xi Jinping presided over a forum of experts on the economic situation and stressed that to adhere to and develop a socialist political economy with Chinese Attributes. We should be guided by Marxist political economy, summarize and refine the tremendous practical experience of China's reform and opening up and socialist modernization while drawing on the beneficial elements of Western economics.

Scholars have engaged in lively discussions on building and developing a socialist political economy with Chinese Attributes (Hu, 2021). In May 2017, the Central Committee of the Communist Party of China issued the Opinions on Accelerating the Construction of

Philosophy and Social Sciences with Chinese Attributes, proposing accelerating the construction of the disciplinary system of philosophy and social sciences with Chinese Attributes. Xi Jinping's critical statements have provided fundamental guidelines for developing a socialist political economy with Chinese Attributes.

First, it is about the basic principles that should be adhered to in developing a socialist political economy with Chinese Attributes. Scholars have proposed that it must be based on the primary stage of socialism and reflect the characteristics of the times, which is the general basis for building socialism with Chinese Attributes and the theoretical basis of socialist political economy with Chinese Attributes. Moreover, it is necessary to be guided by Marxism, absorb the significant achievements of the economic theory of socialism with Chinese Attributes, and reasonably draw on the economic theories from foreign countries. Some scholars suggest that adhering to the principle of the liberation and development of productive forces is the fundamental approach and principle for developing and applying a socialist political economy with Chinese Attributes. Moreover, they emphasize that the theory of a socialist market economy should occupy an important position in the theoretical system of socialist political economy with Chinese Attributes.

Second, it is about the research object of socialist political economy with Chinese Attributes. Some scholars believe that a socialist political economy with Chinese Attributes should be consistent with the classical Marxist political economy by taking the relations of production as the object of study. Some advocates take the mode of production as the object of study. At the same time, some emphasize the country-specific nature of socialism with Chinese Attributes. Others hold that a socialist political economy with Chinese Attributes is the science of production, exchange, and distribution laws in the primary stage of Chinese socialism, including country-specific and historical features.

Third, it is about the theme and theoretical logic of a socialist political economy with Chinese Attributes. According to some scholars, the socialist political economy with Chinese Attributes intends to solve a series of great contradictions and problems faced by China's development, with development as the core theme. The principal components of Xi Jinping's Socialist Economic Thoughts are one philosophy plus seven insistences, which is also the theoretical logic of socialist political economy with Chinese Attributes. People-centered development philosophy should serve as the mainline for developing the socialist political economy with Chinese Attributes. The ways to deal with the relationship between government and market should be used as the primary paradigm for investigating resource allocation in a socialist political economy with Chinese Attributes.

Fourth, it is about the function of a socialist political economy with Chinese Attributes. Some scholars point out that there should be a clear division of labor and boundary between some disciplines in the theoretical system of socialist economic construction with Chinese Attributes. Moreover, to achieve a breakthrough in the theoretical system, defining the boundaries between the guiding ideology, basic principles, and realistic economic policy research is necessary to boost the socialist economy with Chinese Attributes (Liu & Li, 2019).

Conclusion

China is a leading socialist developing country. The Communist Party of China is the core leader of the Chinese people, and the Chinese people themselves choose the social system of China. Adhering to the leadership of the Communist Party of China is the essential feature of the socialist economy with Chinese Attributes. In recent years, China's economic and social development has made spectacular progress under Xi Jinping's leadership. The consensus of Chinese economic theorists is that the brilliant achievements of China's economic development have been attributed to a large extent to the guidance of Xi Jinping's Socialist Economic Thoughts. Xi Jinping's Socialist Economic Thoughts inherits and evolves Marxist economic thought, represents a high summary and sublimation of China's economic and social development practice, and provides some reference and theoretical guidance for other developing countries' economic and social development.

In recent years, the economic theorists in China have made significant progress in interpreting and theorizing Xi Jinping's Socialist Economic Thoughts from different perspectives in terms of both its breadth and depth, following the path of its formation and development. The review of Chinese scholars' research results on Xi Jinping's Socialist Economic Thoughts is helpful for the international scholars on economics theories and thoughts to gain a profound understanding of the core meaning and the essence of Xi Jinping's Socialist Economic Thoughts. At the same time, it is also valuable for accurately grasping the value pursuit and practical significance of Xi Jinping's Socialist Economic Thoughts to effectively understand and grasp the internal logic of China's rapid economic development in recent years.

The logical starting point of Xi Jinping's Socialist Economic Thoughts is that socialism with Chinese Attributes has entered a new era, featuring the new development philosophy as the main content, emphasizing the principle of seven insistences. The people-centered approach is the value orientation of Xi Jinping's Socialist Economic Thoughts, which gives a clear answer to who the socialist economy with Chinese Attributes is developing for in the new era. It is the heart and soul of Xi Jinping's Socialist Economic Thoughts to recognize and understand the new normal. Xi Jinping's Socialist Economic Thoughts on supply-side structural reform further refine the Marxist political economy's theory on productive forces and relations of production and a new theory to promote the advanced development of productive forces. The main content of Xi Jinping's Socialist Economic Thoughts is one philosophy plus seven insistences, which is the theoretical logic of socialist political economy with Chinese Attributes and is a theoretical thoughtfully in line with China's national conditions. Its logic undeniably shows great reference value and guidance for other countries similar to China.

Chapter 4
Environment and Urbanization

China has set up a master plan to balance resources used and local development in functionally oriented zones. This research examines the concepts of primary regional functions and major functional zones by an empirical approach. It probes the human economic activities and economic constructions in various major functional regions. The analysis underlines the critical role of human activities and the consequences of the activity for the economy in functional regions. Results show that national major functional zone construction is a creative action that demonstrates developmental achievements with Chinese characteristics.

Introduction

China has set up a master plan for further development based on the bearing capacity of natural resources and the environment. The plan combined with the current development status and the potential for future growth with full consideration of the future population distribution, economy layout, land use, and urbanization patterns. It spatially divides the lands into four function zones: optimized, prioritized, limited development, and prohibited exploitation.

Planning and developing the significant functional regions is a new measurement for China's reform and opening-up policy in the 21st century and creating a stable economy with Chinese characteristics. The Chinese State Council determined to exploit the land resources scientifically and improve economic construction benefits. It synthesized numerous factors, such as the bearing capacity of the resources and environment, the current development degree, and potentials for future development, to put forward the new development plan strategy for the land (Liu, Liu, and Kuang et al., 2017).

We can divide the land into four functional zones: the optimized zone, the prioritized zone, the limited development zone, and the banned exploitation zone. Each takes advantage of the function orientation in perfecting the regional policy and the performance evaluation, regulating the order of spatial development, and then forms the type of "joint effort" devoted to spatial development structure (Pan, Wu, and Zhang et al., 2011). Conclusion this plan of scientific development and practice is challenging to fulfill and an innovation policy regarding reform and opening.

For example, the Guangxi Zhuang Autonomous Region does not belong to the optimized development region at the national level. Nevertheless, the Zhuang ethnic group has seized the historical opportunity of the "Pan-Pearl River Delta Region" cooperation, undertaken many industry projects that transferred from Guangdong province, such as the Liuzhou Motown project. This practice made the backward economic development regions enter the optimized development region ranks (Wei and Wei, 2014). In Guizhou Province, the central economic zone is the optimized area. This area is centered on Guian New District, forming a metropolis group with intense radiation and driving forces, thus promoting Guizhou Province's urbanization (Feng, Shang and Zhang, 2021).

The Tibet Autonomous Region is the main body of the Qinghai-Tibet Plateau. Although Xiangxi Tujia and Miao Autonomous Prefecture in Hunan Province are not included in the limited development regions at the national level, this prefecture's limited development area is not included in the thoughts of main function regionalization construction is in progress. The decision highlights the idea of people getting along harmoniously with nature and has already won a superior performance in custom tourism. The ecological process of Tibet plays a unique shelter-zone role in protecting the environmental security of China and East Asia. Therefore, it is better to classify most parts of Tibet as prohibited exploitation zones. The people of all ethnic groups in Tibet start to explore constructing Carbon Sink Functional Areas, making the snow area plateau a cheerful home for the local people (Wang and Tian, 2014).

Construction of Major Functional Zones

The vast Chinese land territory and marine territory are home for Chinese people to survive and reproduce. Moreover, it is the most precious wealth for our descendants. It is modern people's sacred duty to develop our homes scientifically, to build a more comfortable environment with a more transparent sky, greener ground, and cleaner water. According to the resource environmental carrying capacity in specific areas, it is necessary to make an overall plan for the population distribution and determine the developing direction in the targeted region. There is no doubt that the categorization of major functional zones is a leading strategic action to speed up China's economic and social development and strengthen national power and prosperity.

On December 21, 2010, The State Council of China formally issued The National Main Functional Zones Plan: Construct Efficient, Coordinated, and Sustainable Spatial Development Model (hereafter referred to as "the Plan"). The Plan has drawn a blueprint of the national spatial development model, namely the parallel development among the population, the economy, and the eco-environment. The plan points out that it is necessary to spatially divide the national territory into different main functional-oriented zones in diverse ways. According to the methods of development standard, there are four types of zones: the optimized zone, the prioritized zone, the limited development zone, and the prohibited exploitation zone. According to the content of the development standard, there are three types of regions, respectively, the urbanization area, the primary production area of agricultural products, and the main ecological function area. According to level classification, there are two national and provincial levels. In China's major functional-oriented zones, the plan and practice are historical examples of innovation and development. Following this plan, the government scientifically arranges the spatial productivity layout conducive to narrowing the gap between regional development and livelihoods (Waxman, Rivera and Linn et al., 2016).

Any spatial region is not isolated but marked by different resources and environmental features. We can differentiate spatial regions in terms of what is primary from what is secondary. Therefore, when the problem comes to playing a different role in taking advantage of endowments, the theory of major functionally oriented zones is an in-depth and comprehensive elaboration. To take advantage of the regional system's potential energy, the prerequisite is to know the natural characteristics of differentiation and combination well (see Figure 4.1).

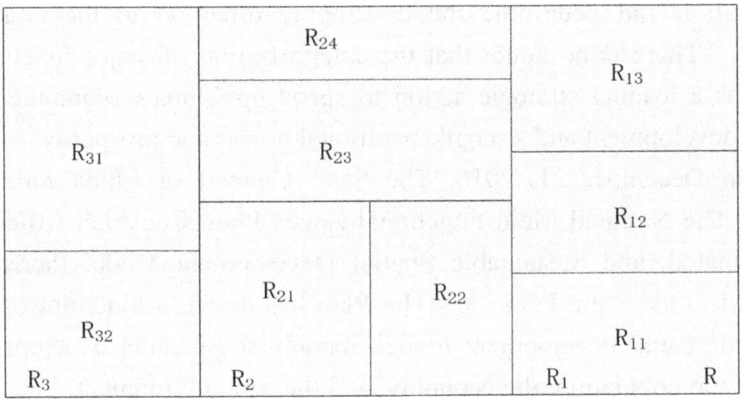

Figure 4.1 Regional system sketch

Firstly, as shown from the perspective of regional differentiation, R is categorized into R1, R2, and R3, according to different actions of regional differentiation factors. Furthermore, R1 is categorized into R11, R12, and R13 under the act of similar regional differentiation factors. Likewise, R2 is categorized into R21, R22, R23, R24, and R3 is categorized into R31 and R32.

Secondly, when looking from the perspective of regional combination, R11, R12, and R13 can be combined into R1, considering the active factors of regional combination. Similarly, R21, R22, R23, and R24 can be incorporated into R2, R31, and R32 into R3.

Thirdly, R1, R2, and R3 can be combined into R under regional combination factors. In short, the regions can constitute various differentiation and combination forms, which will lead to different economic productivity within the entire system. The theory extracted from other records can guide the actual industrial layout and help achieve overall economic performance.

The geographic and geological conditions are different from one region to another. The differences can be shown as the capacity of resources and environment, the degree of development, and the potentiality exploited. Besides, every territory has some environmental and natural resources better than others. It is necessary to concentrate the workforce, the physical resource, and the financial resource to fully exploit the advantages, to achieve the maximum benefit from the agriculture and animal husbandry, the mineral industry, the tourism industry, and some other industries. Combined with adopting a development model that would adjust measures to local conditions, these resource advantages form the major functional zone (Fan and He, 2017).

According to the specialty of China's land territory, the plan emphasizes the necessity of adjusting measures to local conditions during project construction and implementation. The plan points out that some areas are not suitable for the high intensity of industrialization and urbanization on a large scale. Those areas have the characteristics of high elevation, complicated terrain, adverse climate, and fragile ecosystem. Some areas are not even suitable for high-intensity farming and animal husbandry development. Otherwise, it will bring severe damages to the ecosystem and the ability to provide eco-friendly products (Fan, 2015).

Therefore, we must respect the spontaneous circulation of ecosystems; identify the different development contents based on other spatial environment conditions. For another example, the Plan points out that humans require agricultural products, industrial products, and service products and need eco-friendly products like fresh air, clean water, and a pleasant climate. It is based on the new concept of providing the community with eco-friendly products in contemporary society. In a certain sense, these natural elements also have the nature of the product on the demand side (Sleeter et al., 2017).

The process of protecting and expanding the natural world's capacity to provide eco-products is creating new value, so the practice of offering eco-friendly products is a kind of progress. The fact is, by planting trees and grass, there will be more fresh air and pure water. The fresh air and pure water themselves are eco-products that contain human's abstract labor. According to the spirit of the Plan, the process to advance and implement the major functional zones is likely to be a long-term process, which will accompany China throughout building a well-off society in an all-around way (Gao, 2008). As global warming intensifies, environmental deterioration endangers human survival and becomes a severe problem. On the contrary, improving the productive capacity of eco-products can reduce carbon dioxide emissions to a certain extent. Therefore, implementing the project of curbing greenhouse gas emissions through the construction of the major functional zones is of great significance and high operability (Fan and He, 2017).

The Characteristics of Major Functional Zones

The plan has determined four types of major functional zones, with each is clearly defined according to different objective laws standards.

Optimized Development Zone

The optimized development zone refers to the urbanized area with an instead developed economy, high population density, high development intensity, and more prominent problems in resources and environment. Moreover, this area needs to optimize the development process of industrialization and urbanization. The Plan indicates that the functional orientation of the optimized development zone is a critical area to improve national competitive power. It is the leading area to drive the national economic and social development; the innovative site on a national scale; the economic zone with global influence and can participate in the international division at a higher level; the crucial national area concentrated with population and economy. The three pieces of optimized development regions at the national level are the Yangtze River Delta Economic Zone, the Pearl River Delta Economic Zone, and the Bohai Rim Economic Zone (Fan, 2015).

Prioritized Development Zones

The prioritized development zone refers to the urbanized area with a satisfying economic base, relatively valuable resources, and environment carrying capacity. Moreover, it has excellent potential for future development, strong population gathering capacity, and reasonably good economic conditions. These areas need to be prioritized for the industrialization and urbanization development process. The functional orientation of the prioritized development zone is the critical growth pole to support national economic growth. Implementing the general regional development strategy and promoting coordinated development among regions, the public key area is concentrated with population and economy (Fan, 2015).

There are 18 pieces of prioritized development areas at the national level, including eight pieces belonging to the eastern and central regions and ten pieces belonging to the western regions. The first eight regions of economic development are located respectively in the central and south areas of China, such as Mid-South Region of Hebei province, Taiyuan urban agglomeration of Shanxi province, Harbin of Heilongjiang province and Changchun of Jilin province, eastern Lianyungang city of Jiangsu province, and Lanzhou city of Gansu province, an economic zone of west coast Taiwan Strait, an economic zone of Chinese central plains region and the middle region of the Yangtze River. The last ten zones of the Western Ethnic Areas are respectively located in regions such as Hu-Bao-E-Yu areas, Beibu Gulf region, the central part of Guizhou province, the central part of Yunnan province, the middle and southern zone of Tibet, the middle part of Shanxi province and Tianshui city of Gansu province, Lanzhou city of Gansu province and Xining city of Qinghai province, an economic zone of Ningxia Hui Autonomous Region along the Yellow River, and northern slope economic zone of the Tian Shan Mountains in Xinjiang Uygur Autonomous Region (Wang and Fan, 2019).

Limited Development Zones

It is essential to divide the limited development area into two sides; one is the main producing area of agricultural products; the other is the critical ecological functional area. The principal restricted producing areas at the national level in agricultural production refer to the regions with good agriculture production conditions. It is along with the supply function of agricultural products as the primary function, eco-products, services products, and industrial products as the auxiliary function. It is unreasonable for high-intensive industrialization and urbanization development on a large scale in these areas. It is better to maintain and improve the productive capacity of agricultural products in this type of area. The practical orientation of the main producing area of farm products is a significant area to ensure the supply safety of the agricultural products, the beautiful home for people to live and work, also the demonstration zone in building the newly developed countryside (Jiang, 2017).

The critical ecological function area refers to the region with a fundamental environmental system, and it concerns the ecological security on a wide range, even the whole nation. This area also refers to the ongoing degradation of ecosystems. It is also unsuitable for high-intensive industrialization and urbanization development like the first one. However, it can maintain and improve the production capacity of agricultural products. The practical orientation of the critical ecological function area is significant to ensure national ecological security; also, the demonstration zone represents the harmony of man with nature. There are 25 pieces of the key ecological function areas, such as the ecological function districts in the Da Xing' an Mountains and Xiao Xing' an Mountains, the ecological function areas of grassy meadow ecosystem in the "Three River

Sources," the ecological functional regions of soil and water in the "Three Gorges Reservoir," and so forth (Huang and Zhou, 2016).

Prohibited Exploitation Zones of National Level

The prohibited exploitation zones of the national level refer to the representative natural ecological system, which has a concentrated distribution of rare and endangered wild animals or plants and refers to some natural and cultural sites of exceptional value. The practical orientation of the forbidden exploitation zone is the critical area in protecting the natural and cultural resources and the sheltered ground for rare animals and plants. This area needs to prohibit the development process of industrialization and urbanization. According to the regulatory requirements and the relevant provisions, 1,443 pieces of the prohibited exploitation zones by 2010. The total area approximates 120 km2, accounting for 12.5% of the total land area (Chen, 2022).

The plan has divided the land space into four functional zones: optimized, prioritized, limited development, and prohibited exploitation. Besides, it is a significant innovation in the mechanism of national land space development. We can understand that different functional zones have different localizations in area division. Accordingly, we should implement different performance measurements about regional policies (China's Development Plan Research Center of Tsinghua University, 2009). Meanwhile, Plan has pointed out that different functional zones are equally important in social and economic development. They are not the same because of the differences in major functions, development approaches, and protected contents.

China is speeding up the economic growth mode transformation, laying a foundation for stable and rapid economic growth over the long term. The great strategic significance of the major functional region is to promote the formation of the land development pattern, which includes joint development of the population, the economy, the resources, and the environment. What is more, the functional orientation can effectively promote social harmony and stability, ultimately achieving the grand goal of building a well-off society (Jiang, 2017).

Industry Transfer to Western Ethnic Regions

The western nationality regions in China do not have suitable physical geography, economy, and technology conditions, which are essential for the optimized development zones. However, some industries in optimized development zones have transferred from the east coast to western regions. This trend of industrial transfer provides western nationality regions a new impetus to speed up economic development (Samuel, 2017).

Industries Transferred from the Optimized Development Zones

The government cannot push regional economic development in an all-around way. In other words, the regions should use the industrial cluster to promote industry optimization, to enhance the real economy's competitiveness. In the end, we can construct a scientific industry zone backed by industry optimization to promote the economic development of the whole region. In 1995, the world-famous French economist Francois Perroux (1903-1987) came up with a "Growth Pole Theory," which believes the major driving forces of economic development are technological progress and innovation (Guo and Li, 2021).

At present, it mainly focuses on innovations in the propulsive industry that has a larger scale and a faster growth pace. Besides, this type of industry has a more substantial related effect with other types. In operation, the propulsive sector will lead the chain effect on both forward and backward areas and better promote the development of the whole region. The practices have proven that the entire region can finally realize balanced development through unbalanced development. The Growth Pole Theory and Incubator Theory refer to the construction of major functional zones; therefore, it is conducive to the industries' transfer in the optimized development zones under the major functional zones plan (Weil, 2011).

Outward Industries Transfer of the Optimized Development Zones

The optimized development zones determined by the Plan are almost all located in the east coast regions. Although the western regions are unconditioned for constructing this area, some industries can be transferred from the optimized development zones. On January 23, 1979, Guangdong Provincial Party Committee decided to launch a pilot project of economic construction in a poor small village adjacent to Hong Kong. This pilot project aimed at constructing an exclusive zone for export. Deng Xiaoping, the general designer of China's reform and opening-up policy, strongly supported the innovative strategy in building a Special Economic Zone in southern China, Guangdong province (or referred to as Guangdong), Shenzhen city. He made "Shenzhen Special Economic Zone" clear that running a special economic zone is better. In the past, the Shaan-Gan-Ning Border Region was a special economic zone. There is no money in the Central, but one earns it by oneself, so one is exactly on one's way toward a bright future. It has been more than 30 years since the city was established as the "Shenzhen Special Economic Zone" has created the construction miracle recognized around the world. The Shenzhen Special Economic Zone is a leading Guangdong province, or even the whole country (Xiao, Huang, and Luo, 2017).

The Yangtze River Delta Economic Zone and Pearl River Delta Economic Zone have entered a new construction period in the optimized development zones. According to the Law of Comparative Advantage, many industrial enterprises are transferring into the western regions. The Pan-Pearl River Delta Economic Zone cooperation is going into the best time. In China, Guangxi Zhuang Autonomous Region (referred to as Guangxi) has seized the "golden opportunity," undertaking many industrial projects transferred from Guangdong. These industrial projects can continuously expand the areas of

Guangxi-Guangdong's strategic cooperation (Du, Feng, and Zhang, 2017).

In May 2012, some enterprises in Chongqing Municipality (referred to as Chongqing) signed a "largest contract since the founding of the People's Republic of China." It was signed with the central enterprise group in the Bohai Rim Economic Zone. There were 72 items included in this contract, and the cumulative investment could reach up to 350.6 billion RMB (1 RMB=0.156 USD in 2012) when the whole project is finished. This group consists of more than 30 large enterprises directly under the central state-owned, for instance, China National Petroleum Corporation, Sinopec Group, China Huaneng Group, and China Datang Corporation.

Chongqing municipality will continue extending the industry chain in state-owned companies by undertaking optimized development zones projects. Therefore, the economy in Chongqing will enjoy an even faster development. The area will be built into a "Growth Pole" in this way, and we can see this fantastic profit clearly through analyzing an example (Li, 2017).

Inheritance and Innovation of Industrial Development

The western ethnic region can undertake the industries transferred from the optimized development zone, which often refers to the east coast areas. This approach will boost the region's economic strength and improve employment. It is an effective way for the undeveloped part to narrow the economic gap with the developed area. Liuzhou city is in Guangxi Zhuang Autonomous Region. Before the reform and opening-up policy, Liuzhou was a low-ranking region in China's economy. Since then, Liuzhou has taken advantage of geography to undertake the enterprises that transferred from Shenzhen Special Economic Zone, Guangzhou city, and Dongguan city. In September 1992, Liuzhou established a High-tech Development Zone, with a total plan area of 110 hectares. On this ground, Liuzhou raised any external funds, and the economy in this district has developed fast. In 2000, through the discussion of "thought liberation," the overall thought of

"Industry makes Liuzhou city rich and brings benefit to the residents" was put forward in the 9th Party Congress report of Liuzhou Municipal Committee (Li, 2015; Ruan and Wei, 2021).

Deepening structural reform brings about significant economic benefits. Under this guideline, Liuzhou' GDP was 20.701 billion RMB, and the per capita GDP was 11,202 RMB in 2001. Liuzhou made unceasingly significant efforts to expand the scope of opening-up, introducing the capital, technology, and projects available outside the city. The local enterprises could utilize these new and high technologies to transform and upgrade traditional industries and then expand the amount and increase in the industry (Zhang, 2017). In 2020, Liuzhou' GDP was 317.694 billion RMB（46.045 billion USD; 1 RMB=0.145USD in 2020）, an increase of 1.5% over the previous year, and the per capita GDP was 77,148 RMB(Liuzhou Bureau of Statistics, 2021).

Liuzhou has actively implemented the strategy of "Enriching People and Prosper Guangxi." After several years of effort, Liuzhou has set up an Automobile Industry Base. On November 18, 2002, the joint venture, SAIC-GM-Wuling, was officially launched in Liuzhou. General Motors (GM)invested in this three-way venture, jointly operated with Shanghai Automotive Industry Corp (SAIC) and Wuling. That month, SAIC-GM-Wuling' intermediate cars named Baojun 630, the "first self-produced car in the joint venture," rolled off the production for the first time. The cars caused full public attention. They looked like galloping horses with more power and movement with smooth lines and dark gray interior design. At the same time, there was another joint venture invested by Wuhan Dongfeng Motor Corporation and Japan's Nissan Motor Corporation established in Liuzhou. It is named Dongfeng Nissan Motor Company Limited. Soon after, this joint venture built up a subsidiary, Dongfeng Liuzhou Automobile Co, Ltd, whose shares are held by Dongfeng Motor Corporation and Liuzhou Industry Holding Corporation together.

Furthermore, this subsidiary specializes in making commercial vehicles (Li and Luo, 2015). Moreover, hundreds of Auto Parts

Companies are clustered in Liuzhou city, including Yuchai Dynamics and Ling Long tires. The automobile industry has led the entire industrial economy in Liuzhou city to realize the leap-forward development for years. In 2009, the industrial output amounted to a new level of 200 billion RMB, and in the next year, it rose to 240 billion RMB there. Moreover, it was over 300 billion RMB in the city in 2011, which accounted for one-quarter of Guangxi's industrial output(Zhang, 2017). After years of effort, Liuzhou has set up an Automobile Industry Base. The reputation of "Industrial Liuzhou" is getting loud soon.

The Motor City Construction in Liuzhou

The "Pan-Pearl River Delta" regional cooperation is vital for developing major function zones. Moreover, multiply investing construction and quickly forming a large automobile-make base in Liuzhou is a classic case of this kind of cooperation. Only after the framework agreement on a period of The Strategic Cooperation between the Guangxi Zhuang Autonomous Region and Guangdong Province in the Eleventh Five-Years Plan (2006-2010) was implemented, the Guangxi region collaborates with Guangdong province in multiple fields (Yan and Hu, 2012). On April 13, 2021, The latest Collaborative Framework Agreement between the Guangxi Zhuang Autonomous Region and Guangdong Province in the Fourteenth Five-Years Plan (2021-2025) was formally signed in Beijing. Both Guangxi and Guangdong are dedicated to exploring a new model of regional cooperation and promoting the coordinated development of regional economies once again (Governmental Informational Office of Guangxi Zhuang Autonomous Region,2021). Guangdong has attained significant achievements during the reform and opening-up policy. One primary reason is the abundant raw material and labor from neighboring provinces, including Guangxi (Yu, 2012). For example, Guangxi exported 5.34 million rural laborers to Guangdong in 2018 alone, and they worked in various industries, becoming an indispensable productive group for adjoining local economic prosperity(He,2019).

With a relatively developed economy, Guangdong assists Guangxi in the capital, technology, and other aspects. From 2019 to 2021, Guangdong's 141 enterprises had invested 4.519 billion RMB in Guangxi's construction, and Guangxi had also invested 24.861 billion RMB of supporting funds. The two sides had jointly completed 156 projects, including a batch of industrial parks, productive agricultural bases, cold chain logistics systems, etc. Giving full play to the advantages of the geographical environment, Guangxi's 37 high-standards agricultural productive bases were recognized officially by Guangdong as commercially supplied model bases, 80 agricultural products as high-quality goods. The goods mainly supply rich international color cities like Shenzhen and Hong Kong. Guangdong formulated 13 preferential policies for anti-poverty cooperation to open its markets to neighboring Guangxi. Guangdong purchased and sold 22.057 billion RMB of agricultural and animal husbandry products and specialty handicrafts from Guangxi in 2021. The preferential policies were effective. In the same year, relevant 730100 rural laborers were employed in Guangxi, including 196900 persons who had been lifted out of poverty（Ying and Wang,2021）.

The facts have shown a collaborative win-win result. Since Guangdong's economy has developed well and become the "well-off earlier" region, it is incumbent upon Guangdong to take responsibility for helping the poor areas. Meanwhile, Guangdong faces the pressures of industrial transformation and upgrading. Therefore, Guangdong has set up a new development strategy, namely the "dual-transfer" in industries and labor forces. Guangxi Zhuang Autonomous Region and Guangdong province are neighbors linked by mountains and rivers. They are ubiquitous in cultural backgrounds and linked very closely in population. Over the years, Guangdong and Guangxi have maintained a long-term cooperation relationship. Guangxi has offered enormous support to Guangdong's rapid economic and social development, especially in ecological conservation in the Xijiang River.

In the next period, Guangxi needs to enhance cooperation with Guangdong in industrial transfer and collaboration, economic circle construction, and regional eco-environmental conservation. There are still high cooperation potentials in Guangdong "dual-transfer" and Guangxi industrial transfer. Besides, the existing mechanism for cooperation is nearly perfect in a mature operating model. Therefore, the economic integration in southern China will be significantly improved, so of the development level (Zhao and Yang, 2017). Under regional cooperation, another new domestic large automobile-make base rises rapidly.

Liuzhou took bolder steps on industrial development as early as the "Twelfth Five-Years Plan (2011-2015)." The goal of it is to construct a "Motor City." On the one hand, it is a way to undertake the industrial transfer from the optimized development zones; on the other hand, it is an excellent opportunity for enterprises to absorb and innovate through a joint venture. This combination leads to a higher level of coordinated development of regional economies.

On September 28, 2010, the State Council of China agreed to upgrade "The High-technology Industries Region of Liuzhou City" in the Guangxi Zhuang Autonomous Region into the national rankings. On January 31th, 2011, the government of Guangxi adopted The General Plan for Motor City Construction in Liuzhou, a significant project that would influence the future development of industry in Liuzhou or even in Guangxi. The targeted positioning of Motor City is "the new platform for technological strategy and the growth pole for economic development." According to that general plan, the Motor City is located in the northeast of the urban district in Liuzhou, covering a planned area of 203 square kilometers (Zhang, 2017).

The Motor City is surrounded by rivers, west of the Liujiang River and east of the Luoqing River. The Motor City was constructed by clean energy technology abandoned the traditional production way with black smoke issuing from the chimneys and loud roaring noise. Since the supervision and administration, combined with the productive system to compensate the ecosystem, are essential parts of major functional zones' construction, the management department has set up a strict regulatory regime (Wang, 2009). The Motor City under the building is next to the highway that runs from Guilin to Beihai. This highway is one of the national highways about "five vertical and seven horizontal trunk lines" and the body part of the thoroughfare to the sea in Southwest China. There are eight functional areas and nineteen functional blocks included in the plan structure of the Motor City in Liuzhou. The eight functional regions refer to the industrial area, residential area, business area, and cultural tourism area. The nineteen functional blocks include auto production, commerce and service center, auto financing, and auto sports.

Motor City's constructional framework was completed in 2012. The annual scale of car production was 0.75 million units through the joint efforts by SAIC-GM-Wuling, Dongfeng Liu steam, and Yuchai Dynamics. Among those companies, SAIC-GM-Wuling has adhered to the principle of "People-oriented, Safety first" over the years and achieved remarkable results. In May 2012, the company was awarded the "National Model Enterprise for Safety Culture Construction" by the State Administration of Work Safety. Over the years, the company has made persistent efforts without arrogance or rashness. SAIC-GM-Wuling's annual sales volume exceeded 1.6 million vehicles, achieving the double growth of year-on-year and link relative ratio for nine consecutive months in 2020(Weng,2021).

Furthermore, Liuzhou has gathered three whole vehicle enterprises that quickly manufacture automobiles. At the same time, four special vehicle enterprises and 308 parts enterprises were established above the national specified capital scale. The main products of these enterprises are multi-functional passenger cars, sedans and a series of trucks. In 2020, Liuzhou produced 1.74 million automobiles, and the total industrial output value of the automobile industry reached 174.66 billion RMB(23.315 billion USD), accounting for 54.98% of the city's total GDP. In the same year, SAIC-GM-Wuling exported 77,376 vehicles, and spare parts gained a total sales revenue of 501.478 million USD in overseas markets, covering 40 countries in Central and South

America, Africa, the Middle East and Southeast Asia. The municipal government also formulated a series of new policies, such as Several Opinions on Promoting the Development of New Energy Vehicles in Liuzhou. Supported by flexible policies such as government-enterprise cooperation and market forces, the productive quantity of clean energy vehicles has grown rapidly. Also, in 2020, Liuzhou produced 182,000 pure electric vehicles, 190.6% more than the previous year, accounting for 16.5% of similar products in the country (Liuzhou Investment Promotion Bureau,2021). The construction of Motor City has a multi-win-win result by the joint efforts of all the parties. It is also the best example for the coordinated development of regional economies (Huang and Hu, 2017).

Under the direction of Plan, Liuzhou has become the right place for venture development, also a livable landscape city. Liuzhou has undertaken the industries transferred from the optimized development zones. In the future, the city of Liuzhou will be expanded, and economic power will be increased. The "beautiful landscape" is the city brand of Liuzhou, and the lives of people of all nationalities driven by Zhuang ethnic groups will be more productive and more colorful (Yuan, 2017).

The Construction of Prioritized Development Zones

"The Qianzhong Economic Zone" in Guizhou province (referred to as Guizhou) is one of the eighteen prioritized development zones set by the Plan. It is located in Sichuan province, Yunnan province, and Guangxi Zhuang Autonomous Region. Therefore this economic zone has a critical strategic position in China. According to the document titled Some Views Concerning the In-depth Implementation of the Western Development Strategy by the CPC Central Committee and the State Council, the central government has officially incorporated "the Qianzhong Economic Zone" into the prioritized development zones. The central government decided that this Economic Zone should be developed first, becoming a new growth engine for Guizhou (Jiang, 2017).

The Construction of New Towns

The plan has pointed out that China is still in the process of urbanization, with so many people from rural areas are rushing into urban areas. This movement increases the demand for the expansion of urban space and brings about the unoccupied housing problems in rural areas. Therefore, we need to optimize the structure of residential space in both rural areas and urban areas, increase space utilization efficiency. For the prioritized development zones at the national level, the most critical development direction and principle are to adjust and expand the urban structure, to form a central city with a powerful motive force as soon as possible. Then this central city can promote the development of other cities, including the urban agglomeration characterized by the division of labor and cooperation and complementary advantages, with intensive and highly efficient development. Only in this way can we accelerate the forming of population accumulation and improve the urban carrying capacity in population. As one of the prioritized development zones at the national level, Qianzhong Economic Zone is developing fast under the Plan's guidance (Huang, 2016).

The Integrated Development between Guiyang and Anshun Cities

Both Guiyang and Anshun are the cities (referred to as Guiyang and Anshun) in Guizhou province. The unified development of these two cities will be crucial for developing the Qianzhong Economic Zone following an essential scheme of "Integration of Guiyang - Anshun cities," which is expected to be a new growth platform for the economic growth in western China. As an essential part of the Qianzhong Economic Zone, Guiyang city (referred to as Guiyang) is also the provincial capital of Guizhou province. This capital is the political, economic, and cultural center of Guizhou; most important, it is a basement for attracting talented people. Therefore, Guiyang should take advantage of the provincial capital effect; have the industrial distribution and division into full consideration. Then it can expand the construction scale of infrastructures to lead the way towards developing the information-sharing network quickly (Deng, 2017).

Anshun should concentrate efforts on infrastructure construction that focuses on transportation equipment, especially for the urban arterial roads. It is necessary to make full use of the comparative advantages in Anshun. For instance, it can develop the industries by exploiting the unique resources in the local area. We need to accelerate the development of the "Guiyang-Anshun Industrial Corridor" in the Qianzhong Economic Zone. At the same time, establish the bases of advanced equipment manufacturing, strategic emerging industries, circular economy, and the modern logistics industry, which can be the demonstration zone for coordinating urban and rural developments. The Guiyang-Anshun belt is Guizhou's primary bearing area for industrialization and urbanization. It can be the critical growth point for developing the Qianzhong Economic Zone and the supporting point for developing between regions.

When it comes to constructing regional economic "integration of Guiyang and Anshun Cities," the first is to focus on completing the "New Guiana District." The construction orientation is "the demonstration district of opening up and development in the inland cities," which is a developing new district at the country level in the future. According to the General Plan for New Guiana District, this area includes eight towns in Guiyang and fourteen towns in Anshun. The total spatial space of this area is about 2000 square kilometers, with a planned population size of 4 million people and a land-use scale of about 500 square kilometers. Through the construction of this new district, Guiyang and Anshun can be connected into a more significant spatial area to form a growth pole of the city cluster development in the Qianzhong Economic Zone (Fan, 2017).

The Development Guiyang – Anshun Economic Belt

The economic developmental construction of the integration of Guiyang and Anshun Cities is the principal strategic direction of the optimized development zones in Guizhou province. The advantages of developing this economic belt are as follows. Guiyang is an essential central city among the "Qianzhong Economic Zone," "Nan-Gui-Kun Economic Region" (NGKER), and the "Pan-Pearl River Delta Economic Zone," and Guiyang is also an industrial city known for the development of the resources. The city has already constructed a complete industrial system containing 34 industrial sectors and 165 industry categories. The industrial products from this city have been playing an incredibly crucial role in the national economy. Guiyang city is one of the biggest aluminum industry bases in China.

A precision optics instrument is one of the three industry bases. The production of electronics instruments is one of five. At the same time, the aerospace industry is one of China's three international industrial bases. Anshun city, which has long been known as "the abdomen of Guizhou province, the throat of Yunnan province, the lip, and teeth of Sichuan and Guangdong provinces," is the node city for China to connect with the international passageway of Southeast Asia. Guiyang and Anshun are neighbors linked by mountains and rivers, the distance between the two city centers is less than 90 kilometers, and they are also ubiquitous in cultural backgrounds. So, it has distinct advantages for developing together (Xiao, Huang, and Luo, 2017).

The economic strength in Guiyang city is reliable, but the supply prices of all the resources are too high because of the development of the long-time resources. Anshun has a large area of plains linked together, the scale effects are apparent, and the considerable exploration potential. Besides, this area has flat open land and convenient traffic. All these above features make Anshun comparative advantages in Qianzhong Economic Zone. Anshun has a more habitable environment, the climate is mild wet, and the radiation is low. Above all, the relaxing time can last for eight months. Guiyang and Anshun can compensate each other with their advantages, leading to the development process of Guizhou (Huang, 2016).

The development conditions and status in the Qianzhong Economic Zone administration cells are different. So, we need to take the construction of the New GuiAn District as the breakthrough to speed up the integrated development in Guiyang-Anshun areas. Now, there are two kinds of actions that we need to take. One is to compile and improve the general plan of the urban-rural integration for the demonstration zone of the emerging industry in the Qianzhong Economic Zone, which is the guideline for the administrative controls of the integrated development in Guiyang-Anshun cities. The other is to attract capital and investment by constructing the urban roads from Pingba County to Huaxi District and Xixiu District (Gao, 2017).

The Urbanization in Guizhou Province

Urbanization is an inevitable trend in constructive modernization, and it is the material basis for forming the growth pole. Specifically speaking, the labor demand for urbanization mostly comes from rural areas to create the so-called group- "migrant workers."

The Problems and Challenges

The extent of industrialization in Guizhou province is low, so is urbanization. In the eastern Yunnan-Guizhou Plateau, most areas are characterized by hillside ecology and unreasonable urban structure. In big and medium-sized cities, the development lags. It is an apparent contradiction in urbanization. According to the "Sixth National Population Census 2010," the population in Guizhou province is more than 34 million, among which almost 23 million people are farmers. The urbanization rate in Guizhou is 33.81 %, more than 15 points lower than the national average level(National Bureau of Statistics, 2011). On one side, there are only four prefecture-level cities and 19 county-level cities, which respectively account for 44.4 % and 21.6 % of the administrative districts at the same level in Guizhou. On the other side, more than 50 poverty counties at the national level, and the development level lags. As the only big city with more than 1 million people in Guizhou province, Guiyang city can hardly improve the urbanization level with little radiation and leading power (Wang, 2017).

The Potential and Direction

Economic theory suggests that when the urbanization rate rises to 50%, this area will soon achieve an economic and social development boom. According to the comparative data, if the urbanization rate of Guizhou province is 50%, at least 5.7 million farmers will become residents soon as the land space is relatively flat in Guiyang-Anshun areas with a geographical space capacity of about 1 million people. It provides an excellent geographical condition for the mass migration in the urbanization process in New GuiAn District.

The New GuiAn District construction promotes the interactive development of industrialization and urbanization. The mission is to construct the New Guiana Regional city and industrial belts by promoting " two-in-one " integration of industrialization and urbanization through building the Industry Park and Urban District. It aims to achieve the "three-in-one" model: modern industry, modern life, and modern city. The construction of the New Guiana District is a way to expand the new space for the development of industries and populations, which will improve the economic potential for future development (Su, 2016).

The Supporting Policy

In narrowing the gap between urban and rural areas, we need to increase rural incomes. It is better to reduce the rural population and speed up urbanization than provide subsidies to farmers only. Industrialization is the fundamental way to solve " the three agriculture-related issues," It strikes a balance between efficiency and equity. It is far from enough to rely solely on improving the logistics and the hardware environment. Urbanization is a crucial factor that cannot be ignored. If the city scale is not expanded, the level of social and economic development can hardly be improved. So, in terms of strategy, it is critical to deal with the development issues in Guizhou province by shifting the rural population into cities orderly and adequately.

According to the local conditions and the development direction of Guizhou, the strategic focus and the main task in the "Twelfth Five-Year Plan" period is, the urbanization rate of the whole province should be 36 to 38% by 2015, and 46 to 48% by 2020 (Huang, 2017). This task has been exceeded through the peoples' concerted efforts of provincial all ethnic groups. According to the "Seventh National Population Census 2020," there were an urban population of 20.4959 million and a rural population of 18.0662 million, with the urbanization rate reaching 53.15% in Guizhou. Compared with the above situation of 2010, the urbanization rate increased by 19.34 percentage points. The urbanization rate jump of Guizhou province increased by 5.13 percentage points higher than the same of national level. From 2011 to 2020, the number of rural residents decreased by 4.9325 million there (Statistics Bureau of Guizhou Province,2021). Most of those former peasants left the fields and moved into cities. Some found their trading and technological companies, some became industrial workers in different industries, and some bought new houses and lived in cities. They all started a brand new life.

Construction of Limited Development Zones

The plan for the major functional zones has presented two design ideas, referring to the national and provincial levels. When it comes to the economic construction at the provincial level, it is necessary to consider the restrictions of resources and the environment, to implement the limited development policy according to the provincial standards. Xiangxi Tujia and Miao Nationalities Autonomous Prefecture in western Hunan province are located east of the Wuling Mountains, with complicated natural conditions and fragile ecosystems. This region is the central part of the protecting forest system in the Middle-Lower Yangtze River, so the ecological function plays a crucial role. Although this autonomous prefecture is not included in the limited development zone at the national level, it is included in the plan of major functional zones at the Hunan level. Therefore, the development of this area should insist on the principles of giving priority to protection, following appropriate development mode, and developing in critical spots (Wu, 2002).

Xiangxi Tujia and Miao Autonomous Prefecture

Xiangxi Tujia and Miao Nationalities Autonomous Prefecture (here shortened as Xiangxi) lies in the northwest of Hunan province, in the hinterland of the Wuling Mountainous area. This region belongs to the traditional area of " long history, ethnic minority, poverty, and remoteness. " In August 1952, national, regional autonomy was instituted in this region. Jishou city is the capital of Xiangxi Tujia and Miao Nationalities Autonomous Prefecture. The entire territory of this region is about 15000 square kilometers, has seven counties and one city, the whole population is about 2.68 million, and the minorities make up about 73.5% of the total population. So Xiangxi prefecture is a mountainous agricultural region inhabited by multi-nationalities. Because of historical reasons and the restrictions of natural conditions, the infrastructure in this whole region is relatively backward. The rural population accounts for 85% of the total population scale, and the economic basis is weak (Wu, 2009). Although there are many problems in Xiangxi prefecture, there are also some advantages to another side. Such as the spectacular natural landscape, famous places of historical interest, the mysterious cultural and historical backgrounds, enthusiasm and strong ethnic folk customs, and so on forth. All these above advantages can be the tourism resources, which endow this enormous area potential for developing tourism.

In recent years, the economic development speed of Xiangxi Tujia and Miao Nationalities Autonomous Prefecture has accelerated a lot, but still lower than the average level of Hunan province, or even lower than the national average (see Table 4.1). In 8 years, from 2004 to 2011, the speed of GDP in Xiangxi prefecture is almost all lower than Hunan province, except only one year, 2010. Besides, for about eight years, the province's economic output has been hovering at a low level of about 2%. Meanwhile, the per capita GDP gap between this region and the whole province is widening year by year. For example, in

2004, the gap of per capita GDP between Xiangxi prefecture and Hunan province was 3300 RMB, and it rose to almost 8500 in 2011 (Zhu, 2016).

Table 4.1 GDP-linked data between Xiangxi and Hunan Province (2004-2011)

GDP-linked data (every year)	The total amount of GDP (hundred million yuan)		The increased speed of GDP (hundred million yuan)		Per capita of GDP (yuan)	
	Hunan	Xiangxi	Hunan	Xiangxi	Hunan	Xiangxi
2004	3831.9	75．7	9.0	8.0	6054	2746
2005	4151.5	83.4	9.0	4.1	6565	2827
2006	4633.7	91.1	9.6	8.1	7147	3100
2007	5641.9	111.4	12.1	9.6	9117	4042
2008	6511.3	123.3	11.6	10.6	10366	4991
2009	7568.9	148.8	12.2	11.3	11830	5910
2010	9145	190.7	14.5	16.0	14405	7445
2011	11156.6	226.7	12.8	8.2	17521	9081

Sources of the data:

1. Hunan Province Bureau of Statistics, 2012.
2. Xiangxi Tujia and Miao Nationalities Autonomous Prefecture Bureau of Statistics, 2012.

To achieve faster development, Xiangxi Tujia and Miao Nationalities Autonomous Prefecture has created four parts of tourism resources combination based on its environmental resources. They are the historical and cultural tourism in Fenghuang Town, the ethnic, cultural tourism in Dehang Village, the ecological tourism in Meng Dong River, the ancient city tourism in Liye Town. This Autonomous Prefecture has become a high tourism growth rate in Hunan province, even China. In 2011, the ratio of the industrial structure of Xiangxi prefecture in three industries was 18.6% in the primary industry, 41.6 in the secondary industry, and 39.4 in the tertiary industry, respectively (Lu, 2009). Tourism in this Autonomous Prefecture has boomed over the years. Xiangxi prefecture was named one of "National Top Ten

Charm Cities" by 2006, also named one of the "China's Top Tourist Destinations" by the Pacific Asia Travel Association, the International Tourist Chamber of Commerce, and the Tourism Cooperation Organization by Ethnic Chinese in the world (Pan, Cai and Wang, 2017). In 2020, the number of domestic and foreign tourists received was 55.3425 million person-times. The touristic incomes calculated in RMB were 47.785 billion(6.926 billion USD) in Xiangxi, which were 5.47 times and 11.4 times higher than the same items in 2007, respectively (Xiangxi Tujia and Miao Autonomous Prefecture Statistics Bureau,2021). Tourism has made great progress.

Implementing the policy of a limited development zone is not equal to limiting development. On the contrary, the state and province-level management agencies encourage active developments in every local place. Based on the local resources, the government of Xiangxi Tujia and Miao Nationalities Autonomous Prefecture has promoted the development of the tourism industry and has scored notable achievements. On the one hand, based on the local resources, the government sectors of Xiangxi prefecture have promoted the development of the tourism industry, finally scoring notable achievements in this region (Zhu and Wang, 2020).

On the other hand, tourism in Xiangxi prefecture leads to the development of related industries. The development of tourism can give an impetus to the rapid growth of related industries, creating new employment opportunities for native residents (See Table 4.2). The available data from the World Tourism Organization suggests that the tourism industry is a broad concept; it refers to the actual consumption of food, shelter, and transportation and involves traveling shopping, and entertainment. The departments related to tourism, directly and indirectly, are more than 100, citing figures from the National Tourism Administration. According to the statistics, by the end of the "Eleventh Five-Year Plan" period, the employment workers related to tourism were around 150 thousand in Xiangxi Tujia and Miao Nationalities Autonomous Prefecture. Take Fenghuang county of Xiangxi prefecture as an example. More than 15 thousand jobs related to tourism in 2007 accounted for around half of the total employment and re-employment (Li, 2017).

Table 4.2 Tourism employees in Xiangxi (2004-2011)

The data concerned	2004	2005	2006	2007	2008	2009	2010	2011
Tourism employees (10 thousand people)	2	4.2	6	8	9.7	12.1	13	15
Guides with Tour guide certificate(one person)	86	273	400	520	607	850	723	800

Sources of data:

1. Xiangxi Tujia and Miao Nationalities Autonomous Prefecture Bureau of Statistics, 2012;
2. Yearbook of Xiangxi Tujia and Miao Nationalities Autonomous Prefecture, 2011.

The number of tourists coming from developed regions is more significant than undeveloped areas. Because of the historical, geographic, and other factors, places of the right natural and ecological environment and rich folk customs are primarily distributed in remote and deprived areas. So, when the tourists from developed regions come into these deprived areas with abundant tourism opportunities, it is "an economic injection of resources into the local economy" for the weak areas. This kind of "economic injection" can stimulate economic development; speed up the poverty reduction in these regions. For instance, in Wang Cun, Yongshun County, Xiangxi Tujia, and Miao Nationalities Autonomous Prefecture, the economic development was extremely backward. Besides, people's living standards in those regions were superficial.

Afterward, owing to tourism development, a host of hotels, tourism production enterprises, and shops have sprung up in Wang Cun town. This kind of business service amounts to 872 units, and the monthly operating income is more than 10 million RMB. The fiscal revenue in this area has increased around 5.8 times in ten years. Due to tourism development, more than 85% of people in Wang Cun town are out of poverty. Like Wang Cun town in Xiangxi Prefecture, many villagers have built new houses, and the overall living standards are close to the municipal levels (Long, 2017).

In Xiangxi Tujia and Miao Nationalities Autonomous Prefecture, ethnic cultural tourism is a long-term process. Therefore, we should set up a sustainable development strategy tailored to local conditions to develop a particular industry to carry on the green economy and resources (Wu, 2002). Following the rules of the economy, we need to prioritize the protection of the environment and do appropriate exploitation, which is also one of the principles for ecological functional zones at national levels.

Construction of Prohibited Exploitation Zones

As the unique natural region unit, the Tibet plateau is also the body part of the Qinghai-Tibet Plateau. This unit has many types of individual ecological systems, which play a protective role in the ecological security of China, even in East Asia. Because of these characteristics of the particular geographic location, the unique and fragile ecological environment, and the undeveloped economic society, it is necessary to plan Tibet as a functioning zone based on the eco-economic area and major functional zone principles.

Construction of Ecological Barrier in Tibet

The Tibet Autonomous Region (or from now on referred to as Tibet) locates at the body part of Qinghai-Tibet Plateau, which is not only the "Ecological Source," but also the "River Source" of Eurasia. Since the 1990s, the Chinese State Council has increased its spending on protecting and constructing the eco-environment in Tibet. The government has carried out many ecological conservation projects in this area, and environmental protection and economic construction have made positive progress. For example, in February 2009, the State Council of China executive meeting examined and approved the Plan for Ecological Security Protection and Construction in Tibet, which determined the protection of ecological security in Tibet as the critical ecological project of China. During the period 2008 to 2030, the total planned investment of this project was 15.5 billion RMB. According to the plan, the contents of ecological security protection and construction in Tibet can be summarized as the following three parts: ecological protection, ecological building, and supporting system. Moreover, the above three parts contain ten projects (Huang, Cao, and Xu et al., 2017).

At the starting year of the "Twelfth Five-Year Plan," Tibet listed the nature reserve area as the "prohibited exploitation zone" following the Plan. This area covers about 408.3 thousand square kilometers of land is the most significant area that accounts for 34.03% of the total area of Tibet Autonomous Region. The "prohibited exploitation zone" contains 40 natural reservation zones, 21 ecological functional conservation zones, and seven forest parks. Besides, the forested upland areas in the southeast plateau edge of Tibet and Qiangtang highland desert area in the northwest of Tibet are listed in the "prohibited exploitation zone."

The Tibet Autonomous Region plays a vital role in China. The people of Tibet have done an excellent job improving the regional "carbon sink" function (Yang, 2016). The Opinions on Better Development and Stability of Tibet by the Central Committee of the Communist Party of China, the State Council (2005-09-02) emphasized that it is essential to construct the ecological barriers for Tibetan Plateau, pushing the stability and "great-leap-forward development" in Tibet.

A Good Start on the Construction of Ecological Security Barrier

The natural grassland has the highest contribution rate at 48.3 % among the various ecosystems in the Qinghai-Tibet Plateau. Also, natural grassland is an essential source of carbon sink. In 2007, the grand project Plan for National Ecological Security Protection and Construction in Tibet Plateau (2006-2030) was formally implemented. The nation will invest more than 10 billion RMB in carrying out the projects involving three parts: natural grassland protection, artificial grass growing, and the construction of the natural protection area. More specifically, in the plan period, the areas of returning farmland to the forest will reach 14.96 million hectares, the grassland rehabilitation 4.2 million hectares, and the controlled areas of vacant lands 306 thousand hectares. These specific measures will put more than 77% of moderately and heavily degraded grassland under effective control. Undoubtedly, the function of the carbon sink in the Tibet Plateau will be enhanced. Therefore, it is beneficial to construct this area into the ecological security barrier of China, even Asia (Fan and He, 2017).

The Project for Returning Farmland to Forests is Beneficial to Farmers and Herdsmen

The Tibet Autonomous Region has the largest primeval forest in China. The existing forest area in Tibet is about 13.8961 million hectares, and the growing stock volume is 2.091 billion cubic meters. Tibet has strengthened forest and meadowy protection so that the forest coverage rate has increased steadily. In the 1950s, Tibet's forest coverage rate was less than 1 percent (Jiang and Wu, 2017). People of all ethnic groups have been continuously planting trees on a large scale for several decades. Many farmers and herders have received considerable labor rewards by taking part in the constructions such as artificial afforestation, returning farmland to forests, etc. For example, from 2016 to 2020, a total of 397,700 hectares of artificial afforestation (including projects of returning farmland to forest and preventing and controlling desertification) were achieved (Yuan and Zheng,2021). So, Tibet's forest coverage rate increased to 12.31 %, the comprehensive vegetation coverage of natural grasslands lifted to 47 %, and the wetland areas reached 6.529 million hectares by 2020(China Radio and Television Network Station,2021).

Through the compensation fund for the benefit of the forest ecology, the construction of returning farmland to forests, and the Natural Forest Protection Program, the cash income of farmers and herders in Tibet is over 180 million RMB. More specifically, in the project of the compensation fund for the benefit of the forest ecology, about 16,000 forest rangers are local farmers and herders, with about 98 million RMB yearly incomes in total. In the project of returning farmland to forests, the income is 57.5 million RMB in total. In the Natural Forest Protection Program, the yearly revenue is 17 million RMB in total (Peng, 2017). The actual implementation has far exceeded expectations. For example, from 2019 to 2020 only, Tibet accumulatively allocated funds 3.182 billion RMB (461.186 million USD) in compensation and subsidies for forest ecological benefits and 274 million RMD in subsidies for ecological forest rangers, supported hiring competitively 78200 forest rangers (State Council Information Office, 2021).

All the types of incomes mentioned above can improve the living conditions for the residents. Other approaches can improve the residents' income, such as the payments to keepers for the Nature Reserve and the Wildlife Protection, which amounts to 18 million RMB; and the costs for engineering forestation, combines with the individual income in the nursery garden, totally amounts to 12 million RMB (Zhang and Lü, 2020). Meanwhile, the energy to construct the function of the carbon sink zone will be enhanced too.

Benefits of Clean Energy Project

To reduce pollution, Tibet is making efforts to construct the project of clean energy. The long-term constructive plan of biogas digesters and solar stoves has taken Tibet for a while. It sets the goal for ten years from the starting year in "Twelfth Five-Year Plan": to fulfill the construction of biogas and solar energy tasks for about 250 thousand households and provide clean energy for about 1.25 million residents (Yu, 2012). This goal is in progress and promoted continuously, and notable benefit has been achieved. For example, in 2006, the nation invested more than 19 million RMB in the construction projects of rural biogas and solar energy in Lhasa city, Shanna area, and Chengdu area in Tibet.

In 2007, Tibet promoted the biogas model of high efficient, new energy sources vigorously, which could be summarized as "one pool, one greenhouse, and three transformations." These mean one biogas digester, one sunlight greenhouse, and three transformations, pigsty, bathroom, and kitchen for every household, respectively. At the end of 2007, more than 25 thousand households were using biogas. According to the calculation, for a household with 3 to 5 people, one biogas pool, about 8 to 10 cubic meters, can satisfy 80% of the energy consumption. Suppose 25 thousand households are using the biogas pools. In that case, the annual output of biogas is more than 9.6 million cubic meters, which can substitute the standard coal for over 6,800 tons, reduce the sulfur dioxide emissions by about 270 tons, and the carbon dioxide by over 13,700 tons. Moreover, the residue fluid and sludge can replace the chemical fertilizer for about 42.7%.

In 2008, Tibet attained the goal of 30 thousand households using the biogas pools again. About 150 thousand farmers and herders can use solar energy cookers and biogas digesters. According to the " Implementation Scheme of the Substitute Energy Construction Project for reducing Firewood" approved by the government in Tibet Autonomous Region in 2007, combined with the conclusive results, this project has brought noticeable ecological benefits. Two hundred ten thousand biogas digesters were completed accumulatively, and 395,000 solar stoves were promoted in Tibet in 2013(State Council Information Office, 2013). When this project is fully completed, the calculation results show that all the residents in the County towns of Tibet will use alternative energy. About 50% of the herdsmen can use this new energy (except for the solar cooker) too.

At last, Tibet can reduce about 1.32 million tons of firewood consumption per year and 1.412 million tons of animal wastes, saving about 183 thousand hectares of forest from being destroyed. This seasonal storage of this forest area is about 82 million cubic meters. This area can also bring about 1.67 million tons of carbon sequestration, 64.1 million tons of sand consolidation, and 0.134 million tons of oxygen gas every year. In Tibet, the function of the carbon sink zone will be enhanced, and the blue sky, white cloud, and forest landscape will be more charming (Yang, 2016).

In 2008, a guiding policy stressed that the farmer is the main body to build the new and robust country; the government should give full attention to their crucial role and initiatives. This policy is contained in the documentation titled The Decision on Some Critical Issues about Promoting the Construction of Rural Reform and Development by the Communist Party Central Committee. Before the Peaceful Liberation of Tibet, the rural areas were poor and neglected. However, now, in terms of environmental quality, Tibet is one of the best areas in the world. Every year, there are thousands of tourists from all over the globe visiting Tibet. The remarkable result is the contribution of the local people's reform and innovation, especially of the rural farmers and herders that continue to explore and practice. Finally, Tibet has found economic and social development with its actual conditions (Wang, 2009). The experience is precious for Tibet and worth carrying forward in the future.

The construction of the Tibet Autonomous Region must accord with the actual local conditions; namely, take the region feature of the undeveloped economy into full consideration. The most important reason is that the natural conditions in the snow-covered plateau are incredibly adverse. In the guiding plan of the Program "State's Storming the Fortifications in the Work of Helping the Poor (1994-2000)," there were five poor counties assigned by the government. By implementing a guiding plan National Program for Rural Poverty Alleviation (2001-2010), the central government made a new policy of "treating Tibet as the special concentrated poverty areas to support." All 74 counties in Tibet were included in this new policy. Other guiding plans that The National Program for Rural Poverty Alleviation (2011-2020) that approved by the Chinese State Council points out, in the next decade, national poverty alleviation measures should focus on the following areas: These are 14 of "concentrated poverty areas" such as the four clustering areas of Tibetan population including Tibet Autonomous Region, Qinghai Province, Sichuan Province, and Gansu Province, and the three regions, minority prefecture of south Xinjiang Uygur Autonomous Region (Zhang, 2017).

The poverty alleviation efforts for years have had a remarkable social effect. In 2011, the per-capital net income of farmers and herders in the Tibet Autonomous Region was 4,904 RMB, 2.5 times larger than that in 2001, with an annual growth rate of about 13.3%. Meanwhile, according to the 1,700 RMB poverty baseline determined in 2006, 560 thousand people broke out of poverty, accounting for 52.8% of the sparse population (Shen, 2017). The central government and people all over the country have supported Tibet in various ways. All ethnic groups have united and waged an arduous battle against poverty. The result is exciting. By the end of 2019, all 628,000 registered poor farmers and herders in Tibet had overcome poverty, and all 74 impoverished counties and districts had eliminated poverty. Absolute poverty has been eradicated historically in Tibet (State Council Information Office， 2021). However， It is still challenging to eliminate the social, natural, and economic factors that underlie poverty. More significant challenges exist in a new round of preventing the recurrence of poverty factors, and the challenges can be summarized as four points.

Firstly, the degree of poverty is higher. In 2011, the per-capital net income of farmers and herders in Tibet Autonomous Region accounted for 70 % of the national average level, making this area the only province with a large area of concentrated individual poverty.

Secondly, the impoverished scope is more significant. There are many poor people with various difficulties in Tibet. The new national poverty line calculation shows that almost 830 thousand people now live below the poverty line, accounting for 34 % of the total population in agricultural and pastoral areas.

Thirdly, the reason for poverty is more complicated. Due to natural and historical factors, Tibet's economic and social development is still in the primary stage with a weak foundation. The infrastructure in agricultural and pastoral areas is inadequate, and the insufficient supply of public services is prominent. What is more, natural disasters are frequent in this area, leading to the very fundamental problem of the return-to-poor phenomenon.

Fourthly, the management of poverty is complex. Tibet faces many mixed contradictions, such as the contradiction between concentrated poverty and great-leap-forward development, the contradiction between stabilization of sufficient food and clothing and production restructuring, the contradiction between poverty alleviation, and comprehensive well-off. In a word, the main and the particular contradictions of economic and social development are intertwined in Tibet. So, under this circumstance, poverty alleviation in a new stage calls for innovative ideas and new methods. One exploration and innovation is constructing the "carbon sink function zone."

Carbon Sink Function Zone

The term "carbon sink function zone" means a constructive new-style area of the carbon sink economy. The area's characteristic is that giving full play to its resource advantages gets economic efficiency by the relevant resolutions of the United Nations in law enforcement, such as building a carbon sink forest to reduce carbon emissions. It is an effective way to increase the income for the farmers and herders. Tibet Autonomous Region has a unique natural and geographical environment conducive to constructing the "carbon sink function zone" in the Tibetan area.

During the "Tenth Five-Years Plan (2001-2005)," the Chinese Academy of Sciences carried out a National Key Basic Research Development Plan of China. We call it research on the "Formation and Evolution of Qinghai-Tibet Plateau, the Environmental Effect and Resource Effect." This study showed that the ecosystem of Qinghai-Tibet Plateau created services value about 936.39 billion RMB every year, accounting for 16.7% of the national level and 0.61% of the global level. Qinghai-Tibet Plateau is the most significant carbon sink area in China, and it is an essential base for the environmental system of China Mainland and East Asia. This first source is the basis for a new round of development and can make breakthrough progress in sustainable development (She, Wu and Huang et al., 2017).

The Report of the "17th Communist Party of China National Congress" pointed out clearly that we must enhance our capacity to respond to climate change and make new contributions to the protection of the global climate. A stretch of frost and plains in the Tibet Autonomous Region is the carbon sink zone with enormous potential, reducing the gas concentration in the atmosphere. Therefore, we need to take the scientific view of development as the guideline, take advantage of the resource environment in Tibet, to construct the carbon sink function zone, which is an effective way to implement the mission of relevant policies (Wang, Wang and Cheng et al., 2017).

To construct the carbon sink zone, we should take the Outline of the "Eleventh Five-Years Plan (2006-2010)" of China as the guideline, and take The National Programs on Coping with Climate Change (2007) issued by The State Council of China as the standard for action. Then, we can use the power of "energy-saving and emission reduction" promoted by the State Council of China to make the overall arrangements, pushing forward steadily (Yan and Hu, 2012).

Firstly, do the overall plan and conduct a demonstration pilot project for carbon sink construction. It is difficult to construct the carbon sink function zone, so we must make a comprehensive practical plan with "government guidance, multi-units participation" (The National Programs on Coping with Climate Change 2007). Furthermore, we should start with the more manageable tasks before moving on to the more difficult ones, putting efficiency first.

Secondly, focus more on the unique features of the nature reserve. According to the geographical environment and outstanding climate, and within the framework of natural resources that have already been approved, we should take measures in the light of local conditions. Moreover, we need to pay more attention to the standard of vegetation coverage choose the area with the healthy function of carbon-oxygen transformation, thus conducting a demonstration pilot project for carbon sink construction.

Thirdly, combine ecological protection and economic development. The goal for constructing the carbon sink function zone is to create the necessary conditions for human beings, leading to lasting stability and sustainable development in Tibet, even in China and the world. Therefore, it is required to set the right direction. Developing ecological economics and the environmental resources industries are the right things we need to do. Only when we coordinate the enrich measures and environmental protection can we arouse the people's enthusiasm in urban and rural areas.

The more forest grasslands, the stronger the function of carbon-oxygen transformation will be. For a time, the Tibetan public gave this kind of evaluation to the forestation: "plant trees in spring, no greens in summer." It sounds like this project is wasting money and time, so we need to take adequate measures to change this inefficient situation.

It is undeniable that some regions taking the "vanity projects" blindly pursue the forestation size. On the one hand, we should conduct the forestation with a liberated mind and initiative spirit. To improve the survival rate of trees, we need to comprehensively implement the policy that the Forestry Department made of Tibet Autonomous Region by 2008: "Forbid to conduct the forestation beyond the range, forbid to misuse the project funds, and forbid to change the design operation casually."

Everybody should remember that planting a tree is equal to constructing a carbon sink. In a word, we must end the flashy actions to effectively assure the survival rate of trees at an elevated level. On the other hand, we should ensure that the public can benefit from the forestation. The relevant department should properly use the project funds and promptly pay the workers' salaries. Meanwhile, the department can try to use part of the fund as an investment in science and technology, which will make a long-term benefit for the local farmers and herders.

Conclusion

It is necessary to make plans and implement them efficiently to make profound progress for social development. For most people in the world, settling down usually comes first, and then they can engage in productive activities as soon as possible. This kind of "settling down" applies to many human activities, like eating, housing, wearing, and so on. It has been a necessary condition for human society for thousands of years and the precondition for beautifying and purifying the environment in modern times.

The housing project has benefited the public directly, so the farmers and herders welcome it. Forestation should be the main task of local construction. Firstly, accelerate the pace of building new countryside. Firmly establish the grand goal of making a pristine countryside, prioritize developing production, and mobilize the masses to plant more trees.

Secondly, construct houses with energy efficiency. We should continue to use new and green materials for building, reducing the usage of wood. At the same time, the plan and layout of the village are also essential; the housing can be appropriately concentrated so that we can protect farmland and save environmental resources.

Thirdly, give full respect to people's willingness. The houses are exceptional with people's features, which reflect the wisdom of people's intelligence and high creativity. When building homes, the government should consider the cultures and styles and let people enjoy the fruits of re-construction and transformation.

The project to construct functional zones is not only to plant trees. This construction has so much content, as the low-carbon lifestyle is precisely a critical aspect. Besides, some enforcement laws should be continuously reinforced, and more steps should be taken to construct function zones. According to the Plan to consider ecological environment characteristics of Guangxi Zhuang Autonomous Region, Tibet Autonomous Region, and Guizhou Province, and within the overall plan of the national main function zones, the goal of national strength and prosperity will soon be achieved by the measures discussed. The Chinese people must form a rational layout of productive forces, take full advantage of the natural resources, and contribute strengths to society's development.

Chapter 5
Urban Agglomeration Coordinated Development

The pursuit of modernization is one of the essential activities for human society. Urbanization is seen in China as the main path to modernization. Urban agglomerations are an important symbol in the development of modernization. This study attempts to utilize the establishment of National Urban Agglomeration (NUA) as a quasi-natural experiment in the Chinese scenario and construct the difference-in-differences (DID) model to examine the effect of NUA implementation policy on economic development and environmental pollution in China. It adopts 280 cities from 2005 to 2018 in China as the research samples. The result shows that the NUA policy can deliver a win-win situation in boosting economic growth and reducing environmental pollution, which still holds after the robustness test. The heterogeneity analysis showed that compared to the central and western regions, the curbing effect of the NUA policy on SO2 emissions is apparent in the eastern region. It is essential to strengthen regional cooperation and establish the community of interests' development concept between cities.

Introduction

Regional development planning is playing an influential role in China's modernization process. In particular, China developed and implemented the National Urban Agglomeration (NUA) policy in 2015. In this context, we analyze the theoretical relationship between the NUA policy and the regional economy and environment and use the NUA policy as a quasi-natural experiment in the Chinese scenario to explore the effect of the NUA policy on regional economic development and pollution emissions. Existing studies on regional integration typically use the price approach to measure the degree of regional integration rather than focusing on regional integration policy. This chapter aims to examine the NUA policy impact at a macro level, rather than being limited to the level of a particular economic zone. We can broaden the spatial scale of policy evaluation, enrich the research on coordinated regional development, and provide meaningful international lessons for other emerging countries. Cities have increasingly become the center of human production and life, a significant characteristic of modernization.

It can be said that urbanization is essential for realizing modernization, and the city is the spatial expression of modernization. In China's practice, urbanization is seen as an important approach to modernization. China must learn from the advanced experience of the first modernization transition in developed countries, such as the labor transfer and forming a unified factor market. Also, China must face the new situation of the second modernization transition, such as the information technology revolution and the regional eco-environmental problems. Urban agglomerations are an important symbol of the improved level of modernization in China. Examining the future trends regarding China's modernization through urban agglomerations will support the judgment that China is on the " last leg " of modernization while highlighting development uncertainty.

An urban agglomeration is a group of cities with a compact spatial organization. It closes economic ties, generally with mega-cities as the core and three or more large cities as the constituent units, formed within a specific geographical area and relying on well-developed transport and communication networks (Fang and Yu, 2017). Agglomeration benefits are key drivers of economic growth and prosperity in large cities (Rosenthal and Strange, 2004). Labour productivity and wage premiums perform better in densely populated and larger cities (Combes et al., 2015). Yet, despite the higher productivity of larger cities, city size has not been the key to its growth of welfare in recent years (Camagni et al., 2016). Metropolitan functions rely more on inter-city network embeddedness than city size (Meijers et al., 2016).

Urban agglomerations are among the most important geographical units for countries to participate effectively in the global economy, process information and allocate capital (Friedman, 1986). The development experience of developed economies shows that dense urban areas represented by urban agglomerations can effectively promote regional development through knowledge spillover and industrial clustering. The Great Lakes urban agglomeration in North America is a good example. Other examples include the Atlantic Coastal Urban Agglomeration in the Northeast of the United States, the Pacific Coast agglomeration in Japan and the British Urban Agglomeration. Competition between regions is increasingly concentrated on the combined power of urban agglomerations. Regional planning policy has effectively reduced inter-regional disparities and promoted economic and environmental development (Saunavaara, 2017; Randolph, 2019).

Over the past 40 years, China has carried out several regional adjustment policies at different stages of development. The "Reform and Opening-up" policy was implemented in China in 1978, focusing on establishing special economic zones in the eastern coastal areas to attract foreign investment and develop the productive forces of society. The "Western Development" policy was approved and implemented by the State Council in 1999 to narrow the economic gap between the western region (involving 12 provinces or autonomous regions) and the eastern coastal region and improve people's living standards. The "Revitalization of Northeast China," proposed in 2003, aims to support the restructuring and transformation of industries in the Northeast and support the development of sustainable industries in cities where resource extraction is the main focus. The "Rise of Central China" was approved in 2006 to explicitly build a national grain production base, energy and raw material base. It also serves as a modern equipment manufacturing and high technology industry base and a comprehensive transportation hub in the central region (including six provinces) to promote the common development of the central region. The "One Belt, One Road" was introduced in 2013 to strengthen economic ties among countries along the route, explore the potential of intra-regional markets, create demand and employment, and enhance cultural exchanges among people along the route.

From the implementation of the "Reform and Opening Up (1978)" to the gradual promotion of the "Western Development (1999)" to the "Revitalization of Northeast China (2003)", the "Rise of Central China (2006)" and the "One Belt, One Road" (2013), indicating that the national development planning has become an effective means of promoting China's regional economic and social development. The term urban agglomeration first appeared in the outline of China's 11th Five-Year Plan in 2006. The National New Urbanization Plan (2014-2020) and the 13th Five-Year Plan (2016-2020) have explicitly proposed urban agglomeration as the main form of promoting new urbanization. These policies have coordinated regional development. During this period, China's State Council has approved ten national urban agglomerations. According to the China Urban Agglomerations Development Report in 2019, the 19 urban agglomerations generated more than 85% of the country's GDP with an area of about 25%.

The urbanization rate reached over 61% in these regions. For a long time, for the GDP race and political advancement, local officials' protectionism and rent-seeking behavior aggravate regional market fragmentation (Young, 2000), distorting market resource allocation, environmental pollution, and other problems. As an important tool for modernization in China, can implementing the National Urban Agglomeration (NUA) policy bring about coordinated development of the economy and environment? Accurate evaluation of the effects of the NUA policy has become a hot issue of concern for government agencies and academics.

Urban development planning involves a complex relationship between economic growth, environmental protection and social equity in cities (Campbell, 1996). Many scholars have conducted numerous researches on the definition (Gottmann, 1957; Kipnis, 1997; Kanemoto,

2002; Steiner, 2003), spatial organization (Lang, 2009; Wu, 2015), and spatial distribution (Lin and Chen, 2003) of urban agglomerations. Many kinds of literature have focused on the impact effects of regional integration, which fall into two main areas.

On the one hand, it has been found in the literature that urban integration can enhance economic productivity by accelerating factor mobility (Jeanneney et al., 2006), promoting industrial upgrading (Aghion et al., 2015), and strengthening regional cooperation (Brakman et al., 2012), among others. Meijers (2017) examined whether the urban integration consisting of the polycentric urban region (PUR) in Europe affects the performance of PUR; and found that functional and institutional integration of PURs positively affects the economic performance of PURs. He (2019) pointed out that the spatial organization of the Chang-Zhu-Tan urban agglomeration has a marked concentration trend. The agglomeration effect has an important role in its integrated development process.

Li (2017) found that regional integration has a significant positive influence on the energy and CO2 emissions performance. He (2018) found that China's regional economic integration gradually increased over 2002-2011, contributing to the marginal abatement cost of CO2. He's study (2020) showed that regional integration has a significant inhibitory effect on transboundary water pollution. On the other hand, urban integration enhances using environmental resources and thus reduces total regional pollution emissions (Chen and Huang, 2014). In addition, urban regional integration buffers the role of environmental regulation (Sheng, 2021), which can cause a decline in regional environmental quality (Surya, 2021).

The literature has studied the relationship between regional integration and energy, carbon emissions and economic growth. Although the NUA policy has existed for many years, most studies have only focused on individual city clusters or economic zones. Most of these studies have used the price approach to measure the degree of regional integration rather than focusing on regional integration policy, neglecting to examine the impact of NUA policy at the macro level.

The reasons for using China as our setting for our empirical study are as follows. First, as the second-largest economy in the world, unlike developed economies, China is still in the transition phase from the central-planned to the market economy. In the context of China's transition from the "administrative economy" to "economic integration," it is critical to scientifically assess the economic and environmental effects of the NUA policy, especially for emerging economies. Second, as an old Chinese saying goes, "It is impossible to have a good plan for the present without any long-term strategy." Planning policy has become an essential tool for macroeconomic regulation by the Chinese government (Fan et al., 2013).

China has drawn up and implemented fourteen consecutive "The Five-Year Plan," which have played an irreplaceable role in guiding development, allocating public resources and achieving strategic goals. China's HDI (Human Development Index) has risen from 0.41 in 1978 to 0.758 in 2018. According to the World Bank's international poverty standards, seven hundred forty million people have been lifted out of poverty in China, accounting for around 70% of global poverty reduction. The 13th Five-Year Plan (2016-2020), which has already been carried out, and the 14th Five-Year Plan (2021-2025), which is currently being implemented, focus on NUA as an important spatial vehicle for promoting coordinated development of the economy and environment. China's policy system provides an ideal condition for testing the effects of NUA policy.

Our study's marginal contribution is summarized: First, existing studies on regional integration typically use the price approach to measure the degree of regional integration rather than focusing on regional integration policy. In contrast, this chapter uses the NUA policy as a quasi-natural experiment in the Chinese scenario to explore whether the NUA policy can deliver the dual dividend of promoting economic development and reducing environmental pollution. It can provide meaningful international lessons for other emerging countries. Second, we examine the heterogeneity of NUA policy at the regional and scale levels, providing an empirical experience for further understanding of the role of NUA policy.

Economic and Environmental Effect of the NUA Policy

At the factor allocation level, the center-periphery and free capital models in the new economic geography explain how regional integration shapes the spatial distribution of economic activity based on factor mobility (Krugman, 1991). Regional integration facilitates market competition and promotes the free flow of innovation factors (including the capital, resources, talents, technology, knowledge, information, etc.). It is guided by the market competition mechanism to achieve an optimal combination in a larger space (Grossman, 2015), putting the endowment structure between cities in dynamic change. The efficient allocation of production factors can enhance the coupling between the industrial system and the innovation system among cities, leading to the positive convergence effect, thus helping to stimulate technological innovation and economic growth. On the other hand, local governments will break down barriers to market entry under integrated development. Market integration can facilitate the development of the industrial division of labor system within urban agglomeration. It will bring about the regional industrial agglomeration (Commendatore, 2014; Hong, 2019). In addition, based on the theory of circular cumulative causality, the industrial linkages, spatial overflow and input sharing generated by the integrated development can effectively accelerate the process of inter-city knowledge transfer and innovation diffusion, which enhance the efficiency of economic growth.

Urban agglomeration integration can influence urban pollutant emissions through energy consumption. First, the regional development planning can strengthen the relationship between local governments and reduce internal administrative barriers, integrating energy markets (e.g., establishing the regional pollution emission trading market) and improving the efficiency of using environmental factors. In this context, market integration brings specialization according to comparative advantages (Grossman and Helpman, 2015). It promotes upgrading industrial structure (e.g., cooperating to establish industrial parks, industrial development zones, etc.). Also, it can improve regional resource utilization, reduce the cost-sharing of polluting facilities and generate economy of scale in pollution control. As such, it is thereby incentivizing enterprises to reduce emissions. Second, it has been shown that the diffusion of technological progress and management experience can be limited by regional market segmentation (Peluffo, 2013). With the implementation of the NUA policy, regional market integration has been strengthened. Market competition motivates enterprises to innovate green technologies and adopt more environmentally friendly production techniques. In addition, market integration can speed up the diffusion and application of energy-saving and emission reduction technologies and decrease the transaction costs of environmental protection technologies, improving the efficiency of energy factors and reducing pollution emissions.

Research Design and Process

The regional and temporal variations in implementing the National Urban Agglomeration (NUA) policy provide an opportunity for a difference-in-differences (DID) analysis. Since 2015, China's State Council has approved a total of 10 national-class urban agglomerations, namely: the Yangtze River Midstream City Cluster, the Ha-Chang City Cluster, the Chengdu-Chongqing City Cluster, the Yangtze River Delta City Cluster, the Central Plains City Cluster, the Beibu Gulf City Cluster, the Guanzhong Plain City Cluster, the Hubao-Egyu City Cluster, the Lanzhou-West City Cluster, and the Guangdong-Hong Kong-Macao Greater Bay Area. Considering the Guangdong-Hong Kong-Macao Greater Bay Area was approved in 2019. The remaining nine city clusters were selected for this chapter due to the sample period and data availability constraints. In our study, the sample consisted of 280 cities in China. Specifically, the sample is divided into two groups: the treatment group comprising 143 cities designated as NUA cities and the control group comprising 137 cities from the non-NUA cities. We set the dummy variable NUAi depending on whether the city belongs to the

NUA or not. NUAi indicates city i's NUA status, i.e., NUAi =1 if city i is an NUA city and = 0 if city i is a non-TCZ city. We set the dummy variable Timet according to when the city was approved. Timet indicates the post-treatment period, i.e., Timet = 1 when the city was approved as an NUA and in subsequent years and = 0 otherwise. We can then compare environmental pollution and economic development in NUA cities before and after implementing the NUA policy with the corresponding change in non-NUA cities over the same period.

To ensure the quality of the sample data, the study sample was screened in the following manner: (1) Excluding cities with changes in administrative boundaries (e.g., Sansha, Haidong, etc.) and cities with serious data missing (e.g., Bijie, Tongren, Lhasa, etc.) in the period 2005-2018. (2) Excluding areas with different social regimes (Macau, Hong Kong, and Taiwan). We finally selected 280 cities in China from 2005 to 2019 for our study. The data used in our research are drawn from several sources. Information on the timing of the approval of NUA and the cities included was obtained from the Central People's Government of the People's Republic of China website (http://www.gov.cn/index.htm). The remaining data were collected from the China City Statistical Yearbook from 2005 to 2018. In addition, taking 2005 as the base period, all price-specific data were adjusted to remove the influence of price fluctuations.

The dependent variables include economic development (pcgdp) and environmental change (SO_2), measured by Per Capita GDP (logarithm) and per capita sulfur dioxide emissions, respectively. In the robustness testing section, we also use employment (employment), per capita smoke (smoke) and per capita wastewater (wastewater) in place of the above variables. We chose the per capita emissions of pollutants (logarithm) as a proxy for the environmental variables.

The core explanatory variable in our study is the NUA*Time, an interaction term of the dummy variables, equals 1 after the city i is approved as NUA city, otherwise 0. Following previous studies (He et al., 2018; He and Lu, 2020), the characteristic variables include Con, GI, Sec, Gov, Inv, Hum and Fin. Specifically, (1) social demand includes consumer demand (Con), measured as the ratio of total retail sales of consumer goods to GDP, and government demand (Gov), measured as the share of local government expenditure in GDP; (2) governance intervention (GI), measured by the ratio of fiscal expenditure to fiscal revenue; (3) the level of human capital (Hum), measured by the number of people employed in the city (taken as a logarithm); (4) industrial structure (Sec), measured by the ratio of secondary sector value added to GDP; (5) financial development (Fin), measured by the ratio of total deposits and loans of urban financial institutions to GDP; (6) the share fixed asset investment (Inv), measured by the ratio of the amount of fixed asset investment to GDP. In addition, we have industry and year dummy variables in the regression model. The descriptive statistics for the variables are shown in Table 5.1.

Table1 5.1 Descriptive statistics

Variable	NO. of obs.	min	mean	max	S.D.
pcgdp	4756	4.595	10.231	15.675	0.849
So_2	4562	-1.304	6.773	10.241	1.228
Con	4473	0.0001	0.349	5.671	0.293
Gi	4479	0.649	2.198	39.031	1.836
Gov	4479	0.031	0.142	6.041	0.205
Sec	4479	2.660	48.510	90.970	11.022
Fin	4479	0.245	1.144	24.800	1.089
Hum	4452	1.399	3.415	6.895	0.817
Inv	4476	0.087	0.616	10.979	0.648

The DID estimation model in our study is as follows:

$$y_{it} = \beta_0 + \beta_1 did_{it} + \sum \gamma_j x_{it} + \mu_i + \eta_t + \varepsilon_{it} \quad (1)$$

Where y_{it} is the measurement of dependent variables, including environmental pollution (SO_2) and economic development (pcgdp), in the city i at year t; β_0 is constant term; did_{it} denotes the interaction term of the dummy variables (NUAi*Timet), the coefficient β_1

indicates the net effect of NUA policy on economic development and environmental pollution; x denotes the matrix-vector of the control as mentioned above variables; μ_i denotes the city fixed effect. η_t denotes year fixed effects, representing yearly factors common to all cities, such as industrial policy, monetary policy, macro uncertainty, etc., and ε_{it} denotes the random error term.

Findings and Empirical Analysis

We conduct the DID estimation model, controlling for year and individual fixed effects, to examine the NUA policy on economic growth and environmental pollution. Table 5.2 reports the regression results for equation (1). The coefficients of did are positive and significant at the 5% level in columns (1) and (2) when employing pcgdp as the dependent variable, indicating that the NUA policy positively affects urban economic growth. The results suggest that cities approved as NUA can achieve relatively faster economic growth in integrated regional development. The coefficients of did are negative and significant at the 1% level in columns (4) and (5) when employing SO_2 as the dependent variable, indicating that the NUA policy has a negative effect on SO_2 emissions. Compared to cities that have not been approved, the results suggest that cities that have been approved as NUA can decrease urban SO_2 emissions. Overall, the NUA policy has effectively promoted economic growth while curbing the emission of environmental pollutants.

Table 5.2 Baseline regressive results

Variables		*pcgdp*			*SO_2*	
	(1)	*(2)*	*(3)*	*(4)*	*(5)*	*(6)*
did	0.099***	0.038**	0.031**	-0.183**	-0.196***	-0.145**
	(3.38)	(2.98)	(2.33)	(-2.13)	(-2.30)	(-3.36)
Con		-0.396***	-0.322***		-0.097	0.011
		(-10.18)	(-8.10)		(-0.60)	(0.09)
Gi		-0.026***	-0.037***		-0.087**	-0.053***

		(-6.50)	(-7.04)		(-2.14)	(-3.20)
Gov		0.093	0.600***		2.126**	1.043***
		(1.18)	(-4.83)		(2.55)	(2.60)
Sec		0.015***	0.016***		0.014***	0.017***
		(26.06)	(25.18)		(3.10)	(8.40)
Fin		-0.070***	-0.061**		-0.016	0.045*
		(-9.41)	(-7.41)		(-0.34)	(1.72)
Inv		0.076***	0.097***		0.016	0.055
		(4.90)	(5.55)		(0.17)	(0.98)
City fixed	Yes	Yes	Yes	Yes	Yes	Yes
Time fixed	Yes	Yes	Yes	Yes	Yes	Yes
Observations	4477	4378	4016	4397	4306	3959

Notes: *, **and *** respectively denote the significance level of 10%, 5% and 1%, and the value in brackets is t value.

To test the robustness of the model results, we relax the assumption of individual randomness and apply the PSM-DID method for estimation. In the following way, we first use the control variables as matching variables and calculate the propensity score for each city using the logistic model and match the scores. Next, we estimate the impact of NUA policy on economic development and environmental pollution using the DID method. The estimated results are in columns (3) and (6) in Table 5.2. The coefficients of did were 0.030 and -0.148, respectively, and significant at the 5% level in columns (3) and (6), indicating that the NUA policy can significantly enhance urban economic development and reduce pollutant emissions. This finding is generally consistent with the baseline model, i.e., the conclusion that NUA policy can deliver a win-win situation for their cities is robust.

We also use employment, smoke (dust) and wastewater in place of the above variables. As shown in Table 5.3, the coefficient of did is significantly positive at the 5% level in column (1) when employment is the dependent variable. The coefficients of did are negative and significant at the 10% level in columns (2) and (3) when employing smoke (dust) and wastewater as the dependent variables. The NUA policy has a positive effect on employment and a negative effect on urban smoke (dust) or wastewater emissions, suggesting that the findings of the baseline model still hold after replacing the dependent variables.

Table 5.3 Baseline regressive results

Variables	*employment* (1)	*smoke (dust)* (2)	*wastewater* (3)
did	0.038***	-0.230***	-0.058*
	(2.91)	(-5.21)	(-1.79)
controls	Yes	Yes	Yes
City fixed	Yes	Yes	Yes
Time fixed	Yes	Yes	Yes
Observations	4630	4479	4494

Notes: *, **and *** respectively denote the significance level of 10%, 5% and 1%, and the value in brackets is t value.

In addition, according to Chinese geographical divisions, we divided the sample cities into three regions: eastern, central and western. The estimated results are shown in Table 5.4. The coefficients of did are positive and statistically significant at 1% in columns (1), (3) and (5), indicating that the NUA policy has a significant positive effect on urban economic growth in all regions. The coefficient of did is significantly negative at 1% in column (2), significantly negative at 10% in column (4), and negative but insignificant in column (6), indicating that compared to the central and western regions, the curbing effect of the NUA policy on SO2 emissions is apparent in the eastern region.

Table 5.4 The heterogeneity test at the regional level

Variables	Eastern		Central		Western	
	pcgdp (1)	*So_2 (2)*	*pcgdp (3)*	*So_2 (4)*	*pcgdp (5)*	*So_2 (6)*
did	0.414***	-0.323***	0.375***	-0.143*	0.456***	-0.064
	(5.37)	(-4.68)	(8.13)	(-1.88)	(4.56)	(0.67)
controls	Yes	Yes	Yes	Yes	Yes	Yes
City fixed	Yes	Yes	Yes	Yes	Yes	Yes
Time fixed	Yes	Yes	Yes	Yes	Yes	Yes
Observations	4378	4306	4378	4306	4378	4306

Notes: *, **and *** respectively denote the significance level of 10%, 5% and 1%, and the value in brackets is t value.

Conclusions and Policy Implications

Based on the panel data of 280 cities from 2005 to 2018, this study evaluates the effects of NUA policy on economic growth and environmental pollution by using DID model. The main findings are as follows. First, the NUA policy has effectively promoted economic growth while reducing environmental pollutants. Second, this study examines the heterogeneity of NUA policy at the regional level, showing that the effects of the NUA policy are more evident in the eastern region.

The revelations are as follows. Firstly, Regional development planning ensures policy continuity at the macro level and contributes to long-term stable economic development, which is one of the concentrated manifestations of the Chinese model. For developing countries, in particular, it is important to strengthen inter-city linkages and develop a sustained and coherent regional development policy that plays its role in leading the direction of development and allocating public resources. In addition, the decisive role of the market in resource allocation should be brought into play to promote the full flow of factors. The authorities should break down barriers between cities through institutional reform and give cities of different levels a relatively balanced right to development. According to local conditions, the construction of communities of interest should be promoted in key areas (transport integration, ecological and environmental protection, and industrial docking and collaboration).

Secondly, the management should promote the transformation and upgrading of the city's industrial structure by implementing differentiated industrial policies. Credit and financial incentives should be implemented to attract qualified enterprises and talents. It will improve the R&D capability of enterprises to ensure the wide application of green technology.

Finally, the environmental protection sector should strengthen the synergistic management of environmental pollution emissions between cities, such as further promoting joint prevention and control of air pollution and increasing the comprehensive management of transboundary water pollution. Market-based "green technology + finance"' integrated solutions should be explored, and the concept of community of interest development should be established.

Chapter 6
Integration of Industries and Rural Economic Revitalization

Integrated development between the primary, secondary and tertiary industries is an important means of promoting the transformation and upgrading of agriculture and revitalizing rural areas. Scholars have paid much attention to the research on the model integrating the primary, secondary and tertiary industries. Based on the field survey of Yongan village in Fujian Province, it was found that Yongan Village made a new attempt to integrate the primary, secondary and tertiary industries. It first developed agriculture in the primary industry. The tertiary industry is based on the study of tourism flourishing around the flower culture, and finally, the processing of flowers and other agricultural products for tourism. It creatively moves from the development of primary industries to tertiary industries and then to secondary industries, i.e., the "1+3+2" development model. Thus, it provides a new path for integrating the primary, secondary and tertiary industries. Based on the empirical exploration into Yongan Village, an experience program with distinctive themes, which integrates the primary, secondary and tertiary industries, was first designed from the perspective of the experience economy. Second, the infrastructure construction was reinforced, and the personnel security system was enhanced to advance the steady progress in integrating the primary, secondary and tertiary industries. The development model of such integration in Yongan Village was studied to provide theoretical guidance and practical reference for other rural areas in China and even other parts of the world.

Introduction

China's economy has undergone tremendous changes over the past 40 years of reform and opening-up. At the same time, China's rural areas have also undergone farmers' aging, rural hollowing-out and other rural recession, the root cause of which is the lack of sustainable factor supply for rural industrial development (Kong & Xia, 2019). Based on the reality, the industrial prosperity in China's rural revitalization should be achieved by strengthening agriculture, developing related industries around agriculture, extending the agricultural industrial chain, and developing agricultural and rural service industries (Kong et al., 2018). In 2015, the Chinese government officially proposed a strategic plan to promote the integrated development of the primary, secondary and tertiary industries in rural areas. In the following five years, the government has given clear instructions on the integrated development between the primary, secondary and tertiary industries in rural areas.

The integrated development between the primary, secondary and tertiary industries in China's countryside is also developing very rapidly under the high emphasis of the government. At the end of 2015, the national operating income of leisure agriculture was 440 billion yuan (Zong et al., 2017). In 2017, the national operating income of leisure agriculture and rural tourism was 740 billion yuan (Zhang, 2019). In 2018, the National Development and Reform Commission released a report on integrated development between the primary, secondary and tertiary industries, summarizing the typical experiences in this aspect. It sets the main idea for constructing modern agriculture in China, marking the rise of integrated development between the primary, secondary and tertiary industries to the national strategic level (Xiong & Zhang, 2019). It can be seen that integrated development between the primary, secondary and tertiary industries is an important means to promote agricultural transformation and upgrading and rural revitalization, among which leisure agriculture plays an important role. In the era of the experience economy, it is characterized by the fact that goods and services are endowed with experience value and enable consumers to be physically and mentally delighted (Yu, 2017). Experience economy provides new ideas for the implementation path of integrated development between the primary, secondary and tertiary industries. Therefore, from the experience economy perspective, it is important to integrate with the primary, secondary and tertiary industries to promote rural revitalization. This study will conduct in-depth research on the case of Yongan village in Fujian Province to analyze and discover the model integrating the primary, secondary and tertiary industries in this village, which is different from other Chinese villages. Thus, it provides theoretical and practical references for the research field of integrated development between the primary, secondary and tertiary industries for rural revitalization in China and the integration of the primary, secondary and tertiary industries in other villages in China.

The concept of integrated development between the primary, secondary and tertiary industries in rural China comes from the "sixth industry" abroad. In the 1990s, Japanese scholar Naraomi Imamura first proposed the concept of "sixth industry," which means the integration and penetration of rural primary, secondary and tertiary industries to form a complete industrial chain integrating production, processing, marketing and services. And the sixth industry is the multiplication effect of the primary, secondary and tertiary industries (Imamura, 1996). The sixth industry specifically encourages farmers to engage in agricultural processing (secondary industry) and agricultural marketing or services (tertiary industry) based on the primary industry. "1+2+3" equals 6, and "1×2×3" also equals 6, and Japanese scholars call it "sixth industry" (Kong et al., 2018). On this basis, different aspects of the sixth industry have also been studied in various countries. Chaniotakis pointed out that integrating primary, secondary, and tertiary industries can help develop the rural economy and protect the rural ecosystem (Chaniotakis, 2017). Donaubauer J. and Meyer B. et al. point out that infrastructure, human capital and investment environment will directly affect the benefits of rural-related integration, so the government should increase financial investment in these areas (Donaubauer & Meyer, 2016). Compared to foreign studies, studies started late in China but have developed very rapidly. The current research on integrated development between the primary, secondary and tertiary industries in rural areas is mainly focused on the following aspects:

First, the research is about the connotation and development stages of integrated development between the primary, secondary and tertiary industries in rural areas. According to Wang Lejun et al., integration of the primary, secondary and tertiary industries refers to the process of relying on agriculture and realizing the extension of the agricultural industry chain, the leap of the value chain, the expansion of functions and the win-win situation of multiple subjects using industrial linkage, factor accumulation, technology penetration and institutional innovation. It also allows farmers to participate in the secondary and tertiary industries and share the value-added income (Wang, 2017). Xiao Weidong et al. proposed that integration of the primary, secondary and tertiary industries is to establish new agricultural organizational modes and develop new agricultural sectors, formats and modes by reorganizing various sectors within agriculture and integrating agriculture and rural secondary and tertiary industries (Xiao & Du, 2019). Yang Yanfeng et al. proposed that industrial integration refers to the synthesis of two or more industries into a new one, which gradually reveals new industrial attributes (Yang et al., 2020). Wan Baorui divided the history of integration of the primary, secondary and tertiary industries in China into three stages: the initial stage of agro-industrial joint operation, the primary stage of agricultural industrialization, and the stage of integrated development between agriculture and information, tourism, culture, and education, where the agricultural chain is extended (Wan, 2019).

Second, the research is related to the model integrating the primary, secondary and tertiary industries in rural areas. Jiang Gaoming proposed that the primary task is to create jobs for farmers around their residence and develop primary processing industries, commerce, tourism, and culture around agriculture to promote the development of primary, secondary, and tertiary agriculture (Jiang, 2019). Sun Jingmiao et al. proposed that we should fully utilize the unique resource advantages, human conditions, ecological scenery of rural areas and integrate the primary, secondary and tertiary industries through industrialization. We may develop modern farming, rural industry, rural service industry, leisure agriculture and smart agriculture based on modern agriculture (Sun et al., 2018). Cheng et al. proposed the concept of "secondary agriculture" in the integration of the primary, secondary and tertiary industries, which utilizes various organic residues or wastes mainly from agriculture to produce and sell high value-added biofuels and biosynthetic materials, thus forming a new "secondary agriculture" (Cheng & Zhu, 2020). Wang Jingyi proposed that the development model integrating the primary, secondary and tertiary industries in China includes industrial link extension, leading enterprise-driven, regional industry cluster and leisure countryside tourism (Wang et al., 2018). Jiang Tianlong et al. proposed that industrial integration can be divided into three types according to the categories of industries included: the first is the integration between the primary and secondary industries, i.e., the "1+2" model that uses processing technology and manufacturing technology to enhance the added value of agricultural products; the second is the integration of primary and tertiary industries, i.e., the "1+3" model that utilizes the catering, wholesale, retail, tourism, and recreation industries to expand and enhance the added value of agricultural products; the third model is the "1+2+3" model that integrates these three industries (Jiang & Shu, 2020).

Third, the research is on integrated development between the primary, secondary, and tertiary industries from the experience economy perspective. Taking Guangdong Province as an example, Pan Ling proposed five development models of rural tourism products in Guangdong from the perspective of functional value, enjoyment value and conformity value of experience demand based on the characteristics of rural tourism in Guangdong (Pan, 2020). Zhang Liqiong proposed that to get out of the green marketing dilemma of ecological agriculture, we could optimize the structure of agricultural products and cultivate green and organic brands. Also, we may build a platform for tracing the origin of products to transform agriculture into a green and low-carbon industry in the context of an experience economy (Zhang, 2021). Wang Yueqi suggested that the combination of study tours and experience economy can lead to profound impressions from the problem of traditional study tours in which participants do not have a perception of participation (Wang, 2021). Focusing on the ranch, Wang Zhanlong and Zhang Guocheng proposed that leisure experience modes such as science popularization and education, animal husbandry and labor, characteristic homestay, and DIY experience are the future development orientations of leisure tourism ranches (Wang & Zhang, 2018).

Fourth is the theoretical study of integrated development between the primary, secondary, and tertiary industries. Lu Qianwen divided Chinese scholars' research on the integration of primary, secondary and tertiary industries into three stages: the first stage before the introduction of foreign industrial integration theories, the second stage when successful foreign theories were introduced, and the third stage when integrated development between the primary, secondary and tertiary industries rose to a national strategy and gradually matured (Lu, 2016). In addition, Chinese scholars have studied the integration of the primary, secondary and tertiary industries based on different theories. Liang Weijun analyzed whether the integration of the primary, secondary and tertiary industries is horizontal or vertical. He suggested that both approaches eventually evolve into a block-like industrial chain development form of horizontal industry widening and vertical industry lengthening (Liang, 2011). From the perspective of cultural science, Li Bing proposes to refine rural cultural imagery. Since the tertiary industry is a way to recover the real cultural imagery to realize the intergenerational transmission of regional culture, the cultural imagery should be developed in conjunction with the tertiary industry (Li, 2019). Based on the opportunity cost theory, Ren Liang et al. argued that the opportunity cost of agricultural land for ecological construction such as afforestation and grass planting is less than that of agriculture. They proposed building an integrated system that prioritizes the development of ecosystems and considers the development of agricultural sectors (Ren et al., 2021). Tan Mingjiao proposed a three-dimensional theory of integrating the primary, secondary and tertiary industries (Tan, 2020). Wang Chao et al. proposed a comprehensive layout and arrangement of integrated development between the primary, secondary and tertiary industries in rural areas based on the system engineering theory's system elements and structural relationships (Wang et al., 2021). Chen Yangfen and Wang Guogang compiled theories of rural industrial development in China and revealed that they were based on economic, sociological, and geographic perspectives (Chen & Wang, 2020).

Through a review of foreign and domestic studies on integrated development between the primary, secondary and tertiary industries, we found that foreign studies started earlier than China and mainly focused on the integrated development of industries in various countries. The research on integration of the primary, secondary and tertiary industries in China has not yet reached the stage of vigorous development. It mainly focuses on the connotation, development stage, development model and theoretical research of such integration in rural areas. Among these studies, the study of the development model for such integration is particularly important as it has an essential role in guiding and providing a reference for the integrated development between the primary, secondary and tertiary industries in rural areas. From the studies mentioned above, we can find that the research on the model integrating the development between the primary, secondary and tertiary industries based on industry types is mostly focused on the "1+2" model, "1+3" model, or "1+2+3" model and few studies on other models. Based on the experience economy perspective, most studies focus on a specific field such as agricultural products, ranching, and study tours. However, few studies on the overall development model integrate the primary, secondary, and tertiary industries. Therefore, this study attempts to study the integrated development between the primary, secondary and tertiary industries from the experience economy perspective, using the case of Yongan village in Fujian Province. In addition, the "1+3+2" upgrading path is proposed to offer some insights to the research on the integrated development between the primary, secondary and tertiary industries in China, compared with the existing models in China.

Case Selection and Research Methodology

The research team selected the case based on three criteria: First, the case village must represent the development model integrating the primary, secondary and tertiary industries in its natural and geographical environment. Second, the village organization in the case village must attach great importance to the integration of the primary, secondary and tertiary industries. It must formulate a detailed development plan and implement it in an orderly manner. Third, the case village should achieve some social benefits and influence.

Case Selection

This study analyzed Yongan Village in Majia Town, Luojiang District, Quanzhou City, Fujian Province based on three criteria above. First of all, the natural and geographical environment of Yongan village has a typical feature of integrated development between the primary, secondary and tertiary industries. With convenient traffic, the village is located in the north of Luojiang District, west of Xiangong Mountain and northwest of Majia Township. It is 1 km from Majia Town, 30 km from the downtown of Quanzhou City, 117 km from Xiamen City and 156 km from Fuzhou City, the capital of Fujian Province. With about 3 square kilometers, the village has a river valley basin with an altitude of 80-150 meters, rolling hills and a subtropical monsoon climate. The mountain soil is mainly Lateritic red earth with acidic reaction and high fertility. The village has 729 mu (1 mu = 0.0667 hectares) acres of arable land and 5,686 mountainous lands. Second, the village organization is highly functional and attaches great importance to and solidly promotes the integrated development between the primary, secondary and tertiary industries. In 2013, Yongan Village began developing the flower industry and creating a flower industry chain. In 2016, to provide villagers with a sound village environment and prepare for future tourism development, the village organized the construction of a village activity space of 1,050 square meters and a senior citizens' cultural and sports center of 1,500 square meters. It widened, hardened, greened, and beautified the village's main roads.

In addition, the village sanitation and cleaning in Yongan Village have been outsourced to normalize the cleaning process. Pollution has been resolved by the living pollution pond built. Furthermore, the condition and appearance of the village have been improved in all aspects. After being transformed into a beautiful village, Yongan Village also developed a high-quality route of beautiful countryside tour, linked up with Xiangong Mountain, Huini Reservoir and other tourist attractions. It started to develop the rural leisure tourism industry by organizing the orchid festival, ecological tourism festival, food festival and other thematic activities. Third, Yongan Village has gained certain social benefits and influence. In 2016, Yongan Village was awarded the title of "Beautiful Village" in Luojiang District, and in 2018, it was awarded "Fujian Provincial Civilized Village" and "Environmentally Livable Village in Fujian Province." In addition, the village's orchid planting was reported in the local news many times, and its practices were included in the Selected Cases of Developing and Strengthening Village-level Collective Economy in Fujian, which provided references for other villages.

Figure 6.1 Aerial view of Yongan Village
(Yongan Villagers' Committee, 2021)

Figure 6.2 Zoning plan for the rural revitalization
(Yongan Villagers' Committee, 2021)

Research Methodology

Using an ethnographic approach, the research team conducted field surveys in Yongan village from March to August 2021 and interviewed 20 residents, including the Secretary of Yongan village and other villagers' committee officials and villagers. During this period, the Secretary of Yongan village and other villagers' committee officials came to the school where the research team was working, exchanging profound ideas. At the request of Yongan village, the research team conducted surveys on rural experience programs and led village officials from Yongan village to Fuzhou and Xiamen several times to investigate better-developed experience programs.

The research team and other university teams were commissioned by the villagers' committee of Yongan Village to design flower study tours, herbal medicine study tours, and floral food study tours. Based on thorough surveys, the research team discussed with the officials of Yongan Village many times and finally decided on the proposal according to its actual situation. In July 2021, the research team lived in the village for several days and carried out various study tours according to the proposal. In study tours, the research team consulted and worked with the village cadres and volunteers in Yongan Village to develop close cooperative relationships. During the cooperation, the research team carefully observed their ideas and practical actions regarding the development of the village and the implementation of the experience program. It gained a deeper understanding of their actual situation and the difficulties.

The research team guided and accompanied 32 children to experience each program in the study tour. The team took many photos and recorded what they experienced and felt. Finally, the team produced a short video recording the entire study tour for the children. At the end of the study tour, the research team interviewed the children, asking them to tell their thoughts and expectations about the experience, and took notes. When the team had completed its mission and left the village, it had developed a deep bond with the villagers and children.

The research team acquired a large amount of first-hand information about Yongan Village through a variety of ethnographic research methods as described above, such as in-depth interviews, field surveys, and participant observation.

Integration of Industries from Perspective of Experience Economy

As early as 1970, Alvin Toffer described the experience economy in Future Shock, and again in The Third Wave in 1983, he pointed out that "the next step in the service economy is towards experience economy, where businesses will win by delivering such experience services" (Wang, 2011). In 1998, Joe Pine discussed the connotation of experience economy in his book "The Experience Economy," pointing out that the experience economy is characterized by the experience value given to goods and services, enabling consumers to be physically and mentally delighted. From the standpoint of customers, Japanese researchers Nagasawa, S. and Otsu, S. point out that experience is the value that customers feel and are being touched by when they come into contact with a company or brand, and that it appeals to their senses and feelings (Nagasawa & Otsu, 2010).

Schmitt argues that the dimensions and types of consumer experiences constitute strategic experience modules based on the psychological concept of modules. It consists of five experience dimensions: the sensory experience through the five human senses; affective experience based on internal feelings and emotions; reflective experience through intellectually creating new perceptions or providing solutions; action experience related to the body or lifestyle; and associative experience connected to other people (things) or communities (Schmitt, 1999).

Pine and Gilmore distinguish experiences according to visitors' attitudes of participation and action. Whether consumers are active or passive participants and integrated into a situation or just absorb information, experiences are divided into four categories: recreational experiences, educational experiences, mysterious experiences, and aesthetic experiences. In recreational experience, consumers tend to become passively involved in the activity, absorbing its information invisibly. In educational experience, consumers proactively participate, think and act physically to increase their knowledge, broaden their horizons, and absorb the information obtained through the experience. In aesthetic experience, consumers become obsessed with one thing or environment while having little or no influence on the thing or environment themselves. In evasive experiences, consumers become immersed in the entire activity after actively participating (Pine, Gilmore, 1998).

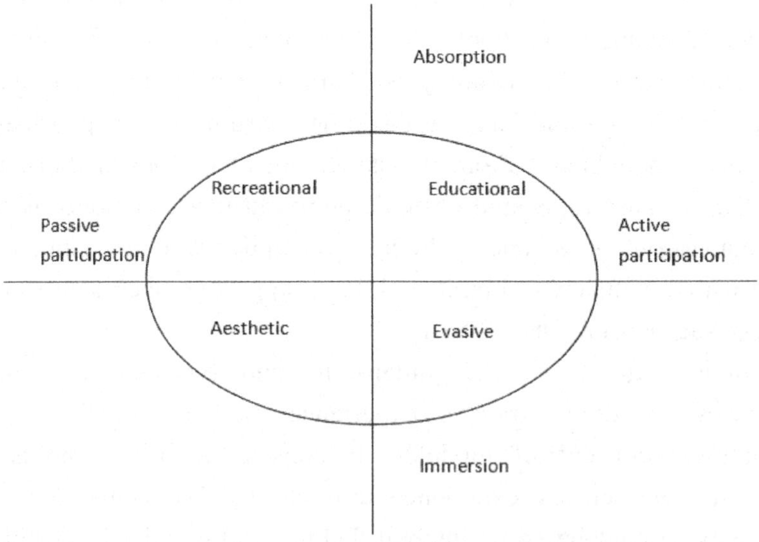

Figure 6.3 Classification of experiences (Pine, Gilmore,2010)

The primary industry in the integrated development between the primary, secondary and tertiary industries is a plantation. Many villages in China have designed some parts of the plantation industry into experience programs. Qiuyang County, Chongqing City, has designed tours and picking activities with fruits, flowers, and vegetables and farming and agro experience activities (Zhou, 2018). Tony's farm regularly invites customers to visit the farm, experience the cultivation of vegetables, and taste fresh vegetables to build their trust in the farm (Ji & Wang, 2020).

The secondary industry in the integrated development between the primary, secondary and tertiary industries is dominated by the processing industry, and programs can also be designed for consumer experience. Mokumoku Farm in Japan has a private meat processing plant. Due to poor transportation, it was difficult to sell the meat at the desired price. The processing plant offered a handmade sausage experience course to attract Japanese homemakers to visit the countryside and participate in sausage making, thus developing a large base of fans and turning pork sausage into a best-selling product with assured quality (Lu, 2021). In China's urban agricultural parks, programs are also available to stimulate consumers to participate in secondary industrial production and processing experiences such as agricultural product processing and handicraft making and drive their consumption (Wang et al., 2017).

The tertiary industry is rural tourism and services. Due to the development of rural tourism, traditional agriculture has been integrated with modern tourism, thus breaking the stereotypes of the traditional farming industry. Also, it has driven the development of rural transportation, commercial and catering services, cultural entertainment and local handicraft production so that the primary, secondary and tertiary industries in rural areas become mutually reinforcing (Zhao, 2009). The Xiaotao Community Field Complex combines idyllic rural scenery, cultural tourism, modern agricultural eco-tourism, and creative activity experience to realize the integration of the primary industry with the secondary and tertiary industries (Ling et al., 2019).

Integration and interaction between the primary, secondary and tertiary industries cultivate new economic growth points by introducing modern industrial organization methods such as industrial chains and value chains into agriculture, forming new industries, new business modes and new models (Li, 2018). From the primary industry to the comprehensive industries of agricultural experience and sightseeing in leisure tourism, the agricultural segment is no longer limited to the cultivation of products. Still, it is also given the function of sightseeing, reflecting the humanistic and technological elements of agriculture (Zeng & Bian, 2019). In the primary, secondary and tertiary industries, the following experience program designs are generally available (Table 6.1).

Table 6.1 Development of primary, secondary and tertiary industries and experience program design

Industry	Development programs	Experience programs developed
Primary industry	Planting of special agricultural products	Experiences or research activities in planting and picking
Secondary industry	Processing of agricultural products and livestock products	Processing experience or study activities
Tertiary industry	Rural tourism, a rural study tour	Study tours of agricultural products, study tours of rural cuisine, rural food, lodging and sightseeing

Source: Compiled by the author from experience programs in all three sectors in China.

History and Issues in Integration of Industries in Yongan Village

With a total population of 3,305 inhabitants in 868 households, Yongan Village has 13 villager groups. There are 32 ancient dwelling buildings of the Qing Dynasty in the village and more than 170 new dwelling buildings with three floors. One thousand fifty square meters of village activity space was built in 2016. Yongan Village has arable land of 729 mu, primarily producing rice, peanuts, sweet potatoes, taro and corn, with tea and fruits and forestry as secondary industries, and a few medicinal herbs such as maitake and tulip, and fruits such as longan, lychee and loquat. Most of the crops grown in Yongan Village used to be basic crops, and the village's collective economic income had been zero for many years. It was once a key village to develop projects for poverty alleviation in Quanzhou City. In 2012, a new election was held in Yongan Village, and the villagers' committee was newly organized. With Secretary Du Zhenzhong as the center, the committee played a leading role in revitalizing the village. By integrating the primary, secondary and tertiary industries, the village has made great achievements in just a few years.

History of Integration of Primary, Secondary and Tertiary Industries in Yongan Village

The first stage is the development of flower cultivation as the primary industry. Yongan Village is blessed with excellent soil conditions. Since the 1980s, many villagers have cultivated various flowers, especially in the Beiqian Group, where almost every household grows flowers. However, these growers have been operating individually and have never developed a large business scale, and they have very little economic benefits.

In 2012, Du Zhenzhong became the Secretary of the CPC Branch of Yongan Village, determined to stop the zero income in the collective economy. Thus, he borrowed the development model of the Beiqian Group and proposed to bring the scattered farmers together to develop the flower industry and establish a flower industry chain. In 2013, Yongan Village's CPC branch took the lead in setting up the Hujing Flower Farmers' Cooperative, adopting the development model consisting of the cooperative, the company, the association and the farmers. The village cooperated with Quanzhou Apollo Horticulture Technology Co., Ltd. to found "Fujian Guoyu Biotechnology Co., Ltd." with a total investment of 8 million yuan and a registered capital of 10 million yuan. The village collectively contributed 1.6 million yuan (51%

of the cooperative's shares) and the villagers jointly invested in the company. Through the development of recent years, the company now has fixed assets of 7 million yuan, liquid assets of nearly 3 million yuan, with a seedling base area of more than 60 mu and a fully automatic standard greenhouse of 11,000 square meters.

The company's main business scope is butterfly orchid seedlings, medium seedlings, flowering plants, and other high-grade potted flowers, with an annual production capacity of 600,000 plants (pots). It has become the largest and most complete standardized production base of butterfly orchid flowering plants in the Quanzhou area, generating more than 200,000 yuan of income for the village every year and driving villagers to increase their income. Today, Yongan Village has formed a new flower industry featuring butterfly orchids. Camellia, osmanthus, banana shrub, podocarpus macrophyllus, rose, and Chinese rose flowers can be viewed. In this aspect, the village is distinctive from the surrounding villages as flowers are highly competitive resources in tourism. The profits of the butterfly orchid base have boosted the village's wealth and the employment of villagers. In 2016, Yongan Village lifted the cap of being a poverty-stricken village and is fully out of poverty. The butterfly orchid has become the pillar industry for Yongan Village to build a beautiful village and an important engine to drive the local rural economic growth. In addition, Yongan Village also supports some villagers in need to transfer more than 200 mu of barren hills and wastelands to develop special industries such as tea-oil trees with the help of the cooperative.

The second stage is the development of the flower culture study tours in the third industry. Driven by the butterfly orchid industry, Yongan Village quickly formulated the next stage of development ideas. Yongan Village combined agriculture and tourism, vertically extended the industry chain, and expanded the business model horizontally. The village extended the industrial chain centering on butterfly orchid planting and promoted the development of the tourism industry at the village level. The village partially transformed the butterfly orchid production base into a butterfly orchid manor. It added a water SPA area and built a fountain accompanied by a light show and other installations.

Meanwhile, the production factory was upgraded into a tourist workshop, which boosted the development of tourism, catering and other related services, laying the foundation for the flourishing of its tourism. Yongan Village followed the national policy and laid out the development of the industry. On March 18, 2016, the Department of Basic Education of the Ministry of Education of the People's Republic of China issued the Notice on the Experimental Zone for Study Tours for Primary and Secondary Schools. The Ministry of Education stipulated that all primary and secondary schools must organize one study tour every year. According to the data forecast by the National Bureau of Statistics, China's youth population will reach a peak of 234 million in 2022, and the huge number of children supports the huge space for study tours in the future. With the release of a series of policies to encourage study tours, the domestic study tour market has soared. The villagers' committee of Yongan Village also fully recognizes the huge market for study tours and has cultivated and developed a diversified study tour industry system driven by "flower culture study tours" using idle mountain and forest land.

With the theme of beautiful Yongan, humanistic style, ancient folklore, floral culture, joyful cooking, interesting knowledge of Chinese herbs, Yongan Village has created a study tour system consisting of flowers, floral food, herbal culture, and Chinese culture.

In the flower study tour, children visit the butterfly orchid manor under the guidance of the butterfly orchid gardener, learn about the butterfly orchid, carefully record their observations in a thread-bound book, and finally draw or write about it. After learning about butterfly orchids, children move on to a floral food program with the same theme. Children are taught to make homemade cookies and ice cream with floral elements to improve their hands-on skills and understand the connection between flowers and food. On the extension of the flower study tour, children are introduced to traditional Chinese culture through the study of Chinese medicine. Children can learn to recognize traditional Chinese herbal medicine, make sachets with herbs, and learn to play the Wuqinxi or make postcards about herbal medicine. The Wuqinxi refers to five-animal mimic boxing, a kind of internal energy training that imitates the movements of the tiger, deer, bear, ape and bird, and was developed by the famous ancient physician Hua Tuo of the Han Dynasty. Yongan Village attracts children consumers and develops tertiary industries by conducting study tours, realizing the " 1+3 " model integrating the primary, secondary and tertiary industries.

The third stage is developing the flower processing industry as a secondary industry. Yongan Village does not stop at the primary and tertiary industries but actively develops the secondary industry on top of them. A professional cultural and creative team is introduced to create an exclusive image of butterfly orchid and cultural and creative derivative products. In addition, the village has further revitalized the image of butterfly orchid and made it known to more people through a variety of interesting activities such as the search for the spokesperson of butterfly orchid, the flower fairy. In addition to the application on the level of physical products, the butterfly orchid is used as a cultural symbol in developing and producing various creative products. Besides, Yongan Village will also process other flowers for study tour purposes. At present, Yongan Village has already renovated the area in the senior citizen center, which is about 500 square meters in size and has two ponds. According to the land and water supply characteristics, the technological specialist appointed by Fujian Provincial CPC Committee has selected the flower varieties suitable for the site to grow for study tours and processing and selling after the study tours. The project will be commenced in the second half of 2021. In addition, herbal medicine and flower cultivation in other places are also under active preparation. The secondary industry is still in the preliminary stage of development, but Yongan Village's innovative model integrating the primary, secondary and tertiary industries has already taken shape. In other words, the primary industry is expanded into the tertiary industry and then developed into the secondary industry, realizing the "1+3+2" model of integrated development between the primary, secondary and tertiary industries (see Table 6.2 for details).

Table 6.2 The process of integrated development among industries in Yongan Village

Year	Event	The process of integrated development between the primary, secondary and tertiary industries
2012	A new village organization was established, and a suitable industrial development model was investigated.	It lays a foundation for the development model integrating the primary, secondary and tertiary industries.
2013	A cooperative was established, and butterfly orchid flower cultivation started.	It started to develop the primary industry.
2016	The village was completely lifted out of poverty, with upgraded roads, improved sewage facilities, and a more beautiful landscape.	It prepared for the development of tertiary industries.
2017	A 50kW photovoltaic power generation project was completed.	It prepared for the integrated development between the primary, secondary and tertiary industries.
2018	The road surface was hardened, and the street lights were illuminated.	It improved the infrastructure for the development of the tertiary industry.
2019	Tourist toilets were built, and tourist events such as the Harvest Festival were held.	It continued to improve infrastructure and started to develop the tertiary industry.
2020	A fitness and recreation trail was built, and four ponds were renovated.	It continued to improve the infrastructure and increase the number of projects in the tertiary industry.

2021	Study tours for butterfly orchid, nature, and herbal culture will be conducted A flower plaza will be built, and flowers will be planned for planting and processing after the study tour.	It will focus on cultural study tours in the tertiary industry It will develop the secondary industry It will fully enter into the development model integrating the primary, secondary and tertiary industries.

Source: Compiled by the author based on the history of Yongan Village.

Issues in Integration of Primary, Secondary and Tertiary Industries in Yongan Village

Although Yongan Village has made innovative attempts to integrate the primary, secondary and tertiary industries and obtained initial results during the research process, many problems have emerged in the actual implementation process. They have caused Yongan Village to consider and adjust the development model integrating the primary, secondary and tertiary industries. According to our field survey and the villagers' committees presentation, the problems include the following:

The experience does not run through the primary, secondary and tertiary industries and the themes are scattered. At present, Yongan Village uses the primary industry to develop the tertiary and secondary industries. The experience program is not integrated into the primary and secondary industries among the three industries. In addition, the orchid-based study tours at Yongan Village are problematic, even though they are mainly experiential programs. The village also added study tours with the theme of Chinese herbal medicine and local delicacy cooking to enrich the content of activities. Despite the richness of these activities, which are an apparent upgrade compared to traditional rural tourism such as agritainment, they lack a distinctive theme throughout the program and seem fragmented. In the children's flower study tour in July 2021, the children engaged in butterfly orchid study, Chinese medicine study, food study, and English song singing.

Although the activities were very lively, the themes were scattered and had no specific focus.

Moreover, the design of different study tours is carried out by teachers from different universities. Although they have communicated in the early stages, the activities' style varies greatly and does not leave a deep impression on children. As the theme is the most important element in the experience, Yu Xiangxian suggests that the theme is the premise and requirement of the experience, which can leave a deep impression on the tourists. Agrotourism products must be based on market needs, regional resources, and other factors to determine the theme of the experience (Yu, 2017). The design of study tours and tourist programs must have a distinctive theme throughout the program. The theme is the foundation and soul of the experience, and a well-defined and distinctive theme may create a monopoly for a longer time (Zou, 2001). According to the theme, it must run through the whole design, and it should present the theme in all the details (Yu, 2011).

Various support facilities for the development of experiential programs are currently unavailable. The infrastructure of Yongan Village is insufficient to meet the requirements for large-scale development integrating the primary, secondary and tertiary industries. First of all, there is no place for accommodation. The completed senior center can supply the remaining two floors of rooms, but with less than 100 beds, so Yongan Village cannot cope with the influx of tourists from study tours. Secondly, there are no support facilities for dining and shopping. Although there were only a few tourists in this study tour, it exceeded the current capacity of Yongan Village. Thirdly, other facilities such as utilities, transportation and medical care services are inadequate. In addition, rural tourism roads, parking lots, and visitor reception centers should be further improved.

There is a shortage of professionals for promoting integrated development between the primary, secondary and tertiary industries. According to the village director Du Zhenxing, although Yongan Village is a relatively affluent village, the young people in the village still choose to go out to work or do business, and most of those left in the village are middle-aged and older adults over 50 years old. In the development of primary industries, middle-aged people and even some older adults can take up the corresponding duties. However, professional talents are needed to conduct study activities, and the villagers who remain in the village alone can hardly undertake them. For the study tour in July 2021, some villagers volunteered to help, but they did not communicate well with the tourists because of their heavy accent, and the villagers were not trained and did not have a sense of service. So far, Yongan Village has conducted small-scale study tour programs, relying on some teachers and students from several universities in Fujian Province, such as Yang-En University, Yango University, and Fujian Jiangxia University, but this approach is not sustainable. Many professionals are needed to integrate the primary, secondary and tertiary industries, including agricultural cultivation, rural processing, rural tourism, research and education, and child psychology. One of the reasons why Yongan Village is currently unable to integrate development between the primary, secondary and tertiary industries on a large scale is the lack of human resources.

Integration of Industries in Yongan Village from Perspective of Experience Economy

Experiential programs on integrating the primary, secondary and tertiary industries with distinctive themes may be designed. Yongan Village can design study programs based on the primary industry, butterfly orchid flowers, and have designed a study program for children with the theme of butterfly orchid. In addition, to increase the number of study programs, other flowers (such as trillium) have been added for planting and viewing. The study of these flowers is an extension of the butterfly orchid study program. Depending on the characteristics of flowers, butterfly orchids and other flowers are immediately sold, while flowers like bougainvillea need to be processed before sales. The "1+3+2" development model integrates the primary, secondary and tertiary industries. A distinctive theme should be used throughout these experiential programs, and Yongan Village can design its experiential programs with the theme of "Recognizing, Returning to, and Enjoying Nature."

Table 6.3 Experiential program design that integrates the industries in Yongan Village

Experience theme		Development program	Developable experiential programs	Experience theme throughout the program
Recognizing, returning to, and enjoying Nature	Primary industry	Plantation of special agricultural products	Planting and picking experience or study tours	Recognizing nature
	Tertiary industry	The rural study tour, rural tourism	Study tours of agricultural products, study tours of rural cuisine, eating, staying and touring in the countryside	Recognizing, returning to, and enjoying nature
	Secondary industry	Processing of agricultural products	Processing experience or study tours	Recognizing nature

Source: Self-made by the author.

In addition to the three industries, Yongan Village can also design programs such as folklore shows and harvest festivals based on the qualities of experience to enhance the village's attractiveness and provide more experiences to consumers. These programs are designed to provide consumers with recreational, educational, evasive and aesthetic experiences with the theme of "Recognizing, Returning to, and Enjoying Nature."

Infrastructure development and human resource security mechanism should be strengthened. In developing the experience-based integration model of the primary, secondary and tertiary industries, the follow-up guarantee mechanism is an important condition for sustainable development and steady operation, mainly including the following aspects:

Table 6.4 Unique experience-based rural tourism study programs at Yongan Village

Experience theme		Developable experiential programs	Experience theme throughout the program
Recognizing, returning to, and enjoying Nature	Recreational experience	Folklore performance, harvest festival	Enjoying nature
	Educational experience	Plant and animal identification, food preparation, participation in farming, a study of food processing	Recognizing nature
	Evasive experience	Rural specialties (food), rural lodging (accommodation), forest bathing, plant-based healing	Enjoying and returning to nature
	Aesthetic experience	Enjoy farmland, vegetable gardens and flower gardens	Enjoying and recognizing nature

Source: Self-made by the author.

Firstly, more infrastructures should be developed. Infrastructure development is an important factor in integrating primary, secondary and tertiary industries. Therefore, local governments should renovate roads and build public facilities such as public toilets, parking lots, and street lights (Zhang & Bao, 2012). Moreover, rural infrastructure should be prioritized and built rationally and orderly (Jiang & Shu, 2020). From the experience economy perspective, priority should be given to developing infrastructures that can enhance consumers' experience, such as boutique B&B, forest trails, and study centers. In addition, attention should be paid to the late maintenance of the infrastructure. Some rural infrastructures are not maintained well, resulting in damage and hygiene problems, hurting the consumer experience.

Secondly, we should ensure the cultivation and stability of the talent team for rural development. First of all, the people who have returned to their hometowns for work and business should continuously improve their professional skills and sense of integration. According to the specific needs of the returnees, they should be trained in various aspects, including modern scientific cultivation, professional knowledge of the processing industry, and professionalism and skills required for the service industry. They should also be encouraged to integrate with the newcomers and enhance the sense of cooperation between them. Second, we should actively guide people outside the village interested in the industrial development of the village, especially those with some professional skills, to become new villagers so that the new villagers can act as an important force in the development of the village.

Conclusion

This study analyzed the history of the "1+3+2" development model integrating the primary, secondary and tertiary industries of Yongan Village in Fujian Province. And the village first established such a development model based on the experience economy. The model that integrates the primary, secondary and tertiary industries in Yongan Village has its unique features. Firstly, Yongan Village has developed its primary industry by growing and selling butterfly orchids in large quantities. Secondly, with the theme of butterfly orchid, Yongan Village has developed the tertiary industry of rural study tours by combining other flowers and traditional Chinese medicine. Finally, other flowers are processed and sold to develop the secondary industry. Thus, innovations are made in the "1+3+2" development model integrating the primary, secondary and tertiary industries of Yongan Village.

Yongan Village develops the primary industry first, followed by the tertiary industry and the secondary industry (the "1+3+2" development model), While other villages in China commonly use the "1+2", "1+3" and "1+2+3" development models. This study provides a new development model for the studies of the development model integrating the primary, secondary and tertiary industries to rejuvenate rural areas, adding to the cases in this field and enriching the research results in this field.

After analyzing the development model and problems of Yongan Village, a path was proposed to integrate the primary, secondary and tertiary industries based on the experience economy perspective. Firstly, it should design the experience programs integrating the primary, secondary and tertiary industries with distinctive themes from the perspective of the experience economy. Secondly, infrastructure construction and human resource security mechanisms should be strengthened to promote the steady integration of integrated development between primary, secondary, and tertiary industries. Previous studies have generally focused on a specific product or field, such as agricultural, livestock, and study tours. This study proposes an experience program based on the perspective of the experience economy, which can be carried out across the primary, secondary and tertiary industries. It provides a systematic and innovative approach to designing experiential programs that integrate the primary, secondary and tertiary industries. Yongan Village is still evolving and will continue to reveal different situations in the future development process. The research team will keep abreast of the subsequent development of Yongan Village to conduct more in-depth research on its development model and mechanism.

The results of this study will provide theoretical guidance and practical reference for the integrated development between the primary, secondary and tertiary industries in similar villages in China and other developing countries.

Chapter 7
Internal Governance of "Double First-class" Universities

Universities in China have been implementing large-scale higher education reform to construct a modern university system with Chinese Attributes. Internal governance structure reform has achieved good results to adapt to the scale expanding. Chinese universities need to legalize governance structures, promote the autonomous operation of universities and the democratization of governance policies, pursue the de-administration of their academic affairs and regulate their academic power in the system. The present study explores the relationships of political, administrative, and academic power based on data analysis of China's first batch of "double first-class" universities.

Introduction

In recent decades, the direction of the educational system and higher education reform has been closely related to economic globalization and market forces. Encouraging academic freedom and reviewing government powers has become the choice of higher education governance reforms in many countries and regions. Braun and Merrien (1999) have conducted joint case studies on the UK, the Netherlands, France, Germany, Italy, the USA, and Switzerland to track state-led higher education's political and internal progress. They believed that modern managerialism is a new type of state intervention, including state, university, and scholar levels.

Government intervention remains the main action in the context of Chinese higher education. In the macro context, a series of projects and policies have been adopted to optimize internal governance structure and improve the efficiency of organizational operations. After introducing into the higher education system, these policies and suggestions have aroused the concerns of Chinese and international academic circles on the quality of Chinese higher education. The main purpose of this study is to analyze the basic conditions and existing problems of the internal governance structure and relationship of Chinese universities and explore the institutional factors and institutional barriers that affect the effectiveness of governance. In the nearly twenty years of development of China's higher education, how does the internal governance structure of Chinese universities work? What is the relationship between political, administrative, and academic powers and other dimensions?

Some researchers pointed out that the US model has been copied and learned much, and the importance of delegating powers to lower levels has been recognized. Sporn (1999) indicated that many higher education systems, especially in Europe and Asia, introduced the Anglo-Saxon and US models to reform the educational systems based on the traditional models, with China and Japan being no exception. Is this real? This chapter aimed to answer this question by exploring the relationship between administrative power and academic power in the governance of higher education in Chinese universities. Meanwhile, many studies remind us that university governance reform aims to improve academic ability and enhance autonomy. Neave (1995) emphasized the importance of university autonomy in achieving its goals.

At the same time, an institution will prove to be more efficient if it gains greater autonomy. The institution mentioned here refers to an organization and its existing practice. Chana and Yang (2018) point out that greater autonomy and flexibility are feasible in the opinions of both governments and universities. Does academic freedom and delegation of academic power to lower levels relate to the development of university reforms based on the experience of the USA, Hong Kong &Taiwan in China? This question has raised the researcher's interest in the current university governance reforms. Especially in China and other parts of Asia, whether empirical support on the practical higher education environment has been obtained?

Decentralization Governance

To pursue the effectiveness of local economic development, the USA has decided to decentralize to lower levels in terms of higher education governance. McLendon and Hearn (2009) concluded that "decentralization to lower levels" would be controlled in all regions. The coordination within the scope of the entire state would be coordinated with loose program control to seek local economic efficiency and effectiveness. Neave (1995) wrote that in contemporary American universities, the traditional governance buildings of a university are its trustees, administrative and teaching staff, other groups, and organizations. In an article, Chana and Yang (2008) wrote that the three Es, namely effectiveness, economy, and efficiency, aim to improve institutional autonomy and enhance government control over the results.

Hong Kong has always been deemed as a regulated region. The government's least intervention and free and unrestrained economic orientation are considered public administration and welfare management (Lo, 2017). Neoliberalism proposed a psychological form in which audit, accounting, and management technology play a positive role in the governance of a state to achieve the goals of freedom, choice, competition, and individual sovereignty. The market has always been regarded as the ultimate solution for social distribution and regulation (Olssen and Peter, 2005). Mok (2008) concluded that the Hong Kong Government operates under the model of economic liberalism by playing the role of the market driver to avoid the intervention with the higher education market. The move attracted both local and non-local students. Students raise tuition fees through private financing such as loans.

However, absorbing too many non-local students increases the difficulty of local students in competing for resources and employment opportunities and creates heavy debt. Thus, the failure of the Hong Kong government to directly provide funds to universities has become a major gap. Lo (2017) summarized that the relatively common role of the government in higher education expenditure had become a major constraint of Hong Kong universities to compete for a large proportion in global higher education. Then, he emphasized the concept of an accountability system and asked China to strengthen its role in monitoring and supervising higher education quality.

Taiwan still maintains a traditional academic culture related to universities and joint governance (Chen, 2004). Chana and Yang (2018) find that teachers and staff chair university committees and councils and hold administrative positions. Academic peers tend to make decisions on major issues and plan for the future; Teachers prefer a bureaucratic environment controlled by the university system, which would give the university a fully self-management capability in legally independent entities. Privatization and commercialization are widely accepted as a philosophy of university governance in Taiwan.

Government Intervention

The main characteristics of China's higher education are still more bureaucracy and political overtones. We have seen a more administrative-oriented higher education institution (Wang, 2011). What should be highlighted is that bureaucracy may lead to university corruption. Osipian (2017) investigated the autonomy of universities in Ukraine. He believes that students from low- and medium-income families are deprived of access to enter top universities due to the higher degree of corruption of higher education enrollment and high tuitions. Lin (2011) emphasized that Chinese higher education is undergoing an audit process. The trend shows that this big country is striving to combine its bureaucratic style of work with auditing techniques to guide the development of Chinese higher education from the perspective of the State's will.

China's higher education features dual governance and collective leadership. The central government leads all institutions in a unified manner and supports the performance of responsibilities (Huang, 2018). Chinese universities have made remarkable visual achievements in building world-class universities through unremitting efforts. However, they are still weak in intangible cultural capital. The cultural construction of world-class universities with Chinese Attributes aims at world-class universities and highlights the ideals and pursuit of Chinese universities (Li and Gao, 2021). It is worth noting that more powers of autonomy are granted to some institutions, especially in providing academic courses and reorganization of academies. The dominant power of the national government has been strengthened, and the diversified and independent development of colleges and universities has been limited (Wang, 2021). To guarantee the quality of educational activities, the Central Government has also introduced the evaluation system for self-assessment and external evaluation to ensure the quality of educational activities and its strong influence on some institutions (Huang, 2006).

Theory of Governance Types

Governance types are categorized in different ways. When studying the governance structure of universities, the international academic circle mainly holds the views of holism, dualism, and pluralism. Holism is represented by the research conducted by Clark (2001), a higher education expert of the University of California, Los Angeles. He believes that the governance structure has the characteristics of separation of administration culture and culture of teachers and students in the academic system. The decision-making institutions and groups at all higher education levels have academic power. Dualism dominates the internal governance of universities. Corson (1961) was the earliest who has focused on and proposed the co-existence of the section-level power structure and professional power structure in universities. Ma (2015) pointed out that the power of the universities is divided into two dimensions, namely administrative and academic, and is enjoyed and exercised by two different types of entities. She also stated that American universities' departments, school, and university levels have a dual governance structure. Based on the dual governance structure theory, the Chinese academic research circle combines the political power of the independent existence of Chinese universities. With the central government as the representative, the internal governance structure of Chinese universities is divided into political, administrative, and academic aspects. Currently, the imbalance between administrative and academic powers is the core issue Chinese universities must face in internal governance.

Based on the above research at home and abroad, this chapter further analyzes China's higher education management. At the same time, 137 double-first-class universities announced by the Ministry of Education in 2017 were selected as the respondents. According to the Higher Education Law of the People's Republic of China revised in 2015, a questionnaire survey was conducted from four perspectives of central government leadership reflecting political power. The principal accountability system embodies administrative power, the function of the academic committee embodies academic power, and the supervision function of the representative teacher committee embodies democratic rights. Ideas and comments were collected from existing university governance teachers, staff members, other administrative personnel, and students of universities. Questionnaire feedback is used to analyze Chinese universities' governance and demonstrate the validity of our theoretical support. Finally, conclusions were drawn.

Research Methods and Process

This study used 137 "double first-class" universities announced by the Ministry of Education of China as the survey objects. Paper and electronic questionnaires, phone and social networking software and other survey forms were combined in this research. "Teachers" and "staff members" were considered analytical units. The surveyed teachers or staff members were requested to respond to university governance structure issues, academic committees' operating status, and teacher's representative committees they considered. The Linkert 5-point scale was used in the questionnaires. Each measurement item scores from 1 (strongly disagreed) to 5 points (completely agreed) and consisted of four parts, namely basic data, governance structure issue analysis, operating status of the academic committee, and operating status of teacher's representative committee.

First, basic data for respondents in an organization was given, such as career type, administrative post, number, and ratios of respondents. Respondents were then requested to comment on the issues regarding university governance structure and adjust the degree. This section consists of 7 items. Next, the respondents were requested to express their opinions and adjust the operating status of the academic committees. There are five items in this section. Finally, they were requested to express their thoughts or feelings on the operating status of the representative teacher committees. There are also five items in this section.

Participants

A sampling of respondents from different types of universities is critical. Teachers of different grades and employees at different administrative levels were included. The survey included one hundred thirty-seven leading universities, with samples from the "985 Project" and "211 Project" universities and other leading universities. The samples included 1,092 teachers from 137 universities. The number of respondents was better, and there were many valid questionnaires. In addition, safeguard measures were taken on the questionnaire quality of this survey. The researchers had confidence in the final results of this research.

All the previous "Project 985" and "Project 211" universities were covered in the 137 universities. It can be seen that the 137 "double-first rate" universities are typical among the survey samples, which can reflect the characteristics of the management system after the further reform of the internal governance system in China since the 1990s. In addition, the origins and development of 137 universities vary. Peking University, Tsinghua University, and other high-level research universities and general industrial universities are among the first-class universities, which can better reflect the requirements of sample coverage required by the survey in terms of type, scale, and level.

Table 7.1 Basic data of questionnaire survey samples

Type of personnel		Number of respondents	Percentage (%)
Teachers	Senior title	146	13.37%
	Vice-senior title	249	22.80%
	Intermediate title and below	93	8.52%
	Subtotal of teachers	488	44.69%
Staff members	University leaders	64	5.86%
	Division-level leaders	158	14.47%
	Deputy division-level leaders	177	16.21%
	Section-level leaders	205	18.77%
	Subtotal of staff members	604	55.31%
	Total	1092	100.00%

Table 7.1 shows the distribution of all respondents. 44.69% of the respondents were teachers, including 13.37% teachers with senior titles, 22.80% teachers with vice-senior titles, and 8.52% teachers of intermediate titles and below. About 55.31% were staff members, including 5.86% university leaders, 14.47% were division-level leaders, 16.21% were deputy division-level leaders, 18.77% were section-level leaders. Respondents were evenly distributed and highly representative, meeting the data integrity requirements required by the survey. The basic information of the questionnaire survey sample is shown in Table 7.1.

Measures

There are two types of questionnaire surveys. First, 1,200 questionnaires were distributed to respondents from 137 first-class universities. After deleting the invalid important data loss from 816 questionnaires, the remaining 758 questionnaires were collected for demographic analysis. Secondly, according to the static analysis of the first survey, 382 questionnaires were obtained using targeted telephone and social networking software. These questionnaires were used to increase and compensate for the respondent information uncovered in the first surveyor that of universities which were insufficiently covered in the first survey to make the survey data complete. Finally, after 48 invalid questionnaires in which answers were carelessly given were removed, the information of 1,092 questionnaires obtained from the two surveys was combined for demographic analysis. It ensures the quality of the questionnaire, ensuring that the survey accurately reflects the credibility of the surveyed project and results.

Findings and Discussion

This section reviews the statistical results of the questionnaire and discusses the findings. The first part focuses on the governance structure of the universities. Degree adjustments are made on different items, and the impacts of government regulation, academic atmosphere, and operation of the party-government system are analyzed. The second part analyzes the operating status of academic committees in Chinese universities through five projects. Finally, the third part analyzes the operating status of the representative teacher committees. The data analyzed below is the average of the data collected from three types of universities.

Findings

As can be seen from Fig.7.1, the operational status of the Chinese university governance structure is generally satisfactory. 70.03%, 25.16%, and 4.81% of respondents respectively believe that they are in good operating condition, average and bad and that some institutional obstacles affecting governance efficiency generally exist. As shown in Fig. 1, the problems are mainly reflected in six perspectives: government regulation, party-government relation, power centralization, lack of system, administrative procedure design, and academic atmosphere. About 27.2% of respondents believe that the government represented by the education authorities exerts excessive control over university affairs, which are not conducive to university development. Nearly 15.78% of respondents believe that the unclear division of political and administrative powers and unharmonious party-government relationship at universities hinder the development of universities.

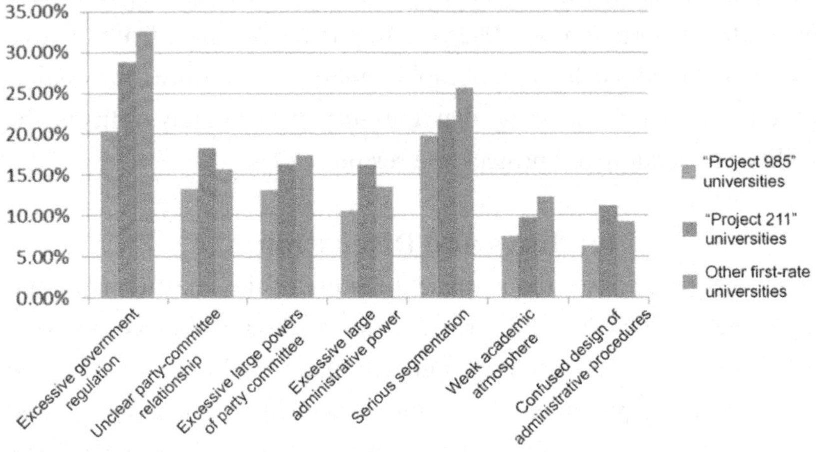

Fig.7.1 Problem analysis of governance structure of universities

Among the respondents, 15.64% consider that the Party secretary, who represents political power, is granted too much power, which will have a negative impact on the administration and academic freedom of the university. About 33.44% of the respondents believed that the university administration interfered excessively in academic affairs and was "offside." At the same time, about 22.36 percent of respondents believe in great differences between central governments and administrative systems. About 9.84% of the respondents believe that universities are characterized as public institutions and lack an academic atmosphere. Around 8.95% of the respondents believe that colleges and universities' problematic administrative procedure design has affected the operational efficiency of colleges and universities. That shows the generally good governance structure and relationship of Chinese universities. There is a large space for them to improve, though.

The second part of the questionnaire focuses on the functioning of the Academic committees (referred to as "committees"). The survey results are shown in Fig.7.2, 27.36%, 56.24%, and 16.4% of respondents believe that the operating status of the committees and their functions are positive, average, and negative. As shown in Fig.7.2, committees have varying degrees of functional orientation, power gaps, rules and procedures, system safeguards, and representativeness of committee members. 26.21% of the respondents believe that the functional orientation of committees deviates from their governance structure orientation, making them play an insufficient role in academic affairs. 18.9% of the respondents believe that academic and administrative power is not equal.

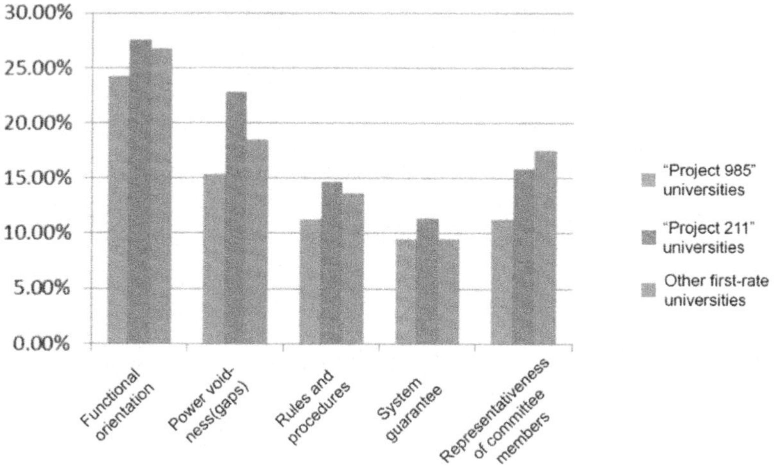

Fig.7.2 Operating status of academic committees

However, the powers of the committees are fully reflected in the university charter. They become void in the actual implementation. 13.16% of respondents believe that the substantial decision-making power is insufficient as the Party committees' decision-making is procedural post-event decision-making. About 10.17% of respondents believe that the organization of the committees is incomplete. 14.9% of the respondents believe that the representatives of the committee members are low, and they are affected and restricted by administrative power, so they cannot fully represent scholars. Overall, the operating status of the academic committees of Chinese universities is not quite satisfactory, and the problems are mainly reflected in the academic decision-making power of committees. 45.11% of respondents believe that committee roles in academic affairs are insufficient due to insufficient academic decision-making power. The above results indicate that the operating status of the academic committees of Chinese universities is not quite satisfactory.

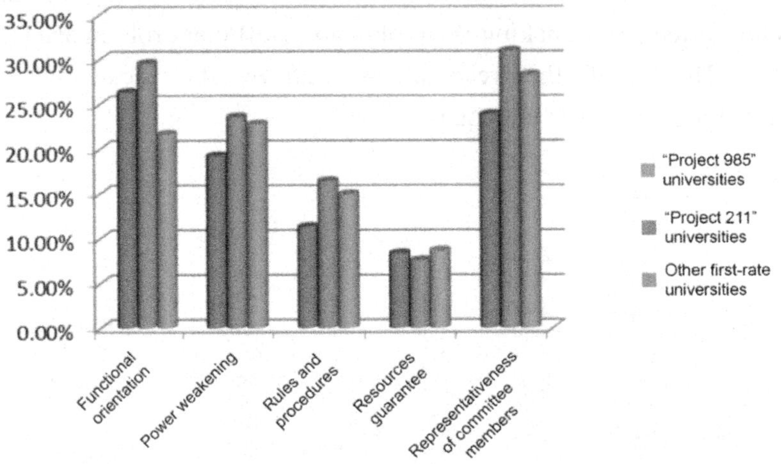

Fig.7.3 Operating status of teacher's representative committees

If turning to the operating status of the representative teacher committees, the survey result is shown in Fig.7.3. The operating status and functions of the representative teacher committees of China are not quite satisfactory. Only 19.5%, 48.6%, and 31.9% of respondents believe the status good, average and bad, respectively. As shown in Fig. 3, the problems are mainly reflected in power weakening, functional orientation, system and mechanism, representativeness. About 25.88% of the respondents believed that representative teachers' committees did not supervise major school reforms, major decisions, and important tasks, and their role was limited. At the same time, 21.89% of the respondents believe that the power of the representative Teachers' committee to represent teachers and staff's rights and interests has been weakened. About 14.25% of respondents believe that the organizational mechanism of the representative teacher committee is incomplete.

While about 27.74% of the respondents believe that the representatives in the representative teacher committee are not reasonable, and the representatives acted by ordinary teachers are insufficient. Another 8.67% of respondents believe that universities fail to exploit the role of the representative teacher committees due to their deficiency of resources.

Discussion

This section discusses the current state of internal governance in Chinese universities. The results show that the internal governance structure of Chinese universities with comprehensive governance characteristics is very different from the internal governance structure of Western universities. In the meantime, the system synergy between administrative and academic powers is also discussed. Results indicate that administrative and academic powers overlap to some extent. Thus, administrative power would undoubtedly affect academic behaviors. However, the party and the state have established a university academic committee supporting academic freedom.

Physical Presentation of the Governance Structure

The governance structure of Chinese universities can be described as an organized non-anarchy. The famous management scientist March (2011) described the governance structure of universities (mainly American universities) as organized anarchy. The governance structure is a relatively fixed main framework formed in the configuration, operation, and supervision of governance power presented as a specific organizational or social relationship. According to modern organizational theory, an organization's governance structure is mainly polymerized and integrated. The former highlights the decentralization, while the latter emphasizes the centralization of power. Both governance structure types vary in organization form, decision-making mechanism, operational procedures, and governance structure. American scholar Birnbaum (2003) previously proposed the organization operation models of universities, including society, bureaucracy, political party, and anarchy. The survey results indicate western universities are aggregative and have obvious characteristics of decentralization. In contrast, Chinese universities have an integrated governance structure with teaching test integration as the main and teaching test separation.

As shown in Fig.7.4, the political, administrative, and academic powers and democratic rights in the governance structure of Chinese universities are implemented via the Party committee leadership, presidential accountability, professorships, and democratic management. Here are corresponding organizations in the four governance dimensions, namely the central government system, the administrative system, the academic committee, and the representative teacher committee, guaranteeing their powers. In addition, the powers of different dimensions are never independent of each other but have the division of labor and cooperation.

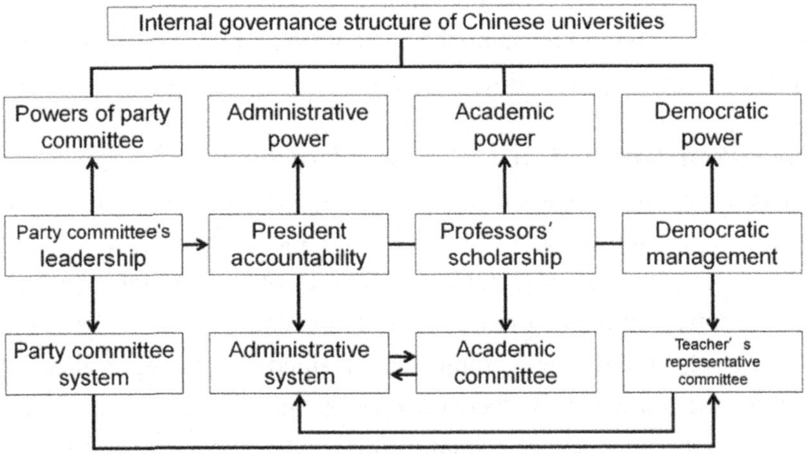

Fig.7.4 Status of the internal governance structure of Chinese universities

More importantly, it must be acknowledged that the integration and polymerization of governance structure only represents an ideal abstract classification. In actual governance, excessively concentrated or decentralized power can affect the effectiveness of organizational operations. Although centralization can improve execution, it can easily lead to power abuse and corruption. It will also increase the risk and uncertainty of decision-making. D. Wrong (2001) pointed out that when sufficient power monopolizes decision-making and actions, power must be dispersed to limit the power and avoid abuse of power.

Universities should establish a long-term decision-making mechanism, support mechanism, evaluation mechanism, supervision mechanism and collaborative innovation mechanism to provide all-around participation space for the internal and external subjects to promote the construction of "double world-class." In practice, colleges and universities must be based on the three levels of value system and behavior and follow the principles of value orientation, standardization, gradualism, multiple cooperation and cross-nationality. It is important to adhere to the basic path of independent management of universities, government guidance, enterprise cooperation and innovation. Through the efforts of scholars, coordination of social organizations and the support of the public, an orderly pattern of diversified social subjects participating in the construction of "double world-class" has been formed (Yang, 2021).

Through the investigation, combined with issued by the competent department of the Ministry of Education and other five about downsizing and decentralized organization, administration, and the separation of higher education, optimizing the combination of several opinions of the reform of service, the guiding principles of Chinese university governance structure to solve the following three questions: one is to strengthen the leadership of the party, the elaboration of the central government and the President's power and responsibility; Second, perfect the academic governance system and guarantee the academic decision-making power of the academic committee; Third, improve the democratic management mechanism, strengthen the supervision and guarantee of the power of the committee of substitute teachers.

Status Expression of Internal Governance Relationship

Through investigations, it is found that the internal governance relationship at Chinese universities is mainly reflected in three aspects, namely division of labor, system synergy, and protection of rights. These three aspects are mutually coordinated and complementary and enable internal governance's consciousness, self-conducting, and autonomy. The structural status of governance reflects the overall pattern of power operation, and the state of governance reflects the expression mechanism of power operation. In the university's internal governance process, the specific governance relationship may be expressed as a complex mode in which power is restricted, the system is restricted by power, and rights restrict rights.

Sometimes, due to a lack of understanding, leadership style, decision-making mechanism, and other factors, it is difficult for central governments and administrative departments to reach an agreement on many specific issues in a short period. According to statistical analysis, 58.9% of respondents believe that the central government plays a big role in core political leadership in many major universities' decisions. About 61.1% of the respondents believe the administrative system represented by the president is entitled to independent execution of the central government's decision, which shows the good relationship between political and administrative powers in Chinese universities. This chapter argues that Chinese universities' political and administrative power is never a restriction but is responsible for different tasks under the same power. This kind of relationship mechanism better solves the problem of power restriction and inefficiency in the decentralization restriction.

According to our survey, the academic committee and their functions are unsatisfactory. Administrative power remains to play a dominating role in the academic affairs of Chinese universities. 43.9% of the respondents believe that academic committees have insufficient decision-making power and play an insufficient role in academic affairs. By the Higher Education Law, the Outline of the National Medium-and Long-Term Program for Education Reform and Development (2010-2020) issued in 2010 and the Regulations on Academic Committees of Higher Education Providers promulgated by the Ministry of Education of China in 2014, the academic power of Chinese universities is realized by teaching and scholarship and in the form of the decision-making power of academic committees in discipline construction, academic evaluation, academic development and learning style building.

In terms of governance structure, Chinese universities' academic and administrative power is mutually reciprocal on the structure level from the perspective of governance structure. The former is restricted by the latter. However, in the process of governance, universities have the characteristics of an academic organization; there is a natural intersection between academic power and administrative power; the academic committee of the university is separated from the administrative system, and there is no condition for independent work. It also shows that in this survey, most of the full-time teachers believe that the internal governance of Chinese universities works well on the one hand, and on the other hand, denies the excessive administrative interference of administrative power in academic affairs.

Another problem reflected in the data is that teachers have less power to represent committees. About 52.0% of the respondents believe that the teacher's representative committee is weak in powers and has an insufficient role. It demonstrates that the representative teacher committee is a weak organization within the internal governance structure of the universities, and the universities fail to implement the provisions of the party and the State on the representative teacher committee. There are specific explanations on the functions of the representative teacher committees in the Trade Union Law, Labor Law, Education Law, Higher Education Law, and Teachers Law of China. The Regulations on the Teacher's Representative Committees of Universities proposes more explicitly the rights of the representative teacher committee to listen to important reforms and tasks of the universities such as formulation of articles of the association, development plan, annual work, etc., and to propose comments and suggestions.

In addition, although most of the respondents believe that the role of the representative teacher committee is too inadequate, the representative teacher committee pays much less attention than administrative and academic power. As a basic form of democratic management of Chinese universities, the representative teacher committee plays an indispensable role in supervising major reforms of universities and needs to attract the attention of universities and the academic circle.

Conclusion and Suggestions

This research is mainly limited to the analysis scale and scope. Only higher education governance of Chinese universities is paid attention to, and other organizations in the education system are not considered. However, the same system enjoys a similar style. Additionally, despite the small scope of the survey, the quality assurance questionnaire design allows respondents to represent the whole better. It shows that China's higher education governance has serious problems such as a low degree of academic autonomy and poor operating status of the representative teacher committee. Government intervention is still the main feature of governance. In the case of separation of powers in universities, the central government and the administrative system lack supervision and full coordination. Universities should further strengthen their leadership. At the same time, follow the central government's Regulations on Internal Supervision and formulate and implement detailed rules for implementing the Presidential accountability system under the leadership of central governments.

According to the analysis and research results, although the status and role of the academic committees of Chinese universities have been improved, there is still a large gap between the existing power operation and ideal status. The main means of solving the institutional obstacle is to strengthen system building. It is imperative to clarify the scope and boundaries of academic power and solve the "offside" problem of academic power. On a global scale, matching executive power and academic power at world-class universities is quite reasonable. According to the articles of association of 114 universities approved by the Ministry of Education in 2015, the universities under the ministries have formulated specific regulations on academic committees' duties, functions, and organizations.

The representative teacher committee is an organization that guarantees and safeguards teachers and staff members' legal rights and benefits. It is an important organization for avoiding power abuse in the integrated governance structure. As far as the internal governance structure of world-class universities is concerned, it is necessary to strike a balance between rights and powers that are restricted by power. In the future, Chinese universities should further highlight and support the work of teachers' representative committees. At the same time, they should strengthen lead group building and faculty team building and ensure the system's implementation and power of teachers' representative committees through internal management.

Chapter 8
Impulsive Consumption Behavior in Rural Tourism

Rural tourism has become an important component of Chinese tourism development. This chapter established a regression model of pleasure and impulsive consumption in rural tourism. It takes Lanzhou City as a case, which obtained 575 questionnaires, to provide a typical case study for sustainable research of rural tourism consumption from tourists' perception. Using regression analysis, regulation effect and intermediary effect, pleasure will stimulate tourists' impulsive consumption behavior in rural tourism. The result indicates: Firstly, the pleasure of the rural tourism process will stimulate the impulsive consumption behavior of tourists; for every 1% increase in pleasure, the actual cost of visitors increases by 16.7%. Secondly, the characteristics of rural tourism resources will become an important factor, and the pleasure stimulates consumption in rural tourism. The empirical results show that when the interaction effect of rural tourism pleasure and the characteristics of rural tourism resources increases by 1%, the actual consumption capacity will decrease by 32.6%. Finally, in the process of rural tourism, rural tourists from Lanzhou city's male groups are more likely to produce impulsive consumption. When researching pleasure influence factors of impulse consumption behavior, empirical results show that rural tourism increases for every 1% increase. We witness increases in foreign tourist consumption capacity by 20%, male consumption capacity by 28.1%, tourists aged 31-40 by 38.4%, and undergraduate and college-educated consumption capacity by 24.8%.

Background of the Study

Tourism development can significantly reduce the urban-rural income gap (Zhang et al., 2021); rural tourism becomes a mass consumption trend (Zhang et al., 2020). Tourist shopping behavior is a mixture of planned, impulsive, and experiential consumption behavior (Fang and Xu, 2012). Eating, living and traveling are often called basic tourism consumption. In contrast, the previous three are called non-basic consumption (Xi, 2003), and impulse purchasing does occur in tourism (Christian L. and Sara D., 2012). At the same time, the development of tourism in rural areas must develop more intelligent and personalized tourism services (Hu et al., 2021). Rural tourism has attracted many tourists returning to nature to become an important form of current tourism consumption type (Wu, 2018). Rural consumer tourism motivation research can effectively predict the needs of rural tourism consumers (Zhai, 2020). Impulse buying is considered an unplanned purchase carried out instantly (Gautam P. and Jenis C., 2018). It is widely believed that impulse consumption can be divided into two major categories: general impulse consumption and forced impulse consumption (Su, 2019).

The impulsive purchase is influenced by economic, personality, time, place and even cultural factors (Stern, 1962). Eleven thousand samples from the China Labor-force Dynamic Survey data reveal that ICT adoption increases the probability of tourism participation among rural Chinese residents by 18.6% but decreases the expenditure of tourism participants by 442 yuan/capita on average (Zhu et al., 2020). However, the motivation of rural tourism is the tourists' homesickness experience (Fang and Dai, 2019), but less research is conducted on rural tourism products and consumption trends (Yu et al., 2007). Rural tourism consumption demand is mainly divided into material demand, experiential demand and spiritual demand (He, 2020). Due to the study of impulsive consumption since the 1950s, it is believed that this study is relatively mature (Xia, 2012). Tourism increases the desire and impulses to repeat tours (Zhou 2020) the appearance of new trends and models of tourism consumption (Masot A.N. and Rodriguez, N.R., 2021). However, the study of impulsive consumption behavior in rural tourism is relatively late and has the unique characteristics of impulsive consumption behavior. Analyzing rural tourism consumption mainly includes experiential context (Chang S. et al., 2014), motivation-based segmentation of rural tourism market (Noel B. L. and Elirehema M., 2020), an exploration of Rural Tourism Segmentation by motivation (Wu, 2020), marketing for 'rural tourism' (Lesley R. and Derek., 2004) and the comparative study of urban tourism consumption behavior (Hui Song, 2015). Rural tourism plays an important role in sustainable development (Kranjčević J. et al., 2020). Can segmentation analysis of the domestic rural tourism market (Celeste E. et al., 2016) become the driving force of their impulsive consumption behavior? Rural tourism lets foreign tourists enjoy the visual impact and the impulse of production and consumption (Yang, 2020), and consumption has the twin characteristics of "situational consumption" and "impulse consumption." It should focus on creating a rural tourism experience (Hou and Gen, 2020).

This chapter takes Lanzhou City in Northwest China to measure rural tourists' consumption behavior. This chapter enriches the empirical research on rural tourism impulse consumption behavior and provides a possible solution for the rational development of the rural tourism consumer market. Therefore, through the regression of the relevant literature, this chapter puts forward the hypothesis of impulse consumption and verifies it by the regression model, analyzes the survey data, and draws the relevant conclusions.

Theories of Rural Tourism

Rural Tourism

The World Tourism Organization defines rural tourism as "the activities of tourists staying, studying and experiencing rural life patterns in and around the countryside. The village can also be used as a tourist base to explore nearby areas." Bramwell and Lane noted that rural tourism is agriculture-based travel and multi-level tourism, including special-interest natural tourism, ecotourism, sports and health tourism, educational tourism, cultural and traditional tourism, and some regional folk tourism activities. Gannon points out that rural tourism refers to the extensive activities, services and pleasant things provided by farmers or rural residents for economic purposes to attract tourists to travel. The study of rural tourism focuses on the concept of rural tourism (WTO,1997； Koscak M. 1998) Study on the Impact of Rural Tourism (Dernoi L. A., 1983; Briedenhann J. and Wickens E., 2004; Slee B. et al., 2010; Oppermann M., 1996), A Study on the Behavior of Rural Tourists (Frovhot I., 2005; Murphy A. and Willams P.W., 1999), Study on Resident and Community Participation (Lankford S.V. and Howard D.R., 1994; Perdue R.R. et al., 1990), Rural Tourism Marketing Research (Lane B. and Kastnhole E., 2015; Fleischer A. and Felsenstein D., 2000; Roberts L. and Hall D., 2004), Management of Rural Tourism (Sharpley R., 2002; Augustyn M., 1998) and so on.

At present, research on rural culture and tourism is mainly focused on rural tourism in China, rural culture as the path of the core competitiveness and sustainable development of rural tourism (Chen, 2017; Xie, 2016; Liang, 2013; Kou, 2013), development countermeasure (Zhu, 2018; Mei and Zhang, 2017) and research on other aspects. The Research on Rural Tourism in China mainly focuses on the definition of Rural Tourism Concept (Yang, 1992; Du and Xiang, 1999; Liu, 2006), Rural tourism tourist motivation (Liang, 2019; Xia, 2017; Zhang et al., 2015; Zang, 2011; Guo, 2011), Impact of rural tourism (Chen, 2019; Liu, 2019; Peng, 2019; Chen and Hu, 2019), Rural Tourism Development Countermeasures and Rural Tourism Planning (Kuang, 2019; Jiang, 2019; Yuan et al., 2019; Hu, 2019) and research on other aspects.

Rural Tourism Consumption

Tourists are the core elements in rural tourism development (Zhang and Yu, 2019), and the demand of rural tourism consumers has become increasingly diversified and differentiated (Liu et al., 2016). Multiple factors underlying China's inbound and domestic tourism development include policies, management systems, tourism demand, tourist attractions, economic level, consumption level, industrial development, investment status, traffic conditions, accommodation services, intermediary services, and degree of openness (Zhang et al., 2020). For rural tourism, consumption presents a high proportion of food consumption (Zhang and Li, 2020). The rural tourism market has undergone several innovations under the changes in consumption patterns and the business environment (Xie, 2020). Of the 128 combinations formed by local emotion, nostalgia, subjective norms, perceptual behavior control, attitude, desire and tourist destination visibility, eight specific combinations can affect the recreation behavior of rural tourists (Zhang and Yu, 2020). The integration of leisure agriculture and the rural tourism industry is helpful to meet the new tourism consumption needs of tourists (Li and Wang, 2019). Research on the consumption of rural tourism mainly focuses on tourists' decision - making (Cui, 2019), influencing factors (Sun, 2019) and age difference (Li, 2017), and discusses the formation model of rural tourists' behavioral intent through quantitative research methods (Liu, 2020). The factors of the tourist satisfaction model are determined by combining the literature of tourist satisfaction models (Yao, 2019).

Rural Tourism Impulse Consumption

Quantitative research of the consumption behavior of rural tourism mainly includes tourism motivation and tourist parade by factor analysis, variance analysis and logistic regression (Zhu, 2018). Establish the evaluation index system of rural tourists' satisfaction coupled with the theory of perceived performance model of TSE and Wilton through questionnaire sampling while using the Likert5 evaluation scales (Fu and Zhang, 2017). Moreover, it is found that these four types of tourism consumers have obvious differences in purchase decision-making (Wang, 2010). Rural tourist characteristics include decision-making and decision-making-behavior" processes (Zhang, 2008). Based on a generalized utility model of customer satisfaction, this infers multiple models of rural tourists' disappointment, regrets, and satisfaction and takes Chengdu's suburban rural tourism destinations as the study objects (Fan, 2007). The measurement of the consumption behavior of rural tourism in the chapter.

Methods and Measurement

Lanzhou City is high in the west and the south and low in the northeast, living deep in the northwest inland in China. It is the provincial capital of Gansu Province, one of the important central cities in western China, an important industrial base and comprehensive transportation hub in the northwest region, and an important node city of the Silk Road Economic Belt. It has many urban natural resources such as Yuquan Mountain, Baita Mountain, Turpan Valley and Xujiashan, urban cultural resources such as Zhongshan Bridge and Gansu Provincial Museum, and intangible cultural resources such as gourd carving. It has continuously developed into Renshou Mountain, Xujiashan urban leisure, the pastoral complex of Li Jia Zhuang, the original settlement, Yuquan Zhuang and wave street。 The folk culture village and different types of rural tourism areas/points show the development of hot spots. Through a questionnaire in the July-September 2020 field survey, Lanzhou City obtained 575 basic data sets using descriptive statistics, correlation analysis and regression analysis.

Research Design

Impulsive consumption behavior is one of the personality traits of tourists (Yu, 2016). Similarly, rural tourism is a pleasant pleasure activity (Tang, 2015). Therefore, impulsive consumption behavior becomes a focus of rural tourists (Teng and Hu, 2017), who have higher pleasure requirements than other tourism activities (Wu, 2010). The chapter proposes three assumptions from the pleasure characteristics of rural tourists and analyzes the impulse consumption characteristics of rural tourism.

Hypothesis 1: Impulsive Consumption Behavior exists in rural tourism.

Hypothesis 2: Tourists' satisfaction/characteristics/ motivation with the process of rural tourism can promote the consumption level of rural tourists.

Hypothesis 3: Impulsive Consumption Behavior in the zone, age, gender, educational background and other aspects will also affect the consumption in rural tourism.

Model

The rural tourism impulse consumption research mainly adopts the questionnaire design, correlation analysis, and regression analysis methods, including personal information, travel mode, travel cost content, and cognition of the tourism purpose. A regression model of rural tourism impulse consumption is as follows:

$$AC_{rt} = \beta_0 + \beta_1 RRP_{rt} + \mu_0 \qquad (1)$$

In Model(1), AC_{rt} for the interpreted variable, the actual consumption amount of rural travel during the travel process. RRP_{rt} is pleasant and excitation in rural tourism, is the more joyful expressed during the trip, 'rt' is the rural tourist. Considering comprehensively, the singularity of rural tourism can form the influence on the impulse consumption of rural tourism, If the β_1 and the equal coefficient is a positive number, which indicates that the pleasure of rural tourism is a positive incentive to the actual consumption capacity. Conversely, the pleasure of rural tourism is a restraining effect on actual consumption capacity.

$$AC_{rt} = \beta_0 + \beta_1 RRP_{rt} + \beta_2 SAR_{rt} + \beta_3 MRT_{rt} + \beta_4 IN_{rt} + \mu_0 \qquad (2)$$

In Model(2),AC_{rt} and RRP_{rt} same as in model (1),SAR_{rt}, MRT_{rt} and IN_{rt} for the interpreted variable. SAR_{rt} represents the resource of rural tourism.MRT_{rt} represents the rural tourist's motivation.IN_{rt}And monthly income structure of rural tourists. It mainly analyzes the pleasure of rural tourism, the overall satisfaction of rural tourists in the process of rural tourism, the facility environment in tourism and shopping. It also analyzes the resource strangeness of rural tourism to analyze the impulse behavior of rural tourism consumption and whether there is impulse consumption behavior. If the β_1 equal coefficients are positive. There is a positive correlation, and vice versa, a negative correlation.

$$AC_{rt} = \beta + \beta_1 RRP_{rt} + \beta_2 RTD_{rt} + \beta_3 RRP_{rt} \times RTD_{rt} + \mu_0 \quad (3)$$

In Model(3), AC_{rt}、RRP_{rt} same as in model (1). The RTD_{rt} is a regulatory variable representing the characteristics of rural tourism resources. We analyze whether there is a regulating role of the characteristics of rural tourism resources in the pleasure and actual consumption process. If β_3 is positive, it indicates a positive regulatory effect, the promotion action, and otherwise a negative regulatory action, the inhibitory effect.

$$AC_{rt} = \beta_0 + \beta_1 RRP_{rt} + \alpha_1 zone_{rt} + \alpha_2 age_{rt} + \alpha_3 sex_{rt} + \alpha_4 ed_{rt} + \mu_0 \quad (4)$$

In Model(4), AC_{rt}、RRP_{rt} it is the same as in model (1). The zone、age、sex、ed、in and mrt is all a control variable. Zone Customer source for rural tourism, age represents the situation of the age structure of rural tourism, sex represents the gender situation of rural tourists, and ed represents the education level of rural tourists. If α is positive, it indicates a positive regulatory effect, the promotion action, and otherwise, a negative regulatory action, the inhibitory effect.

Table.8.1 Main variables and definitions

Variable name	Measurement indicators	explanation
explained variable	AC	"0" represents "≤500/501-1500", "1" represents "1501-3500",and "2" represents "3501-5000 ≥5000"
explanatory variable	RRP	Tourists score the pleasure of the tourism process
	TC	TC: Satisfaction in the experience process of rural tourists（1-10）

	MRT	MRT: The purpose of rural tourism for rural tourists （"0" represents "Sightseeing/vacation," "1" represents" Sightseeing," "2" represents" vacation" ）
	IN	"0" represents "≤ 3500" "1" represents "3501-5000" and "2" represents "≥ 5501"
	RTD	To score the characteristics of the tourism process of resources in the process of tourism (1-10)
	zone	("0" represents rural tourists from Lanzhou, while "1" represents non-local rural tourists from Lanzhou
controlled variable	age	"0" represents "<18", "1" represents "18-30", "2" represents "31-40", "3" represents "41-60", and "4" represents "> 60"
	sex	"1" represents "male", while "2" represents "female"
	ed	"0" represents "High School and Below， " "1" represents "Undergraduate Studies and Junior College， " "2" represents "Postgraduate."

Findings and Discussion

Basic Data Information

From July 2020 to October 2020, investigation in important rural tourism covers Lanzhou Renshou Mountain, Lijiazhuang Pastoral Complex, Qingcheng Town, Yuquan Heights, Langjie village, and Qingwangchuan Folk Culture Village. Six hundred questionnaires were issued, and 574 valid questionnaires were recovered, determining efficiency of 95.67% as a valid questionnaire. According to the sample survey of rural tourists in Lanzhou, it is found that most rural tourists are non-local tourists (56.70%). In terms of the age structure of tourists, most of them are between 18 and 40 years old (80.49%). The monthly income of tourists mainly concentrated in 4,501-5,000 yuan (34.49%, 1 yuan=0.157 USD) and less than 3,500 yuan (31.01%). From the perspective of travel mode, most of them were accompanied by relatives and friends (51.22%). The expected consumption is mainly concentrated in less than 1500 yuan (59.47%) and 1,501-3500 yuan (31.30%). The actual tourism expenditure is mainly concentrated in less than 1,500 yuan (59.31%) and 1,501-3,500 yuan (33.04%).

Table.8.2 Characteristics of Visitors for rural tourism in Lanzhou city

classification	variable	%	classification	variable	%
zone	Lanzhou city	43.30	vocation	student	18.64
	No-Lanzhou city	56.70		other	19.16
		100		salesman	7.49
gender	Female	37.46		teacher	5.92
	Male	62.54		operating personnel	4.18
		100		administrative staff	4.18
age	< 18	4.53		Administration / later	3.31
	18-30	38.33		Civilian staff and other personnel	13.78
	31-40	42.16			100
	41-60	13.24	travel modes	Unit Organization / Business Meeting	5.75
	>60	1.74		travel agency	21.60
		100		Relatives and friends go together	51.22
educational background	High School and Below	26.31		alone	19.86

Table.8.2 Characteristics of Visitors for rural tourism in Lanzhou city

classification	variable	%	classification	variable	%
	Undergraduate Studies and Junior College	67.94		other	1.57
	Postgraduate	5.75			100
		100	Planning for consumption	≤1500	59.47
	≤3500	31.01		1501-3500	31.30
Monthly income	3501-5000	52.61		≥3501	9.23
	≥5501	16.38	Actual consumption	≤1500	59.31
		100		1501-3500	33.04
vocation	customer service staff	23.34		≥3501	7.65

Note: sorting out according to the questionnaire data

Regression Analysis of Pleasure

(1) Regression Analysis

By analyzing the Pearson correlation of the design variables in the model, the characteristics of rural tourist attractions (points) are significantly related to income, region, age, gender and educational background. The actual consumption of rural tourists can effectively promote the actual income of rural tourists.

Table 8.3 Pearson correlation coefficient table

Variables	(AC)	(RRP)	(MRT)	(IN)	(RTD)	(ZONE)	(AGE)	(SEX)	(ED)
AC	1.000								
RRP	0.152***	1.000							
MRT	0.021	0.079*	1.000						
IN	0.391***	-0.052	0.045	1.000					
RTD	0.136***	0.577***	0.058	-0.036	1.000				

Table 8.3 Pearson correlation coefficient table

Variables	(AC)	(RRP)	(MRT)	(IN)	(RTD)	(ZONE)	(AGE)	(SEX)	(ED)
ZONE	0.456***	0.112***	-0.050	0.047	0.137***	1.000			
AGE	0.095**	-0.035	0.093**	0.295***	0.006	-0.059	1.000		
SEX	0.238***	0.128***	-0.014	0.192***	0.089**	0.253***	0.195***	1.000	
ED	0.286***	0.009	-0.045	0.254***	0.038	0.206***	-0.056	0.054	1.000

*** *p<0.01,* ** *p<0.05,* * *p<0.1*

Through the regression analysis of the pleasure of rural tourism and the actual cost of rural tourists, the regression coefficient between the pleasure and rural tourism actual cost is 1%, showing a positive correlation feature; namely, pleasure can promote the actual consumption of tourists. Specifically, for every 1% increase in pleasure, the actual cost of visitors increases by 16.7%. After adding the control variable (rural tourist motivation and income), it was found that the correlation coefficient of pleasure and actual consumption capacity is also negative, 1%, and increases with the no control variable, which will promote the actual consumption of rural tourists. Specifically, for every 1% increase in entertainment, the actual cost of visitors increases by 19.0%.

Table 8.4 Regression Analysis Results

	(1)Uncontrolled variable AC	(1)Control variable AC
RRP	0.167***	0.122***
	(3.69)	(2.62)
TS		0.152*** (3.18)
MRT		-0.00941
		(-0.27)
IN		0.380***
		(10.72)
_cons	0.224***	-0.127

	(2.61)	(-1.57)
N	575	575
R^2	0.023	0.183
adj. R^2	0.022	0.179

t statistics in parentheses $^{*}p < 0.1$, $^{**}p < 0.05$, $^{***}p < 0.01$

(2) Revenue and Purpose Category Regression Analysis Results

In terms of the income level of rural tourists, it is only useful in the pleasure of middle-income groups and shows a significant positive correlation. Pleasure is more likely to stimulate impulse consumption than lower-income groups and higher-income groups in the process of rural tourists. It is mainly because middle-income rural tourism is more vulnerable to the pleasure brought by the environment to improve its consumption. But the process, low-income groups pay more attention to the experience of the product itself, and high-income groups pay attention to the leisure and vacation of this process.

Table 8.5 Category regression analysis of rural tourist' monthly income

	≤3500	3501-5000	≥5501
	AC	AC	AC
RPR	0	0.295^{***}	0.125
	(0.00)	(4.99)	(0.89)
_cons	0.101	0.126	0.613^{***}
	(1.42)	(1.22)	(2.96)
N	178	302	95
R^2	0.000	0.077	0.008
adj. R^2	-0.006	0.074	-0.002

t statistics in parentheses $^{*}p < 0.1$, $^{**}p < 0.05$, $^{***}p < 0.01$

From the purpose of rural tourism, only in the tourist group of tourist pleasure and the process of tourist spending, this presents an obvious positive correlation. That is to say, in the main tourist group for tourist pleasure, it is easier to stimulate impulse consumption, on the contrary, with the dual purpose of tourism and leisure vacation for pleasure and tourist spending in the process of no obvious correlation.

Table 8.6 Category regression analysis of rural tourism motivation

	Sightseeing / vacation	Sightseeing	vacation
	AC	AC	AC
RRP	0.0598	0.355^{***}	-0.157
	(0.70)	(5.65)	(-1.44)
_cons	0.306^{**}	-0.0364	0.617^{***}
	(2.41)	(-0.33)	(3.61)
N	160	305	110
R^2	0.003	0.095	0.019
adj. R^2	-0.003	0.092	0.010

t statistics in parentheses $^{*}p < 0.1$, $^{**}p < 0.05$, $^{***}p < 0.01$

Regulatory Effect Analysis

By observing the coefficient of the characteristic and pleasure interaction items of rural tourism destinations, we found that the coefficient and pleasure level coefficient are 0.370 and -0.326, respectively. As such, the characteristic values of rural tourism destinations will further weaken the payment effect of pleasure in stimulating the rural tourism impulse consumption. The adjustment variable will weaken the main effect. Due to the strong attraction of resources, fewer products attract tourism consumption. Therefore, tourists pay more attention to the landscape appreciation of rural tourism spots in Lanzhou. In other words, the more obvious the resource characteristics of rural tourism destinations, the weaker the consumption of tourism products is.

Table 8.7 Regulation effect results

	(1)
	AC
RRP	-0.326***
	(-2.99)
RTD	-0.457***
	(-4.02)
RRP* RTD	0.370***
	(5.27)
_cons	0.734***
	(5.00)
N	575
R^2	0.081
adj. R^2	0.076

t statistics in parentheses $^{*} p < 0.1$, $^{**} p < 0.05$, $^{***} p < 0.01$

Intermediation Effect Analysis

Zone

From the source of rural tourism, rural tourists show a positive correlation between non-local tourists in rural tourism and their actual consumption capacity. With the increase of the pleasure of non-local tourists in rural tourism destinations by 1%, their actual consumption capacity will increase by 20%. In this process, the pleasure of local tourists is not significantly related to the actual consumption.

Table 8.8 Intermediary effect analysis of the region

	(No-Lanzhou city) AC	(city) AC
RPR	0.201***	-0.0168
	(3.42)	(-0.32)
_cons	0.412***	0.178**
	(4.08)	(2.16)
N	326	249
R^2	0.035	0.000
adj. R^2	0.032	-0.004

t statistics in parentheses $^{*} p < 0.1$, $^{**} p < 0.05$, $^{***} p < 0.01$

Gender

From the perspective of gender characteristics, the fun and cost of rural tourism experience are significantly related. The males are positively correlated in the process, and women in the process are not significantly related to the actual consumption. In other words, men's pleasure in the process of rural tourism is more likely to promote actual consumption. With the increase of male tourists in rural tourism destinations by 1%, their actual consumption capacity increases by 28.1%, which is more likely to produce impulsive consumption behavior.

Table 8.9 Intermediary effect analysis of sex

	(Male)	(Female)
	AC	AC
RPR	0.281^{***}	-0.0868
	(5.02)	(-1.23)
_cons	0.147	0.415^{***}
	(1.53)	(3.74)
N	360	215
R^2	0.066	0.007
adj. R^2	0.063	0.002

t statistics in parentheses $^{*}p < 0.1$, $^{**}p < 0.05$, $^{***}p < 0.01$

Age

From the perspective of the age characteristics of rural tourism, tourists only aged 31-40 are easier to associate the pleasure of the rural tourism process with the actual consumption ability. Specifically, the years between 31 and 40 show a positive correlation, suggesting that rural tourists at this age are more prone to pleasure and consumption. On the contrary, 41-60 shows an obvious negative correlation, suggesting that rural tourists at this age are more vulnerable to pleasure without consumption. It can be concluded that during the ages of 31-40, tourists mainly pay more attention to the pleasure brought by rural tourism resources, and they are more likely to produce consumption. With an increase of the pleasure of male tourists in rural tourist destinations by 1%, the actual consumption capacity of the tourist group increases by 38.4%. Rural tourists aged 41-60 pay more attention to rural tourism's leisure and vacation experience process. They ignore the consumption of this process. With the pleasant increase of male tourists in rural tourist destinations, the actual consumption capacity of the tourist group is reduced by 30.8%.

Table 8.10 Intermediary effect analysis of age

	(<18)	(18-30)	(31-40)	(41-60)	(>60)
	AC	AC	AC	AC	AC
RPR	0.0588	0.0986	0.384***	-0.308***	0.167
	(0.87)	(1.17)	(6.01)	(-2.87)	(0.80)
_cons	-0.0498	0.242*	0.00339	0.769***	-0.167
	(-0.46)	(1.80)	(0.03)	(5.08)	(-0.48)
N	26	220	242	77	10
R^2	0.031	0.006	0.131	0.099	0.074
adj. R^2	-0.010	0.002	0.127	0.087	-0.042

t statistics in parentheses $^{*}p < 0.1$, $^{**}p < 0.05$, $^{***}p < 0.01$

Education Background

From the perspective of the education level of rural tourists, the groups with only bachelor's degrees are more likely to produce better consumption, indicating for every 1% increase of pleasure of rural tourists with this educational background, the actual consumption capacity will be increased by 24.8%. Conversely, there is no obvious correlation between the pleasure of the two tourist groups and the actual consumption ability in the process of rural tourism. It is mainly because the tourists with undergraduate and college degrees are relatively highly educated. The experience process pays attention to the rural tourism resources themselves and is more willing to consume independently. Under this educational background, the other two customers have become more rational in consumption.

Table 8.11 Intermediary effect analysis of education background

	AC		
	(High School and Below 0)	Undergraduate Studies and Junior College (1)	Postgraduate (2)
RPR	-0.0221	0.248^{***}	-0.0915
	(-0.31)	(4.49)	(-0.44)
_cons	0.205^{*}	0.180^{*}	0.835^{***}
	(1.84)	(1.89)	(2.92)
N	151	391	33
R^2	0.001	0.049	0.006
adj. R^2	-0.006	0.047	-0.026

t statistics in parentheses $^{*}p < 0.1$, $^{**}p < 0.05$, $^{***}p < 0.01$

Through the RESET test, the model (below) has F values of 16.45 and P values of 0.0000, indicating the correct model settings used in the article. Similarly, the collinearity detection of the model suggests that the model has no collinearity.

$$AC_{rt} = \beta_0 + \beta_1 RRP_{rt} + \beta_2 MRT_{rt} + \beta_3 IN_{rt} + \beta_4 RTD_{rt} + \alpha_1 zone_{rt} + \alpha_2 age_{rt} + \alpha_3 sex_{rt} + \alpha_4 ed_{rt} + \mu$$

Table 8.12 Collinearar detection

Variable	VIF	1/VIF
RRP	1.58	0.633306
MRT	1.04	0.959371
IN	1.28	0.780908
RTD	1.55	0.646527
1.ZONE	1.17	0.855456
AGE	1.24	0.809379
1	6.54	0.152940
2	7.06	0.141543
3	3.72	0.268676
4	1.39	0.716866
1.SEX	1.19	0.839079
ED		
1	1.50	0.668640

$$AC_{rt} = \beta_0 + \beta_1 RRP_{rt} + \beta_2 MRT_{rt} + \beta_3 IN_{rt} + \beta_4 RTD_{rt} + \alpha_1 zone_{rt} + \alpha_2 age_{rt} + \alpha_3 sex_{rt} + \alpha_4 ed_{rt} + \mu$$

Table 8.12 Collinearar detection

Variable	VIF	1/VIF
2	1.33	0.754352
Mean VIF	2.45	

Conclusion

This study uses 575 sampled survey data in Lanzhou City to build a model of impulsive consumption behavior and studies the correlation between the pleasure of rural tourism and the actual consumption ability. According to the sampling survey of rural tourists in Lanzhou, non-local tourists comprise (56.70%), while local tourists account for a relatively small proportion (43.40%). Tourists who mainly travel with relatives and friends (51.22%) prefer to let men fill in questionnaires to represent common views and ideas; Female (37.46%) and Male (62.54%). At the same time, we find: First, the pleasure of the rural tourism process will stimulate the impulsive consumption behavior of tourists. Second, the characteristics of rural tourism resources will become an important factor, and the pleasure stimulates consumption in rural tourism. Third, foreign tourists and male groups are more likely to produce impulsive consumption in rural tourism. Based on this, the chapter puts forward some suggestions on the transformation and upgrading of rural tourism and hopes to provide some countermeasures and suggestions for the rural development of China and other countries.

In the process of tourism, accompanied by a large number of impulse consumption (Li 2018), rural tourism also has impulse consumption behavior. This study uses 575 sampled survey data in Lanzhou City to build a model of impulsive consumption behavior and study the correlation between the pleasure of rural tourism and the actual consumption ability. It proves the positive relationship between rural pleasure and actual consumption and the impulsive consumption behavior in rural tourism. The results show that the characteristics of rural tourism destinations can weaken in the process of pleasure and impulse consumption, and the origin, age, gender, and educational background of rural tourists will also have different effects on this process.

First, the pleasure of the rural tourism process will stimulate the impulsive consumption behavior of tourists. Seven factors, such as personal perception, positively impact the rural tourism experience (Ge, 2018). Emotional pleasure or tour experience pleasure will also positively impact tourists 'perception value (Teoman D. and Anna S. M., 2018). The process of rural tourism can also further stimulate tourists' perception and stimulate the production of consumption behavior. Through regression analysis, it indicates that impulsive consumption behavior in rural tourism is closely related to the pleasure of the rural tourism process. The regression coefficient between pleasure and actual rural tourism cost is 1%, showing positive correlation characteristics; pleasure can promote the actual consumption of tourists. Specifically, for every 1% increase in pleasure, the actual cost of visitors increases by 16.7%.

Second, the characteristics of rural tourism resources will become an important factor, and that pleasure stimulates consumption in rural tourism. Rural tourism products are satisfied in tourists is the successful rural tourism products (Yuan, 2020). It was also further confirmed, "Local emotion, attitude, subjective norms and other perception control the influence of recreation behavior of rural tourists" (Zhang et al., 2021) and correlation studies. The authenticity of rural tourism has become a new pursuit of regional characteristics, and real experience has become a market trend (Ren and Yang, 2021). Because of this, the resource characteristics of rural tourism need to "Provide visitors with a real rural tourism experience" (Zhang, 2020). From the perspective of rural tourists' rural tourism resources, the chapter further enriches the characteristics of rural tourism resources on rural tourist consumption. The empirical results show that when the interaction effect of rural tourism pleasure and the characteristics of rural tourism resources increase by 1%, the actual consumption capacity will decrease by 32.6%. The characteristics of resource ontology of rural tourism destination resources can restrict the relationship between pleasure and impulse consumption, which shows that tourists are more willing to reflect the real rural tourism.

Third, foreign tourists and male groups are more likely to produce impulsive consumption in rural tourism. Tourism consumption is mainly driven by foreign tourists (Teng, 2020). It further confirms that the foreign tourists in rural tourism are more inclined to produce consumption power, mainly based on the different experiences brought by the pleasure of the non-local landscape, and are more willing to consume. It is often believed that women may usually spend less than men (Yuan et al., 2021). In female college students (Wei et al., 2020), Outbound tourism (Fan and Wang, 2021), females tend to consume more pronounced than men. However, men are more likely to produce impulsive consumption in rural tourism. Age significantly impacts tourism decision-making and consumption behavior (Hu and Huang, 2021). The rural tourism consumer group aged 26-35 is the main consumer group (Lv, 2014), and this group further demonstrates they are more likely to produce impulsive consumption.

Similarly is the correlation between the demand for rural tourism and the educational level of tourists (Bi, 2016). Empirical results show that pleasure influences factors of impulse consumption behavior. Every 1% increase of rural tourism, foreign tourist consumption capacity by 20%, male actual consumption capacity by 28.1%, the actual consumption capacity of tourists aged 31-40 increased by 38.4%, the actual consumption capacity of undergraduate and college education by 24.8%.

Fourth, according to the study of the consumption characteristics of rural tourists, the mode of travel of rural tourists is mainly relatives and friends who go together (51.22%), men are more willing to spend according to their joy during travel. Therefore, we suggest that in the process of rural tourism: First, to improve the richness of rural tourism products, there is a need to attract more tourists to participate in and experience. Second, we should pay attention to the male consumer groups in promoting and marketing rural tourism products. Third, we should constantly optimize and upgrade the service function of existing rural tourism products to meet the higher standards of rural tourists.

Finally, because the male-dominated characteristics of data collection objects may affect the conclusion, the reasons for this phenomenon still need to be further explained in the next study.

Chapter 9
WeChat Users and Their Behavioral Features

WeChat is a social medium for mobile phones developed by Tencent in 2011. By March 2018, there were one billion active WeChat users, making it the social software with the fastest development in China. Most Chinese WeChat users share WeChat Moments, establish WeChat groups, send WeChat red envelopes, and become WeChat Businessman on WeChat. This chapter probes the features of WeChat user behavior in light of the Grounded Theory. The findings revealed four behavioral features: the expression of personality, the connection between individuals, group establishment by individuals, and the connection between individual and group. This chapter analyzed such behavior from interpretivism and found that WeChat users are individuals with different characters. Sharing WeChat Moments enables users to become unique individuals and express their personalities in certain social circles. In addition, people through WeChat Moments and WeChat red envelopes enhance the connections among individuals. WeChat Businessman also develops via the connection between individuals. Different individuals can form WeChat groups according to other contexts, and individuals in different groups can have something in common. The connection between individual and group is also a social need. The virtual world established in WeChat can be called the "WeChat world."

Introduction

In 2011, the Chinese company Tencent launched WeChat, a social medium for mobile phones they had developed for several years. The number of WeChat users has soared since its launch. By March 2018, there were one billion active users monthly (Ma, 2018). WeChat attracted many users so quickly that nearly all the functions based on computers or mobile phones are integrated into the app. With WeChat, users can share their life experiences, thoughts, and photos on WeChat Moments and join or establish different social groups to have real-time interaction with friends on WeChat Moments or WeChat groups. Moreover, users can virtually send WeChat red envelopes (electronica transfer money from one person to others as gifts) and engage in WeChat business transactions.

As WeChat has developed rapidly, increasing research has been done on WeChat in China. The existing studies on WeChat focus on WeChat as software, the social influence of WeChat, the relationship between WeChat and communication, and the connection between WeChat and traditional media (Liu & Hsu, 2014). Some researchers have explored WeChat from a philosophical perspective. Many studies have been conducted on WeChat as software, the relationship between WeChat and sociology, and WeChat and communication. For instance, Chiang probed into the WeChat culture philosophical (Chiang, 2017). Sun studied WeChat technology from existential phenomenology (Sun, 2015). Li researched public opinions on WeChat from the angle of philosophical hermeneutics (Lee, 2015).

However, the studies probing WeChat from a philosophical perspective are relatively limited. This chapter explores WeChat from a philosophical angle. Based on the Grounded Theory, this chapter examines WeChat user behavior by looking at four behavioral features: the expression of personality, the connection between individuals, group establishment by individuals, and individual and group. By studying the behavior of Wechat users in China, the authors conducted further research on the characteristics of Chinese social behavior and consumer behavior. It offers suggestions for enterprises to develop new products, provide new services, and strengthen communication with consumers.

Main Wechat User Behavior in China

WeChat has many functions; however, Chinese users most frequently accessed WeChat Moments, WeChat Group, WeChat Red Envelope, and WeChat Store.

WeChat Moments

WeChat moments refer to a social function on Tencent WeChat. Users can post text and pictures on "Moments" and share articles or music from other applications. Users can "praise" or "comment" on new photos of their friends, while other users can only see "praise" or "comment" from the same friends. This function enables users to share, display, and show what they have (Liang, 2008). They share their experiences and thoughts in daily life in words, photos, or video clips (Wang and Kuan, 2016). It is best to show the We Media function of WeChat (Lee, 2014). Before releasing information, WeChat users can decide on the WeChat friends who can see the information through the app's permission settings. In 2014, Huan Wang and Jing-wen Guan surveyed college students at two universities in Beijing and found that 76% of them shared their life experiences on WeChat Moments and that only a few would share something else.

Moreover, different ages vary in what is shared, and female users are more active sharers than male ones (Wang & Guang, 2016). After users share something on WeChat Moments, their WeChat friends can interact with them by pressing "Like" and making comments. "Like" is set as a thumbs-up sign, meaning: what shared has been read, what shared is agreed, and is highly appreciated. "Comments" refers to the comments on what is being shared. The familiar WeChat friends of the user can only mutually see likes and comments, and knowledgeable friends can make mutual comments.

WeChat Group

One of the primary WeChat user behaviors is joining and forming WeChat groups. This function enables users to locate different groups. WeChat groups can be established by work, life, study, and kinship. Different kinds of WeChat groups can meet different needs. For example, a WeChat group based on life is designed for fun and relaxation, and one based on friendship offers a social sense and a sense of fulfillment featuring self-improvement (Wang & Chu, 2014).

In China, WeChat users tend to communicate to solve unexpected public events. After analysis, Yu-lin Chao pointed out that the general circumstances on WeChat in China arise from the intention to safeguard or seek immediate interests. For instance, the community residents might form a WeChat group to oppose illegal buildings in the neighborhood, or parents might form a WeChat group to discuss the health or study of their children. These groups are established and joined by direct interested parties and are designed to solve group problems. With WeChat Group, they can quickly share information and protect their rights and interests. In addition, they can evade taking responsibility for their actions because they are engaging in collective participation, and the participation is based on a close relationship (Chao, 2018).

WeChat Red Envelope

In 2014, WeChat launched the Red Envelope function. In Chinese culture, "red envelope" refers to the gift money for children during the Spring Festival. As red is an auspicious color in China, the gift money is usually wrapped in red paper or red paper bags. This explanation tells how the "red envelope" got its name. Today, "red envelope" is not confined to the gift money for children; it also refers to giving others a joyful event. It has attracted high user viscosity, featuring easy operation and intense interaction (Chang, 2016). It is a convenient payment, and there had been various methods to make payment before it came into being. Nevertheless, WeChat Red Envelope has many unprecedented functions. It supports one-to-one payments, one-to-group payments, and group-to-group payments.

In addition, the amount can be randomly set in cases of one-to-many payments and many-to-many payments. A red envelope indicates joy and luck; hence, this function quickly prevailed in China. In many WeChat groups, snatching red envelopes has become a phenomenon. A user sends red envelopes (the individual users will determine each envelope and number of envelopes sent out) in a WeChat group. Then other users can snatch one with a different amount according to their speed. In this way, a small amount of money can activate the whole WeChat group. Some users have adopted it as an effective way to release information that requires attention. As is shown in the studies by Peng Lan and other researchers, the top three reasons for users to use WeChat Red Envelope are "to achieve a low-cost social connection," "to be accepted in a group more effectively," and "to enjoy the random competition in the snatching of red envelopes" (Peng, 2017).

Apart from individuals, the media has also adopted WeChat Red Envelope for marketing. In 2014, WeChat Red Envelope attracted over eight million WeChat users within nine days during the Chinese Spring Festival, and more than 40 million red envelopes were received (Tencent, 2015). On February 22, 2018, WeChat released an official report on WeChat statistics during the Spring Festival in 2018. Seven hundred sixty-eight million people conveyed their New Year blessing through the WeChat Red Envelope (TechWeb, 2018). Using WeChat Red Envelope for payment and advertising will become increasingly popular among individuals and media.

WeChat Store

WeChat Store appeared in 2013, and Taoyong Sun, the CEO of Weimob, was the first to propose the concept. According to him, WeChat Businessman has two layers of meaning. First, it refers to a WeChat businessperson who uses a WeChat account for marketing that connects businesses and consumers. Second, it indicates a self-employed businessperson who opens a store on WeChat Moments and directly contacts consumers in individual-to-individual marketing (Sun, 2014). In this chapter, WeChat Businessman refers to a self-employed businessperson who opens and does marketing on WeChat Moments. From 2014 to 2016, the volume of the market transactions by Chinese WeChat businesspeople rose from RMB95.03

billion to RMB360.73 billion, with an annual growth rate of 93.5%. The number of WeChat businesspeople rose from 10,241,000 in 2014 to 12,574,000 in 2015 and to 15,352,000 in 2016 (Hsu, 2018).

According to the survey by Lixia Wang and Yuchi Shih, the commodities most frequently advertised on WeChat Moments are cosmetics and skincare products, accounting for 80.95%. It is followed by clothes and shoes (53.74%), weight loss products, healthcare products, and snacks (about 20%), daily necessities and ornaments (about 11%), and luxury goods (6.12%) (Wang & Shih, 2018). According to some researchers, cosmetics and skincare products, which take the most significant proportion, are sold based on a relatively close interpersonal relationship. For example, Shaohua Li and other researchers stated that WeChat is a platform featuring a solid social connection and that WeChat business is conducted based on a reliable connection. By spreading and sharing information about recommended goods in a circle with a strong social bond, WeChat businesspeople deepen the public understanding of their products and arouse their trust to increase sales volume (Lee & Yang, 2015).

Grounded Theory-Based Summary of Chinese Wechat User Behavior

As WeChat is a new social medium in China, Chinese WeChat users show particular user behavior. The behavior mentioned above, such as sharing WeChat Moments, establishing WeChat groups, snatching WeChat red envelopes, and doing WeChat business, are the primary WeChat user behavior. This chapter investigated if such behavior could reflect any behavioral features of Chinese WeChat users. The authors adopted the Grounded Theory to probe these behavioral features.

We selected 11 people as informants for an in-depth interview in this study. As the Grounded Theory requires that the samples be representative, we chose consumers who used different WeChat functions. All these WeChat users spent over three hours on WeChat per day, and the functions they frequently used were WeChat Moments,

WeChat Group, WeChat Red Envelope, and WeChat Store. Table 9.1 contains the basic information of the interviewees.

The one-to-one in-depth interview method was utilized to collect first-hand data about the interviewees in this study. Each interviewee made an appointment in advance; the interview was made according to the interview plan. Additional questions were asked according to the answers during the interview, and the interviewees were encouraged to give specific examples. Each interview lasted for about an hour, and the records of WeChat use were read, photographed, and stored with the users' permission.

Table 9.1 Profile of interviewees

Name	Gender	Age	Career	Year started	Hours per day	Frequently-used functions
Lin XX	Female	42	WeChat businessman	2011	5	Advertise and marketing tea
Hua XX	Male	46	Company employee	2013	3	Communicate with clients
Lin XX	Female	41	Company supervisor	2011	4	Issue notices and answer questions
Liang XX	Female	21	College student	2014	5	Share things on WeChat Moments
Lin XX	Female	35	Cashier of a drugstore	2011	5	Share things on WeChat Moments
Chang XX	Male	41	College teacher	2011	3	Make confirmations
Yuan XX	Female	19	College student	2016	6	Share selfies on WeChat Moments
Fang XX	Female	42	Company employee	2014	5	Publish advertisements
Chen XX	Male	22	College student	2015	5	Read news and chat with friends
Kao XX	Male	24	College student	2013	6	Read WeChat push notifications
Wang XX	Male	65	Retiree	2015	3	Communicate with children and send red envelopes

Source: From the author's fieldwork notes.

The interviews and WeChat use records were transcribed, and the interviewees confirmed the scripts. As for incomplete information, the interviewees were asked to offer more details for completion. Finally, the collected data were analyzed, and other data were used for the theoretical saturation test. All the collected data were analyzed and summarized in this study, and any invalid information or scripts with little details were eliminated. The valid were used for open coding and were tagged. In the process, 23 ideas were generated (see Table 9.2).

Table 9.2 Interviews Contents Summary

Responding Contents	Main Idea
I often share something about traveling and food on WeChat Moments. Sometimes, I urge to do so even after taking a picture of a beautiful flower. That's because I want to share something extraordinary with my friends. I will feel pleased if my friends like or comment on what I share.	It's a platform where I share something with my friends.
Most of what I share on WeChat Moments is about my child. I want to take photos of my lovely child and share them on WeChat Moments. I do it for two reasons. First, I want to record everything about the personal growth of my child. Second, I will have a sense of achievement if my friends like what I share.	It's a platform to show my child.
I don't like sharing something on WeChat Moments, and I will just do it on several occasions for a whole year. However, I will read what my friends share every day because I want to know what happens in their daily life and clicking "like" on what is shared by my close friends will deepen our friendship.	It's a channel to interact with my friends.
My parents are very strict with me, so I don't talk too much with them at home. I've dreamed of becoming a singer since childhood. But I've never been brave enough to talk about it with them because they would oppose it. I look more attractive in photos, especially in those modified ones. Whenever I share my photos on WeChat Moments,	It helps me become a prominent figure in my life.

all my friends will be amazed. I'm not a singer, but I have gained much confidence on WeChat Moments.	
Some people have mistaken themselves as stars by sharing too many details about their lives, such as having dinner, buying clothes, and running. I read all that was shared, but later I found that it was a waste of time. Now, I only follow some close colleagues and friends.	It creates star effects in the social circle.
WeChat Moment is an extraordinary place where I can say something hard to say in the physical world. On one occasion, our team worked overtime, and we were all swamped. I caught a cold. But as it was not so severe, I didn't ask for leave. I went to see a doctor in a small clinic before working, where I got some medicine and received a nebulization treatment. I took a selfie and shared it on WeChat Moments. All my colleagues showed their concerns when I arrived at the workplace.	It is a particular channel to express my mind.
I don't like sharing anything on WeChat Moments and seldom do so throughout the year. However, I will read what my friends share because I want to know what happens in their daily lives, and clicking "like" for what my close friends shared will deepen our friendship.	It is a channel for me to get news about my friends.
What fascinates me the most about WeChat are the classmate groups, through which I can get in touch with classmates I haven't seen for years. In the classmate groups, we talk about our childhood, which gives us a sense of nostalgia.	It meets the need to contact classmates.
I'm a department supervisor, and there is a WeChat workgroup where our department members can get notices and communicate with each other. I can send all notifications to the group, which has made my work much more efficient.	It meets my work needs in the company.
As a salesman, I need to communicate with clients and answer their questions. With WeChat, I can share with clients regularly. It's very convenient. I could talk with	It meets my needs to communicate

only one client through a phone call in the past. But now, I can communicate with several clients at the same time. It's efficient. Besides, all problems can be discussed, and the frequency of communication with clients has significantly higher.	with clients.
Of all my WeChat groups, my favorite one is the photographer group. In this group, we often share the knowledge and skills of photography. We also go to take pictures together regularly. All my questions will be immediately answered in the group. Moreover, I frequently take photos outdoors with them.	It meets my needs to develop my hobbies.
I've joined many WeChat groups, but I seldom say anything in them because it is a waste of time. However, I will check some main workgroups or liaison groups several times every day for important notices.	It meets my needs to check my work.
Aside from some permanent WeChat groups, I have some temporary ones. For instance, we established a quick group for traveling, through which we got notices and communicated with each other. The group was eliminated right after the trip. Temporary groups are convenient.	It meets our needs for temporary communication.
I have retired. My children are busy with their work and seldom come back home or give me a phone call. So, it is hard for me to know their situation. Now, I've formed a WeChat family group, where I often ask about their lives, and they will respond whenever they are free. I established this group to tell them that we always miss them.	It meets the need to communicate with family members.
Since the WeChat Red Envelope launch, we often snatch red envelopes in our WeChat group for middle school classmates. It's fascinating. The amount in some red envelopes is small, and sometimes it is only RMB0.01. But we all find it interesting and exciting.	It meets the need to activate our social atmosphere.
In the past, elderly family members gave gift money during the Spring Festival. Now we have a WeChat family group where we often send red envelopes. It saves us time.	It is where red envelopes are sent and

But our grandparents don't know how to operate WeChat and thus fail to send red envelopes. WeChat Red Envelope is very convenient, but the sense of ritual in the traditional conduct of sending gift money in red envelopes has been diminished.	snatched up among family members.
As a WeChat businessman, I've joined many WeChat groups for marketing, but many are not active. Sometimes, I send red envelopes to advertise my products, and the red envelopes will be snatched quickly. Then, I can promote my products. By doing so, they will pay attention to my advertisement.	It helps me grab the attention of WeChat group members.
When WeChat Red Envelope started, my children taught me how to operate it, and I found it very interesting. I sent red envelopes in the WeChat groups, but I don't do that now because my children focus on snatching red envelopes back at home and don't talk to me.	It reduces the physical communication among family members.
Since the launch of WeChat Red Envelope and WeChat Transfer, my friends and I have shared the cost whenever we have dinner or buy things together. It's convenient. People competed to pay the parties' bills in the past, and sometimes it would be hard for me to pay if I didn't have any change. I felt tremendous pressure when others paid the bills for me. But now it is a different situation. I can give money to those who pay bills through WeChat, and I don't feel pressure to attend any party now.	It has changed our social connection.
As a WeChat businessman, I put on advertisements and answer customer questions in WeChat groups every day. I focus on old customers, and the sales volume is satisfying. But sometimes I'm afraid that my advertisements may cause disgust from my friends.	I can work as a WeChat businessperson.
I have a job and never thought of becoming a WeChat businessman. But my sister-in-law always encouraged me to join her. As the advertisement pictures all come from her, all I need to do is to forward them. It's very	I can work as a part-time WeChat businessperson.

convenient. If there is an order, I will send the order to her. It doesn't take much time, so I do it.	
Many of my friends are WeChat businesspeople. If some of their products attract me, I will buy some. As we are familiar with each other, I don't think they will cheat me, and I believe that the products they recommend will be good.	I can buy things from friends who are WeChat businesspeople.

Source: Compiled according to the interviewers' answers.

In this study, 23 ideas were generated through the open coding mentioned above. These 23 relatively separated views were analyzed and connected to form four and two main categories. The four categories were the expression of personality, the connection between individuals, group establishment by individuals, and the connection between individual and group. One main category was induced from these four categories (see Table 9.3).

Table 9.3 Category and ideas (individual-oriented interactive social connection)

Category	Corresponding Idea
The expression of personality	"It's a platform to show my child." "It helps me become the main figure in my life." "It creates star effects in the social circle." "It is a special channel to express my mind."
The connection between individuals	"It is a channel for me to get news about my friends." "It's a channel to interact with my friends." "It meets my needs to communicate with clients." "I can buy things from friends who are WeChat businesspeople." "I can work as a WeChat businessman."
Group establishment by individuals	"It meets our needs to contact classmates." "It meets my needs to develop my hobbies." "It meets my work needs in the company." "It meets our needs for temporary communication." "It meets our needs to communicate with family members."

	"I can work as a WeChat businessman." "It's a platform where I share something with my friends." "It meets my needs to check work." "It meets our needs to activate our social atmosphere."
The connection between individual and group	"It is a place where red envelopes are sent and snatched up among family members." "It has changed our social connection." "It helps me grab the attention of WeChat group members." "It reduces the physical communication among family members."

Source: Collected information from the interviewees.

According to the above summarization, Chinese WeChat users show four behavioral features: the expression of personality, the connection between individuals, group establishment by individuals, and the connection between individual and group. These four behavioral features could be summarized as individual-oriented interactive social connections. Each user exists as a different and unique individual, but an individual can't live alone. In society, each individual shows some social behavior. The primary social connections of each individual include an individual's relationships with others, groups of different individuals that form according to different contexts, and the relationship between individual and group.

Interpretivism-Based Analysis of Chinese Wechat User Behavior

The social behavioral features of WeChat users could be analyzed from interpretivism. Derived from hermeneutics, Social Constructivism, Phenomenology, Ethnography, Semiology, Humanism, and other philosophical ideas and research methods, interpretivism has evolved into an independent philosophical idea. The main concepts of interpretivism include the following points (Chu, 2007):

1) It recognizes and respects the existence of individuals.

2) Truth and meaning cannot be generated without a situation or context.

3) Truth or meaning is generated in the interaction between "persons" or "humans and society."

4) There is no objective world because human beings established the so-called world, and the world is projected from human ideas.

5) Understanding things is always a recycling process called a cycle of interpretivism. The relationship between wholeness and individual parts is one featuring cycle and unfolding. Individuals first get to know the details and then understand the whole through the facts, and vice versa (Inagaki, 2013).

In the following section, emphasis is placed on how the philosophical ideas of interpretivism are shown in the social behavioral features of WeChat users.

Recognition of and Respect to Individuals

The fundamental idea of interpretivism is to recognize and respect the existence of individuals. With WeChat Moments, each user can become a star in certain social domains through easy operations to share photos, behavior, and thoughts. According to Jin-feng Yin, WeChat Moments is a stage where users can show rituals to their friends. By shaping their self-image with words, pictures, and facial expressions, they have an opportunity to catch the attention of friends (Yin & Hu, 2018). According to Lingning Wang and Juan Lan, Chinese consumers, especially young people, express their self-consciousness and personality on WeChat Moments. In people's faces other than the target audience, their discourse is self-centered (Wang & Lan, 2017).

Although ordinary users can release information on blogs, Sina Microblog, and other social media, attracting people and maintaining continual attention is difficult. At present, famous bloggers are either stars or those with unique talents, and it is hard for most people to become a star in Sina Microblog. Nevertheless, it is a different story when WeChat is concerned. Ordinary users can receive attention and become a star or central figure by sharing photos or articles. It is safe to say that WeChat has provided everyday users with an excellent stage to show themselves. Each individual is unique on WeChat Moments, and such existence can be revealed and recognized on WeChat Moments.

The Connection between Individuals

According to interpretivism, truth or meaning is generated in interpersonal interaction. It takes time and energy to maintain a friendship. Compared with the exchange in real life, online interaction is more straightforward. Many WeChat functions are designed to facilitate interaction. For instance, users can interact with their friends by clicking "like" or commenting on what they share on WeChat Moments. Such interaction is so convenient that users are more ready to participate. Some users may not click on "like" or make comments, but they can still keep themselves abreast of the life experiences of their friends and then talk about the experiences if necessary. This behavior helps enhance friendship and is also a kind of interaction.

If a salesperson can use WeChat to communicate with several clients simultaneously, the frequency of communication will become high, and their work will become more efficient. The relationship between WeChat businesspersons and clients will become between sellers and buyers due to the frequent interaction. A WeChat businessperson can evaluate the preference of their friends and make timely interactions with them, thus achieving targeted marketing. Those WeChat businesspersons have a closer relationship by interacting more frequently with WeChat users. Therefore, their advertisements will be better accepted (Mao & Chi, 2017). It is safe to say that various Chinese WeChat user behaviors facilitate the interaction between individuals and maintain a close relationship through such exchanges. Moreover, a new value will be created in the interaction. For example, WeChat Businessman is a new marketing model that arose from user interactions.

Group Establishment by Individuals: Situation and Context

According to interpretivism, the world is projected by human beings, and truth or meaning will not be generated without a situation or context. People with different cultures, experiences, or backgrounds will see the world differently. However, for those who share the same culture, experience, or environment (all these can be called the "situation" or "context"), the world they establish will be the same and will have a specific meaning. Take the example of a WeChat class group of middle school students. The group will be formed because the users spend their middle school days together. A WeChat workgroup in a company will be founded on the workplace and the work relations shared by the employees. A WeChat photography group will be built based on the group members' shared passion for photography. In certain WeChat groups, group members share a concept that serves as the foundation of a world where they are intelligible to each other.

According to other reference systems, humans have different forms of existence, mostly in groups and individuals. The WeChat culture is a miniature of these three forms of existence. Meanwhile, these three forms of existence are integrated into the WeChat culture (Chiang, 2017). Humans are creatures that live in groups and cannot live without society. Individuals must relate themselves to social groups bound by specific ties to survive. Individuals will lose the meaning of living if they are separated from a group. Individuals live in different scales and type groups, and such groups can be international, regional, national, or familial. Groups can also be related to career, age, gender, and a common interest (Chiang, 2017).

WeChat social groups enable people to form different groups according to different contexts quickly. These groups have various forms. Some regular and long-term groups feature frequent interaction, such as workgroups and family groups. At the same time, other groups are established for occasional exchange, including class and friend groups. Other groups are temporary ones designed for specific missions. Whatever kind of WeChat group, there is a high degree of freedom to form a group, interact and dismiss.

The Connection between Individual and Group

According to interpretivism, truth and meaning are generated in human-society interaction. WeChat groups also need interaction, and a WeChat group without expression or dialogue would be meaningless. However, WeChat groups are not like society, where a group will be immediately dismissed without dialogue or communication. A WeChat group can stay in a virtual form. Even if it keeps silent for a long time, it will become active when it is needed. WeChat Red Envelope is an excellent tool to active a WeChat group, and it is a unique form of interaction on WeChat. Compared with verbal expression, red envelope-based presentation features less risk.

Moreover, its auspicious symbolic meaning in Chinese culture quickly accepts it in all situations. The red envelope-based payment system has also changed social payment methods among Chinese groups. As mentioned above, the function enables Chinese people to shift from the traditional "bill payment by one" to sharing the cost, allowing people to feel more relaxed about participating in social group activities. As many work teams have formed a WeChat workgroup, users must check their groups to get the latest information or communicate with others. It is safe to say that WeChat has changed how individuals and groups are connected and how the relationship is maintained. For instance, a group that would be immediately dismissed because of zero communication, in reality, can strengthen the relationship between individuals and the group. Moreover, WeChat Red Envelope has made the individual-group relationship more active and even changed the traditional Chinese social connections in a group of people, thus allowing some users to participate in social activities with more ease.

Findings and Discussion

The findings of this study indicate that the Chinese WeChat user behavior can be summarized as " individual-oriented social connection," and WeChat has made such a social connection possible. The virtual world established on WeChat can be called the "WeChat world." As the WeChat world offers many conveniences, it is easy for WeChat users to indulge in it. According to statistics, over 20% of Chinese Internet users check their mobile phone 100 times a day; 23% would feel panic without their mobile phone, and 34% would check WeChat right after getting up in the morning (Iydnews, 2014).

Individual-oriented Interactive Social Connection

As WeChat functions advance, the WeChat world will become better. And the users can lead a basic life as individuals. For instance, they can access various services, such as ordering food, shopping, paying bills, and calling a cab. They can also make friends and interact with friends at any time and place. Much information about work can be obtained and processed in time through WeChat groups. In addition, individuals can collect data from various channels, including news and popular articles. The WeChat world can meet social needs. For some users, the WeChat world can nearly replace the physical world. Nevertheless, there are many problems in an individual-oriented social connection, such as false impressions of individuals and false beliefs of interactions.

False Impressions of Individuals

Some WeChat users are passionate about sharing every detail about their life on WeChat Moments, no matter the significance. What they share can be a photo or a thought. According to Chienkuo Chiang, individuals strive to show their lives and seize all opportunities. Insignificant daily experiences can be shared on WeChat Moments (Chiang, 2014). Such users regard themselves as the center of WeChat Moments and often want to attract public attention. What is shared on WeChat Moments also contributes to shaping their self-image. Some technologies, such as Photoshop and Beauty Camera, can shape and create intended effects to highlight themes. These technologies make it hard for other WeChat users to know the actual image of the users, and even the users themselves may indulge in the false impression.

In addition, WeChat can be as valuable as a dictionary, a book, a teacher, or an older fellow. As an individual, a user can easily access much knowledge and information according to their needs and hobbies, thus acquiring knowledge according to personal demands. However, too much information will distract one's attention. As a result, individuals might not have enough time or energy to digest what WeChat offers. They might scan and forward what is shown rather than deliberating or evaluating it (Wang, 2016).

The closed structure of WeChat Moments allows little space for external information, and the self-correction of data in time and space cannot be achieved. Therefore, the mobile environment and the fragmented time for the use of WeChat make it difficult for users to engage in in-depth reading. Such shallow, fast, and utility-oriented reading can lead to shallow thinking featuring unconditional acceptance of information (Wang, 2014). Such individual-oriented learning and reading on WeChat are false impressions and are not as effective as the physical world.

False Impressions of Interactions

Some users have many WeChat friends and interact with these friends frequently every day. As a result, they mistakenly believe that they have many friends. According to Chienkuo Chiang, the friend circle, which is connected via WeChat accounts, does not consist of friends in the traditional sense but rather as acquaintances in the social mind. It is not a small social circle that is built upon trust. Therefore, there is a significant difference between the WeChat friend circle and a physical, social circle. WeChat-based communication is a kind of restricted and fragmented communication, which lacks complete-textual meaning. The fragmented society established online is loose (Chiang, 2014). The communication on WeChat is done without the physical presence of both parties; therefore, it is not affectionate interaction in an absolute sense.

Those adopting WeChat communication may become involved in the virtual world and pay no attention to the physical world, resulting in a gap between fantasy and reality or understanding misplacement. A high frequency of such absent communication may lower the frequency of face-to-face communication. The social connection may have been widened, but the intimacy has been diminished (Chiang, 2017).

In a physical society, older family members play a leading role in sending gift money in red envelopes during the Spring Festival. They regard it as an excellent chance to show their authority in the family. However, WeChat Red Envelope has taken away the leading role from elder family members who cannot send WeChat red envelopes. As a result, they retreat to a secondary position and are even separated from the ritual. Therefore, the impacts of WeChat Red Envelope on Chinese familial relationships may include shaking the traditional vertical axis-centered family structure, eliminating the boundary between family and social connections, and destroying the family's sacred space during festivals (Chang, 2016). The interaction in a family group without the participation of older family members seems active. Still, it is false that interactions without elders, important family members, are not as meaningful as traditional family interaction.

Conclusion

This chapter analyzed Chinese WeChat user behavior from interpretivism and came up with the following ideas. Chinese WeChat user behavior shows the following features: personality, the connection between individuals, group establishment by individuals, and the connection between individual and group. First, WeChat enables users to become unique individuals and show their personalities in certain social circles. Second, users can use WeChat as a primary social connection tool to communicate with others and establish various WeChat groups according to what is shared among friends. The connection between individuals and groups has become stronger with the launch of WeChat. WeChat user behavioral features can generally be summarized as individual-oriented social connections. To some degree, the WeChat world can substitute the physical world, and some people can choose to live in it. However, the individual-oriented social connection may cause such problems as false impressions of individuals and false beliefs of interactions.

The WeChat user behavior investigated in this chapter could be summarized as individual-oriented interactive social connections. Such a social connection has two essential features. First, it is individual-oriented; second, it connects individuals and between "individual and group." Such new social connections will change traditional Chinese social connections into a new social order and impose challenges on the social system and laws. As for enterprises' marketing, it will bring new opportunities and problems.

Due to the article's length restriction, this chapter could not explore other Chinese WeChat user behavior aspects. What are the behavioral features of WeChat users outside of China? What are the differences in behavior between Chinese and non-Chinese WeChat users? Can such behavior reveal the ideas of interpretivism? How to make an in-depth analysis of other Chinese WeChat user behavior from the perspective of interpretivism? All these issues need to be further discussed in future studies.

References

Aghion, P, J. Cai, M. Dewatripont, L. S. Du , A. Harrison and P. Legros. (2015). Industrial policy and competitionAmerican Economic Journal: Macroeconomics,7(4):1-32.

Augstyn, M.(1998) National strategies for rural tourism development and sustainability: The polish experience. Journal of Sustainable Tourism 6(3),191-209.

Bai, S. J. (2021). A profound understanding of the decisive significance of the major assertion of "two establishments." Jinzhong Daily, 2021-12-10(003).

Bi L.X.(2016) The Market Demand Analysis of Elderly Rural Tourism in Fengman District of Jilin City. Central South University of Forestry & Technology.

Birnbaum, R. (2003). How Colleges Work: The Cybernetics of Academic Organization and Leadership. Translated by Bie Dunrong, Yu Xuefeng & Zhang Jibiao. Qingdao: China Ocean University Press, 143.

Brakman, S, H. Garretsen, C. van Marrewijk and A. Oumer. (2012). The border population effects of EU integration. Journal of Regional Science,52(1):40-59.

Briedenhann, J., Wickens, E.(2004) Tourism routes as a tool for the economic development of rural areas: vibrant hope or impossible dream?. Tourism Management 25(1),71-79.

Camagni, R., R. Capello and A. Caragliu. (2013). One or infinite optimal city sizes? In search of an equilibrium size for cities. The Annals of Regional Science, 51(2), 309-341.

Campbell, S. (1996). Green cities, growing cities, just cities?: Urban planning and the contradictions of sustainable development. Journal of the American Planning Association, 62(3), 296.

Cao, Z. (2007). Promote the Scientific Development of Army Construction at A New Starting Point and Fully Fulfill Our

Army's Historical Mission In the New Century and New Stage. People's Daily, Oct.18, 2007: p.2.

Celeste, E., Maria, J. C., Elisabeth, K., Elisabete, F., Diogo, S. S.(2016) Who is consuming the countryside? An activity-based segmentation analysis of the domestic rural
tourism market in Portugal. Journal of Hospitality and Tourism Management. 31.https://doi.org/10.1016/j.jhtm.2016. 12.006.

Chana, Sheng-Ju and Yang, Chia-Yu (2018). Governance styles in Taiwanese universities: Features and effects. International Journal of Educational Development. Vol. 18 (63): 29-35.

Chang, F. (2016). Study on the Operational Model of WeChat Gift Money for Chinese Spring Festival in Chinese Familial Bonds. Social Sciences in Nanjing, (11), 103.

Chang, S., Stansbie, P., Rood, A. S.(2014) Impulsive consumption in the experiential context. Current Issues in Tourism 17(2). https://10.1080/13683500.2012.749843.

Chaniotakis, I.E. (2017). Innovative Agri-Food Value Chain Financing in Greece.Food Security and Sustainability. Springer International Publishing, 12, 31-35.

Chao, Y. L. (2018). Mechanism and Response: In-depth Analysis of Public Events on WeChat. Journal of Intelligence, 37(3), 131–132.

Chen, B. W. (2021). Study on the Theoretical Origin and Innovation of Xi Jinping's Socialist Economic Thoughts on Socialism with Chinese Attributes for A New Era. Shandong University of Finance and Economics.

Chen, D. (2011). On Zhou Enlai's Contribution to the Theory and Practice of China's Modernization. Journal of Shaanxi Normal University (Philosophy and Social Sciences Edition), 40(04), 154-162.

Chen, J. (2018). On the Rich Connotation of Xi Jinping's Socialist Economic Thoughts on Socialism with Chinese Attributes for A New Era. Journal of Beijing University of Chemical Technology (Social Sciences Edition), 2, 1-5.

Chen, Lei (2022). Research Review on Efficiency for Land Use and Theoretical Logic of Improved Path: Based on the Thinking of Governances in Main Functional Zones. Research of Soil and Water Conservation, 29 (1): 386-393,403.

Chen, N., Hu, T. (2019) Practice of traditional village economic construction with rural tourism as the development path-Take Longtai Village, Guzhang County, Hunan Province as an example. Tourism Overview (05),169-170+172.

Chen, P. (2019) Precision Poverty Alleviation of Scenic Area Driven Rural Tourism: Connotation, Mechanism and Realization Path. Ecological Economy 35(06),120-124.

Chen, S. (2019). The Similarities and Differences of Harmonious Spirit of China and Its Cultural Value of Constructing the Community of Human Destiny. Shanghai Jiaotong University.DOI:10.27307/d.cnki.gsjtu.2019.000083.

Chen, S. S.(2017) The Beautiful Countryside Planning from The Perspective of Rural Cultural Heritage: A Case of Feng He Village in Jiangling County. Yangtze University.

Chen, X and B. Huang. (2014). Club membership and transboundary pollution: evidence from the European Union enlargement. Energy Economics,(53):230-237.

Chen, X. (2020). Let All Chinese Have A Better Life. Beijing Observation, 27(11), 32-33.

Chen, Y. F., Wang, G. G. (2020). Theoretical Perspective and Policy Thinking on Rural Industrial Development. Economic Geography, 40(09): 145-151.

Chen, Zhaotong (2016). The land-use policy's development, mechanism, and status quo in the main functional areas. Guangxi University, 2016.

Cheng, X., Zhu, W. B. (2020). Second Agriculture and Integration of Rural Primary, Secondary and Tertiary Industries. Science & Technology Review, 38(9): 6-12.

Chiang, C. K. (2014). Addiction to WeChat: Social Illusion and Self Loss. Social Sciences in Nanjing, (11), 100.

Chiang, C. M. (2017). A Philosophical Analysis of the WeChat Culture. Journal of Socialist Theory Guide, (7), 41.

China Radio and Television Network Station(2021). Happy New Tibet Beautiful the

Third Pole. May 23. http://news.cnr.cn/native/city/20210523/t20210523_525493831.shtml

China's Development Plan Research Center of Tsinghua University (2009). The policy study on China's main function zones, Beijing, China: Economic Science Press, 2009.

Christian L., Sara D.(2012) Impulse purchasing in tourism – learnings from a mature market study. Anatolia 23(2).https://doi.org/10.1080/13032917.2012.688409.

Chu, H. Y. (2007). Bidirectional Analysis of Educational Organization Research Methodology—Structural Functionalism and Interpretivism in Educational Organization Research. Theory and Practice of Education, 27(1), 15.

Combes, P. P., G. Duranton, L. Gobillon, D. Puga and S. Roux (2012). The productivity advantages of large cities: Distinguishing agglomeration from firm selection. Econometrica, 80(6), 2543-2594.

Commendatore, P., I. Kubin, C. Petraglia and I. Sushko. (2014). Regional integration, international liberalization and the dynamics of industrial agglomeration. Journal of Economic Dynamics & Control,265.

Cui, C. Y.(2019) The influence of social media marketing in rural tourism destinations on self-help tourist decision-making- A comparative study based on Lujia Village and Emerald Village. Anhui Normal University.

Deng, X. H. (2021). Review and Prospect of Research on Xi Jinping's System of Economic Thought on Socialism with Chinese Attributes for A New Era. Journal of the Party School of Guizhou Province, 6, 21-30.

Deng, Zhognyuan (2017). Excavating and utilizing local resources to help the economic and social development of Guiyang. Guiyang daily, 2017-09-08 (007).

Dernoi, L. A.(1983) Farm tourism in Europe. Tourism Management (3),155-166.

Dill, D.D. (1999). Academic accountability and university adaptation: the architecture of learning organization. Higher Educ. 38(4): 127-154.

Donaubauer, J., Meyer, B., Nun-nenkamp, P. (2016). Aid, Infrastructure, and FDI: Assessing the Transmission Channel with a New Index of Infrastructure. World Development, 78(02): 56-62.

Du, Chuanzhong, Feng, Jing and Zhang, Mi (2017). China's Three Primary Economic Circle Technology Transfer Performance Evaluation Research. Research on Financial and Economic Issues, 404 (7): 95-101.

Du, J., Xiang P.(1999). English Abstracts of Selected Articles in This Issue. Tourism Tribune 14(1),15-18.

Fan, G. Z., Wang, Y.(2021). A Comparative Study of Chinese Citizens' Outbound Tourism Consumption Under the Perspective of Promoting Domestic Demand and Consumption-Based on Individual Survey Data from Overseas Countries. Journal of Applied Statistics and Management 40(01),117-134.

Fan, J. P. H., J. Huang and N. Zhu. (2013). Institutions, ownership structures, and distress resolution in china. Journal of Corporate Finance, 23, 71-87.

Fan, Jie (2015). The Planning Schemes of Main Functional Zones in China. *Journal of Geographical*, 70(2): 186-201.

Fan, Song (2017). On China's urbanization and the history of urbanization in Guizhou, Guizhou Social Sciences, 331, (07):87-92.

Fan, X. Q.(2007). Study on the effect of Disappointment and regret on Tourist Satisfaction of Rural Tourism. SouthWest JiaoTong University.

Fan, Xiaosha, He, Ping (2017). Ecological carrying capacity: research progress existing problems corrective countermeasures. Research of Environmental Sciences, 30(12): 1869-1879.

Fang C., and D. Yu. (2017). Urban agglomeration: An evolving concept of an emerging phenomenon. Landscape and Urban Planning, 162,126-136.

Fang M., Xu Y. J.(2012). Tourism shopping behavior: planned, impulsive, or experiential?. International Journal of Culture, Tourism and Hospitality Research,6(3). https://doi.org/10.1108/17506181211246401.

Fang, S. M., Dai Q.L.(2019). Research on Tourist Homesickness Experience Based on Network Text Analysis.Tourism Overview (02),25-26+28.

Fei, H., & Chen, J. (2019). Where is the "New" of New China (Part 1)? Xinxiang Review, 67(10), 34-36.

Feng, Langang, Shang, Shu and Zhang, Zaijie (2021). Research on the Development and Path of Big Data Industry in Guizhou. *Science and Brainpower*, 9, 1-10.

Flescher, A,Felsenstein D.(2000) Support for rural tourism.Annals of Tourism Research 27(4):1007-1024.

Friedman J. R. (1986). The world city hypothesis: Development and change.Urban Studies, 23 (2), 59-137.

Frochot, I.(2005). A benefit segmentation of tourists in rural areas: A Scottish perspective. Tourism Management 26(3),335-346.

Fu, R., Zhang, S.(2017). Study on the Improvement for the Rural Tourist's Satisfaction Based on the Geographical Difference Culture Perspective-Taking the Dihua Ancient Town and the Yuanjia Village as the Examples. Information Engineering Research Institute, USA, Asia Pacific Environmental Science Research Center, Hong Kong: Intelligent Information Technology Application Society.

Gao, Guoli (2008). The Division of Main Functional Zones and the Research of Policies. Beijing, China: Chinese Plan Publishing House, 2008.

Gao, Jiansheng (2017). Optimize the development zone's management system and policy environment: Shanxi people's political consultative conference, 2017-05-26(00C).

Gao, Q. Q. (2021). Study on Xi Jinping's Socialist Economic Thoughts on Socialism with Chinese Attributes for A New Era. BOHAI University.

Ge, Y. N.(2018). Study on the experience and influencing factors of Rural Tourism tourists in Hainan Province. Hainan University.

Gottmann. J. (1957). Megalopolis or the urbanization of the Northeastern Seaboard. Economic Geography, 33(7):189-200.

Governmental Informational Office of Guangxi Zhuang Autonomous Region (2021). Press Conference on Economic Cooperation and Construction in Guangxi. Nanning, July 23. Guangxi Transportation News Center, http://jtt.gxzf.gov.cn/xwdt/xwfbh/t9615336.shtml

Guo Jiajun and Li Qian (2021). Growth Pole Theory and Research on Spatial Distribution of Agricultural Industry. Journal of Agriculture, 11 (1): 85-90.

Grossman, G. M. and E. Helpman. (2015). Globalization and growth. American Economic Review.105 (5),100-104.

Guan, M. (2019). The History of China and the United States, the Future of the Future. Guangming Daily, Jun.03,2007: p.1.

Guan, M. W. (2019). The Historical Thoughts and Future Questions Behind the U.S.-

China Economic and Trade Friction. Guangming Daily, 2019-06-03(001). DOI:10.28273/n.cnki.ngmrb.2019.003538.

Guo, W. R.(2011) Comparative study of rural tourism consumers' behavior in Fuzhou. Fujian Normal University.

Han, H. (2020). Study on the practice of Xi Jinping Thought on Ecological Civilization in Guizhou. Guizhou Social Sciences, 11, 40-47. DOI:10.13713/j.cnki.cssci.2020.11.005.

Han, H. T., Xie, J. Y. (2020). On the scientific connotation of people's aspiration for a better life. Journal of Luoyang Institute of Science and Technology (Social Science Edition), 35(02):81-86.

He, F.(2020) Development Pattern of Rural Tourism Industry under the Context of Changing Consumption Demand. Agricultural economy (11),143-144.

He, H. B. (2021). The People-centered Nature of Xi Jinping's Thought on the Rule ofLaw and Its Theoretical Value. Probe, 6, 1-16. DOI:10.16501/j.cnki.50-1019/d.2021.06. 001.

He, L. and J. Lu. (2020). Can regional integration control transboundary water pollution? A test from the Yangtze River economic belt. Environmental Science and Pollution Research International, 27(22), 28288-28305.

He, Wei (2019). Both Guangdong and Guangxi Deepen Cooperation for Poverty Alleviation and Join Hands to Tackle the Root Causes of Poverty. Huan Qiu, March 14. https://city.huanqiu.com/article/9CaKrnKj1vA

He, W., B. Wang, Danish and Z. Wang. (2018). Will regional economic integration influence carbon dioxide marginal abatement costs? Evidence from Chinese panel data. Energy Economics, 74, 263.

He, X. L., Ye, J. (2021). Review and Prospects of the Research on Xi Jinping's Socialist Economic Thoughts on Socialism with Chinese Attributes for A New Era. Journal of Beijing Jiaotong University (Social Sciences Edition), 20(01):131-138.

He, Y., G. Zhou, C. Tang, S. Fan and X. Guo. (2019). The spatial organization pattern of urban-rural integration in urban agglomerations in china: an agglomeration-diffusion analysis of the population and firms. Habitat International, 87, 54-65.

Hong, T., N. Yu, S. Storm and B. Gao. (2019). How much does regional integration contribute to growth? An analysis of the impact of domestic market integration on regional economic performance in china (1997–2011): Znanstveno-strucni casopis. Ekonomska Istrazivanja, 32(1).

Hou, X. F., Gen, N. N.(2020) The Research of Rural Tourism Creativity Under the Background of Integration of Culture and Tourism. Journal of Jincheng Institute of Technology.13(06),33-36.

Hsu, D. D. (2018). Current Development of WeChat Business People in China and the Analysis of Problems, Brand Research, (4), 94.

Hu, B. M., Huang, X.(2021) Study on the influence of high-speed railway development on post-modern tourism consumer behavior. Journal of Sichuan Normal University(Social Sciences Edition 48(02),92-102.

Hu, J. F. (2021). Study on Xi Jinping's Socialist Economic Thoughts on Socialism with Chinese Attributes for A New Era. Jilin University.

Hu, S. W.(2019). Construction of Key Factor System for Measuring Environmental Carrying Capacity of Rural Tourism Planning. Environmental Science and Management 44(04),165- 169.

Hu, S. Y. (2021). Continuously enhance the people's sense of achievement, happiness and security--Study the spirit of Xi Jinping's important speech during his visit to Hunan. Xinxiang Review, 4, 33-34.

Hu, Y. M. (2021). On the New Realm of Marxist Political Economy. Studies On Marxism, 8, 56-67+163.

Hu, Y., Li, J.(2021). Research on rural tourism service intellectualization based on neural network algorithm and optimal classification decision function. Journal Of Ambient intelligence And Humanized Computing. doi:10.1007/s12652-021-03039-6.

Huang, Futao (2018). University governance in China and Japan: Major findings from national Surveys. International Journal of Educational Development. 63(3): 12-19.

Huang, Guilin (2016). The Building Sub-central City of Economic Zone in Central Guizhou would Need to Make Good for Efficiency. Contemporary Guizhou, 2016, (15):38-39.

Huang, Lin, Cao, Wei, Xu, Xinliang, Fan, Jiangwen, Wang, Junbang (2017). The macro-ecological effect of ecological security barrier protection and construction project in Tibet. Journal of Natural Resources, 2017: 1-13.

Huang, Qin, Zhou, Ting (2016). The main functional area system and the implementation of the 13th five-year plan. Development finance research, 2016,5(01):28-35.

Huang, Xiaoyan (2017). Guian new area: development of service trade innovation with big data strategy. High-Technology & Industrialization, 2017, (06):52-57.

Huang, Xinxian and Hu, Baoqing (2017). Study on the spatial and temporal pattern of economic polarization in Guangxi. Areal Research and Development, 2017,36(05):17-22.

Hui, S.(2015). A Comparative Analysis of Urban Residents' Consumption Decision-making Behavior in Rural Tourism Based on Food Circulation Channels Perspective. Advance Journal of Food Science and Technology.8(11),https://doi.org/10.1016/j.trd.2020.102278.

Hunan Province Bureau of Statistics (2012). Statistics Bulletin of the National Economic and Social Development in Hunan Province (2011), Changsha city, China.

Imamura, N. (1996). Creativity of the Sixth Industry as the Agricultural Industry of the 21st Century. The Japanese Journal of Community Health Care, 1996(1), 89.

Inagaki, Y. (2013). Interpretation of management. Japan: Hakuto publishing.

Iydnews, (2014). Netizens and Their Fingertips—2014 Analysis on mobile network users' behaviors (2014). Available at: http: / /www.iydnews.com/2323.html (Accessed on Feb. 3, 2018).

Jacques, M., Sun, Y. N., Zhang, L., Liu, Q. (2016). When China Rules the World: the end of the western world and the birth of a new global order. CITIC Press Group.

Jeanneney, S. G, P. Hua, and Z. C. Liang. (2006). Financial development, economic efficiency, and productivity growth: evidence from China. Dev Econ, 44(1):27-52.

Ji, L. G., Wang, J. H. (2020). Research on the E-commerce Model of Fresh Agricultural Products Circulation under the Background of 'Internet +' and the Improvement of Quality and Efficiency.

Journal of Hebei University of Economics and Business, 41(01): 67-75.

Ji, Z. J., Xu, X. M., Qin, Y., Pei, W. (2021). Review of Studies on Xi Jinping's Socialist Economic Thoughts. Economic Daily, 2021-11-29(001).

Jiang, G. M. (2019). Vitalization of Rural Areas: The Creative Outlet of Prosperity. Beijing: China Science and Technology Press, 38.

Jiang, H.(2019). Analysis on the Tourism Planning Thoughts of Tea Country from the Perspective of Idyllic Complex.Journal of Anhui Agricultural Sciences 47(08):133-134+139.

Jiang, Hongqiang and Wu, Wenjun (2017). The ecological environment balance sheet promotes the application of green development. environmental protection, 2017, (17):23-26.

Jiang, Li (2017). The research progress and review of the main functional area of China: The enlightenment of "the Belts and Roads" classified regional regulation. Journal of Harbin business university (social sciences),152 (1): 69-78.

Jiang, T. L., Shu, K. L. (2020). The Model, Dilemma and Countermeasures of the Integration of Three Industries in Rural Areas. Taxation and Economy, 2020(5), 57-61.

Jishou City Government (2011). Statistical Yearbook of Xiangxi Tujia and Miao Nationalities Autonomous Prefecture.

Kanemoto, Yoshitsugu and K. Tokuoka. (2002). Proposal for the standards of metropolitan areas of Japan. Journal of Applied Regional Science. (7):1-15.

Kipnis, B. A. (1997). Dynamics and potentials of Israel's megalopolitan processes.Urban Studies,34(3), 489-501.

Kong, X. L., Xia, J. M. (2019). The Value Logic Relationship and Cooperative Path Selection between Rural Revitalization Strategy and Rural Tri-product Integration. Journal of Northwest University (Philosophy and Social Sciences Edition), 49(02), 10-18.

Kong, X. Z., et al. (2018). Nine Dimensions of Rural Revitalization. Guangzhou: Guangdong People's Publishing House, 28.

Koscak, M.(1998) Integral development of rural areas, tourism and village renovation, Trebnje, Slovenia. Tourism Management 19(1),81-85.

Kou, L.(2013) Research on the perspective of the culture of Shaanxi Province Rural Tourism Development. Northwest Normal University.

Kranjčević, J., Stober, D.(2020). Planned Villages as Rural Heritage in the Function of

Sustainable Development: Case Study of Gornji Vrhovci in Slavonia, Croatia. IOP

Conference Series: Materials Science and Engineering,960(4).10.1088/1757-899X/960/4/042045.

Krugman, P.(1991). Increasing returns and economic geography. Journal of Political Economy, 99:483-499.

Kuang, B. Q.(2019). Research on Nanchong Local Landscape Planning and Design under the background of regional tourism. Think Tank Era (21),159-161.

Lan, L. (2021). Comprehensive from Yan Zhi Party is A Great Self-revolution. China Discipline Inspection Supervision, Nov. 09, 2021: p.1.

Lane, B., Kastnhole E.(2015) Rural tourism: The evolution of practice and research approaches- towards a new generation concept?. Journal of Sustainable Tourism 23(8/9),1133-1156.

Lang, R. and P. K. Knox. (2009). The new metropolis: Rethinking megalopolis. Regional Studies, 43 (6),789-802.

Lankford, S.V., Howard D. R.(1994) Developing a tourism impact attitude scale. Annals of Tourism Research 21(1),121-139.

Lee, L. (2015). Foresight and Dialogue – An Introductory Analysis of the Opinions on WeChat from the Perspective of Philosophical Hermeneutics. Journal of Beijing Institute of Technology (Social Sciences Edition), 17(5), 156–161.

Lee, S. H., & Yang, L. (2015). Study on the Factors That Influence Consumers' Decision on Purchase in the C2C WeChat Shopping. Consumption Economy, 31(5), 56.

Lee, Y. (2014). Analysis of the Change to the Interpersonal Communication behind the WeChat Communication Mechanism. Jianghan Tribune, (5), 141.

Lesley, R., Derek, H.,(2004) Consuming the countryside: Marketing for 'rural tourism.' Journal of Vacation Marketing,10(3),37-52.

Li, B. (2019). Refining Cultural Imagery to Help Integrate The Primary, Secondary and Tertiary Industries in Rural Areas. People's Tribune, 2019(24), 64-65.

Li, Chunyan, Sun, Yuan (2017). Analysis of Cultural Industry Development Strategy of Jingchu Cultural Circle Based on Growth Pole Theory. The 3rd Annual International Conference on Management, Economics and Social Development (ICMESD 17), 2017.

Li, D. L. (2018). Agriculture 4.0, the Approaching Age of Intelligent Agriculture. Journal of Agriculture, 8(01): 207-214.

Li, Fanghua (2015). Study on the countermeasures of urban cultural construction in Liuzhou city (Master's thesis). Hunan Normal University, 2015.

Li, J. (2020). Xi Jinping's New Era of Socialism with Chinese Attributes and Mao Zedong's Adherence to the Development and Innovation of Mao Zedong's Thought Five: The Mission of being World-minded: From Self-reliance among the Nations of the World to Building a Community with A Shared Future for Mankind. Xinxiang Comment, 68(01), 41-44.

Li, J., Wang, Q. M. (2019). Scientific Connotation, Theoretical Basis and Realistic Choice of China's High-Quality Economic Development. Studies on The Capital, 15(00):145-156.

Li, Lihong and Gao, Guijuan (2021). Cultural Construction of World-class Universities with Chinese Attributes. Higher Education Development and Evaluation. 37(2): 8-16.

Li, M. Y.(2017) Age Differences based Tourism Appeal Research of Rural Tourists -Take the Shaanxi Province as an example. Chang'an University.

Li, Qing (2017). Regional economic analysis of economic development in Chongqing. Knowledge economy, 2017, (09):41+43.

Li, S. (2017). Deep Understanding of the Comprehensive Strict Treatment of Party Strategic Thinking. Chinese Journal of Control, 28(05), 9-12.

Li, S. H. (2021). A multi-dimensional reflection on the significance of achieving a full victory in the battle against poverty. Journal of Southern China, 8, 12-14.

Li, Y.H.(2018) Research on Personal Loan Marketing Strategy of Changchun Urban District Branch of Bank of China Jilin Branch.Jilin University.

Li, Yonghua(2017). Xiangxi tourism poverty alleviation. China Economic Weekly, 2017, (38):74-77.

Li, Z. H., Wang, X. D.(2019) Development strategies of leisure agriculture and rural tourism of Henan province based on industry convergence. Ecological Economy 15(04):289-295.

Li, Z. S. (2021). Upholding the concept of a community with a shared future for humankind and working together to build a beautiful world where people and nature coexist in harmony--Keynote speech at the Guiyang International Forum on Ecological Civilization in 2021. Ecological Civilization in China, 4, 6-9.

Li, Zhaoyang, Luo, Wenrong (2015). Establish risk prevention awareness and accelerate the transformation of the automobile industry. Journal of Liuzhou Vocational and Technical College, 2015,15(06):6-10.

Li, Zuojun (2017). Ecological civilization was promoted to a millennium high in the nineteenth report. Economic Information Daily, 2017-10-23(008).

Liang, S. S. (2008). Something about a Cyber Catchword – "Sharing." Journal of Xinjiang Education Institute, (6), pp. 97–98.

Liang, W. J. (2011). The Study on China's Agriculture Developing by Converging with Related Industries from the Visual Angle of Industry Convergence. Science Economy Society, 29(04): 12-17+24.

Liang, X.(2013) The Research concerning Development of Rural Tourism by Culture Drive Model.Wuhan Polytechnic University.

Liang, Y.L.(2019) Study on the relationship between tourist motivation, authenticity perception and loyalty-Take the Genghis Khan Mausoleum tourist area of Mongolian folk tourism as an example.China Journal of Commerce (01),203-206.

Liao, L. M., Dai, X. L. (2021). The 11th Plenary Session of the 10th CPC Guiyang Municipal Committee was held. Guiyang Daily, 2021-08-25(001). DOI:10.28295/n.cnki.ngyrb.2021.003334.

Lin, X. and Z. Chen. (2003). Review and outlook for urban agglomeration studies within and without China.Tropical Geography, 23 (1),44-50.

Lin, Y. (2011). Auditing Chinese higher education: The perspectives of returnee scholars in an elite university. Int. J. Edu. Dev. 31(5): 505-514.

Ling, L. H., Yu, Y. Y., Xia, D. Y., Li, J. (2019). Research on the Development of Pastoral Complex Based on the Perspective of Industrial Integration——Taking the Xiaotao Community Pastoral Complex as an Example. Anhui Agricultural Science Bulletin, 25(24): 1-3+31.

Liu, D.Q.(2006) Several Discriminations in Rural Tourism, Agriculture Tourism and Folklore Tourism. Tourism Tribune 21(3),12.

Liu, J. (2019). Great Changes in the Relationship between China and the World since the Reform and Opening-up. Learning Times, Jan. 28, 2019: p.1.

Liu, J. F. (2019). The dramatic changes in China's relations with the world since the reform and opening up. Study Times, 2019-01-28(001).DOI:10.38216/n.cnki.

Liu, J. X. (2020). The Scientific Connotation and Policy Propositions of Xi Jinping's Socialist Economic Thoughts on Socialism with Chinese Attributes for a New Era. Reformation & Strategy, 36(08):16-27.

Liu, L. M. (2021). An exploration of the idea of building a new type of international relations with the concept of "building a community with a shared future for humankind."Academic Journal of Jinyang, 2, 87-94.DOI:10.16392/j.cnki.14-1057/c.2021.02.012.

Liu, L.(2021). On the Idea of Building A New Type of International Relations with the Concept of "Building A Community with A Shared Future for Mankind." Academic Journal of Jinyang, 42(02), 87-94.

Liu, M. Y., Li, B. (2019). A reasonable disciplinary orientation and boundary delineation must construct a socialist political economy with Chinese Attributes. Contemporary Economic Research, 6, 30-37+113.

Liu, R. F.(2020) A Study on the Model of Tourist Behavioral Intention in Rural Tourism: The Role of Nostalgia And Place Attachment. Shanxi University.

Liu, T. Y., & Hsu, C. (2014). The Spreading, Sharing and Meaning Construction of WeChat: A Literature Review. Chongqing Academy of Social Sciences, (1), 97–101.

Liu, W. H. (2019). The Background and Contemporary Value of Xi Jinping's Socialist Economic Thoughts. Journal of Shanxi Institute of Socialism, 4, 55-59.

Liu, Weichao, Liu, Jiyuan and Kuang, Wenhui et al. (2017). Examining the influence of the implementation of Major Function-oriented Zones on built-up area expansion in China. Journal of Geographical Sciences, Vol. 27(6):643-660.

Liu, X.(2019) Study on influencing factors of targeted poverty alleviation in rural tourism industry-Based on the survey of 200 registered poor households in 5 villages in Wuling Mountain area.Modern agriculture (06):58-60.

Liu, Y., Zhang, Z. X, Tian, Y.(2016) Study on the Development of Rural Tourism and Tourist Consumption Behavior Characteristics-Take Suzhou City, Jiangsu Province as an example. Rural Economy and Science-Technology 27(03),40-41+45.

Lo, William Yat Wai (2017). The recalibration of neoliberalisation: repoliticising higher education policy in Hong Kong., High Educ. Vol. 000 (73):759 – 773.

Logan, W. (1961). Review: Governance of Colleges and Universities. By John J. Corson. American Journal of Sociology, 66(1): 541.
Liuzhou Bureau of Statistics (2021). Statistical Bulletin on Liuzhou National Economic and Social Development 2020. Liuzhou, May 31. Liuzhou Bureau of Statistics. http://www.liuzhou.gov.cn/sjzt/sjfb/ndtjgb/202107/t20210723_2874684.shtml
Liuzhou Investment Promotion Bureau (2021). Industrial Economy. Liuzhou, September 14. Guangxi Liuzhou Investment Promotion Agency Official Website. http://tzcjj.liuzhou.gov.cn/wsbs/tzzn/lzgkyys/lzsgk/202109/t20210914_2915006.shtml
Long, Xiaohua (2017). Development of the whole region tourism to promote the precision of Xiangxi poverty alleviation. China national newspaper, 2017-06-02(005).
Lu, C. (2021). Rural Revitalization: Strategy and Practice. Shanghai: Shanghai Academy of Social Sciences Press, 81.
Lu, Mingyong (2009). The Development of Economy and Industry in Xiangxi Prefecture, Changsha, China: National University of Defence Technology Press, 2009.
Lu, Q. W. (2016). Research Review on Convergence Among Primary, Secondary and Tertiary Industries in Rural China. Agricultural Economics and Management, 2016(4), 27-34.
Lv, L.(2014) On the Problems and Countermeasures of Rural Tourism Development in Hangzhou.Guangxi Normal University.
Ma, H. T. (2018). WeChat has over 1 billion monthly active users across the world. Available at: http://tech.163.com/18/0305/09/DC4F9BDR00097U7R.html.
Ma, Mengyun (2015). Analysis on the Operating Mechanism of Administrative and Academic Powers of Universities: With American Universities as Reference. Journal of Swupl. 17(4): 39-46.
Mao, Y. P., & Chi, F. (2017). Influence of the Information Delivery of WeChat Business People on Consumers' Intention of Acceptance. Economy and Management, 31(6), 67.

March, James, G. and Olsen, John (2011). Rediscovering Institutions: The Organizational Basis of Politics. Translated by Zhang Wei. Shanghai: SDX Joint Publishing Company.

Masot, A. N., Rodriguez, N.R.(2021) Rural Tourism as a Development Strategy in Low-Density Areas: Case Study in Northern Extremadura (Spain). Sustainability 13(1).https://doi.org/10.3390/S U13010239.

McLendon, M.K. and Hearn, J.C. (2009). Viewing recent U.S. governance reform whole: decentralization in a distinctive context. In: Huisman, J. (Ed.), International Perspectives on the Governance of Higher Education. Routledge, New York.

Mei, J. Q, Ye, X.L.(2018) Problems and Countermeasures in Chinese Cruise Tourism from the international perspective. Shipping Management 40(01),31-34.

Meijers, E. J., M. J. Burger and M. M. Hoogerbrugge. (2016). Borrowing size in networks of cities: City size, network connectivity and metropolitan functions in Europe. Papers in Regional Science, 2016, 95(1):181-198.

Meijers, E., M. Hoogerbrugge and R. Cardoso. (2017). Beyond polycentricity: does stronger integration between cities in polycentric urban regions improve performance?. Tijdschrift Voor Economische En Sociale Geografie, 109(1).

Meng, N., & Zhang, L., & Li, Z., & Wu, J. (2018). Xi Jinping: The Leader of the New Era. Times Post, 20(01), 9-15.

Murphy, A.Willams P. W.(1999) Attracting Japanese tourist into the rural hinterland: Implication for rural development and planning. Tourism Management 20(4),487-499.

Nagasawa, S., Otsu, S. (2010). A Study on Experiential Marketing - Focusing on Strategic Experiential Modules. Waseda International Management Research, 2010(40), 69-77.

National Bureau of Statistics (2011). Main Data on Bulletin of the Sixth National Population Census 2010 (No. 1), Beijing, April 28. Central People's Government of the P. R. of China http://www.gov.cn/guoqing/2012-04/20/content_2582698.htm

Neave, G. (1995). On living in interesting times: higher education in Western Europe 1985e1995. Eur. J. Educ. 30 (4): 377-393.

Noel B. L., Elirehema M. motivation-based segmentation of rural tourism market in African villages. Development Southern Africa.37(5),773-790.

Oppermann, M.(1996) Rural tourism in southern Germany. Annals of Tourism Research 23(1),86-102.

Pan, Fenping, Cai, Jiaoling and Wang, Huiqin (2017). Research on the integration and development of the cultural tourism industry in the western Hunan province. China famous city, 2017, (07):48-55.

Pan, L. (2020). Rural Tourism Product Development Model from the Perspective of Experience Value - A Case Study of Guangdong Province. Rural Economy and Science-Technology, 31(23): 106-108.

Pan, Yujun, Wu, Youde, Zhang, Qianduo, Hua, Honglian, Yao, hui (2011). The provincial research in main function zones, Beijing, China: Economic Science Press, 2011.

Peluffo, A. (2013). Regional integration and technology diffusion: The case of Uruguay.The Journal of International Trade & Economic Development,22(5), 786.

Peng, Jie (2017). The present situation and countermeasure exploration of natural forest protection. Seeds Science & Technology, 2017,35(03):33-34.

Peng, L. (2017). Social Meaning in WeChat Gift Money. Journal of Shanxi University (Philosophy and Social Sciences), 40(4), pp. 61.

Peng, L. Z.(2019) Realization path of the supply-side reform of rural cultural tourism products.Times of Economy & Trade (15),45-46.

Perdue, R. R. Long P. T. Allen L.(1990) Resident support for tourism development. Annals of Tourism Research 17(4),586-599.

Pine Ⅱ, B. J., Gilmore, J. H. (1998).Welcome to The Experience Economy. Harvard Business Review, 76(4):97-105.

Qiao, H. B., Zhang, K. (2021). The Doctrinal Logic and Practical Progression of Xi Jinping's Socialist Economic Thoughts on

Socialism with Chinese Attributes for A New Era. Reformation & Strategy, 37(05):22-30.

Qu, Q. S. (2019). The original intention and mission of the Chinese Communists. Current Affairs Report (Study by Party Committee Central Group), 4, 20-42.

Randolph, R. (2019). Regional development policies and the challenge to reduce spatial inequalities in brazil. Area Development and Policy,4(3):271-283.

Ren, G. B., Xiao, H. C. (2021). Summarizing and uniting: the winning code of the Communist Party of China. Journal of Hunan Tax College, 34(06):49-55.

Ren, L., Sun, F., Ding, D. (2021). Strategies of Giving Priority to Ecological Construction and Consideration to Agricultural Industry Development in the Agro-pastoral Ecotone of Northern China from the Perspective of Opportunity Cost. Acta Agrestia Sinica, 29(06): 1294-1300.

Ren, X. Y., Yang, H.(2021) Research on the Sustainable Development of Rural Tourism from the View of Labor Investment. Agricultural Economy (04),56-58.

Roberts, L., Hall, D.(2004) Consuming the countryside: marketing for' rural tourism. Journal of Vacation Marketing 6(3):253-263.

Rosenthal, S. S., and W. C. Strange. (2004). Evidence on the nature and sources of agglomeration economies. Handbook of Regional and Urban Economics, (4): 2119-2171.

Ruan, Mengling and Wei, Yuhang (2021). Strategical Research on Improving Urban visual image based on regional cultural elements: A case of Liuzhou City, Guangxi. Popular Arts, 8, 27-28.

Ruan, Z. Z. (2021). The Significance of Xi Jinping's Thought on Diplomacy from the Perspective of Uniting Against the Epidemic. International Studies, 1, 11-28+124-125.

Samuel, Morley (2017). Changes in rural poverty in Perú 2004–2012. Latin American Economic Review, 2017, 26(1):54-61.

Saunavaara, J. (2017). The role of international development strategies in making regional development policies: Hokkaido as a case study. Urbani Izziv, 28(2):122-135.

Schmitt, B. H. (1999). Experiential Marketing. Journal of Marketing Management, 15(1):53-67.

Sharpley, R.(2002) Rural tourism and challenge of tourism diversification: The case of Cyprus. Tourism Management 23(3),233-244.

She, Wei, Wu, Yao, Huang, Huang, Chen, Zhongdu, Cui, Guoxian, Zheng, Huabin, Guan, Chunyun, Chen, Fu (2017). Integrative analysis of carbon structure and carbon sink function for significant crop production in China's typical agriculture regions. Journal of Cleaner Production, Volume 162, 702-708.

Shen, Qiu (2017). The historical evolution of China's rural poverty alleviation policy and research on the practice of poverty alleviation. Journal of Jiangxi University of Finance and Economics, 109 (01):91-100.

Sheng, Y. and X. Chen. (2021). Regional integration degree and its effect on a city's green growth in the Yangtze River delta: Research based on a single-city regional integration index. Clean Technologies and Environmental Policy, 23(6), 1837-1849.

Shi, Z. (2013). "Chinese Dream" Thought: From Mao Zedong to Xi Jinping. Studies on Mao Zedong and Deng Xiaoping Theories, 20(10), 1-7+90.

Slee B., Farr H., Snowdon P.(2010). The economic impact of alternative types of tourism. Journal of Agricultural Economics 48(1/3),179-192.

Sleeter, Rachel, Sleeter, M. Benjamin, Williams, Brianna, Hogan, Dianna, Hawbaker, Todd, Zhu, Zhiliang (2017). A carbon balance model for the vast dismal swamp ecosystem. Carbon Balance and Management,2017, 12(1):66-73.

Song, Z., & Zhai, N. (2020). Mao Zedong's Thoughts on Developing Cutting-edge Science and Technology and Realizing National Defense Modernization: centered on Mao Zedong's Reading of the Soviet Union's Political Economy Textbook. Mao Zedong Research, 07(06), 63-75.

State Council Information Office (2013). Development and Progress in Tibet. Beijing, October 22. Huanqiu, https://china.huanqiu.com/article/9CaKrnJCLSC

State Council Information Office (2021). Tibet Peaceful Liberation and Prosperous Development. Beijing, May 21. Central People's Government of P. R. of China http://www.gov.cn/zhengce/2021-05/21/content_5609821.htm

Statistics Bureau of Guizhou Province (2021). Analysis of Permanent Resident Population and Urbanization Situation in Guizhou Province——Preliminary Results Based on the Seventh National Population Census in Guizhou 2020. Guiyang, September 30. http://stjj.guizhou.gov.cn/tjsj_35719/tjfx_35729/202109/t20210930_70689372.html

Steiner, M. (2003). Urban clustering: The benefits and drawbacks of location.Journal of Regional Science,43(1), 211-213.

Su, C. D. (2019). Adhering to the concept of global governance of extensive consultation, joint contribution and shared benefits. People's Weekly, 6, 58-59.

Su, Jiangyuan (2016). Guian new area: "Trization" helps raise the new high ground. Contemporary Guizhou, 2017, (26):10-11.

Su, Y.(2019) Research on the Influencing Factors of Tourist Impulse Consumption Behavior. Guangdong University of Foreign Studies.

Sun, J. M., et al. (2018). Rural Revitalization Strategy. Hangzhou: Zhejiang People's Publishing House, 133-146.

Sun, R. W.(2019) Study on Rural Tourism Modernity from Tourists perception: Influencing Factors and Measurement Models. Guangxi University.

Sun, T. Y. (2014). Those who sell goods on WeChat Moment are not WeChat business people and will be definitely reshuffled. Available at: http://www.ebrun.com.

Sun, W. (2015). WeChat: The "Living Existence" of the Chinese People. Academic Monthly, 47(12), 5–18.

Sun, Y. (2021). Study on the Originality of Xi Jinping's Socialist Economic Thoughts on Socialism with Chinese Attributes for A New Era. Anhui University of Finance and Economics.

Surya, B., A. Salim, H. Hernita, S. Suriani, F. Menne and E. S. Rasyidi. (2021). Land-use change, urban agglomeration, and urban sprawl: A sustainable development perspective of Makassar city, Indonesia. Land, 10(6), 556.

Tan, M. J. (2020). Rural Revitalization and the Integration Development of the Three Kinds of Rural Industries in China. Journal of Technical Economics & Management, 2020(7), 94-98.

Tang, J. B.(2015) Research on the Marketing Strategy of Rural Tourism under the New Normal. Academic Journal of Jingchu 16(04),49-54.

Tang, Xuan (2009). Internal Power Research of Chinese Public Universities: Based on the Perspective of Governance Theory. University Education Science. 115(3):62-66.

Teng, J. L.(2020) SWOT Analysis and Development Strategy of Phoenix Zhonghua Panda Garden. Journal of Green Science and Technology (10),282- 285.

Teng, Z. J., Hu, W. W.(2017) Research on the landscape building mode of rural tourism under the background of regional tourism. Rural Economy and Science-Technology 28(09),80-83.

Teoman, D., Anna, S. M.(2005) The role of affective factors on perceived cruise vacation value.Tourism Management (26),311-323.

Umair A., Peng H., Muhammad K. K., Chen Y., Zubair A.(2018) Factors Affecting Online Impulse Buying: Evidence from Chinese Social Commerce Environment. Sustainability 10(2). https://doi.org/10.3390/su10020352.

Van de Graaff, J. (2001). Academic Power: Patterns of Autonomy in Seven National Systems of Higher Education. Translated by

Wang Chengxu. Hangzhou: Zhejiang Education Publishing House.

Wan, B. R. (2019). Evolution and Realistic Meaning of the Integration of Rural Three Industries in China. Issues in Agricultural Economy, 2019(8), 4-8.

Wang, C. H. (2011). Case Studies in Experiential Marketing. Nankai University Press, 6.

Wang, C., Jiang, Q. Q., Li, C. (2021). The Path of Revitalizing Ethnic Villages by the Integration of the Three Industries from the Perspective of Systems Engineering: Based on the Experience of Pilin Village in Guizhou Province. Journal of Ethnology, 2021(6), 27-37.

Wang, D. (2018). Reform and Opening-up is the Key to Deciding on the Fate of Contemporary China. Party, 31(04), 11-13.

Wang, F., Yang, Z. S., Zhao, H. F., Zhang, Y. K. (2017). Exploring Industrial Options for Building Urban Agricultural Parks in Small and Medium-sized Cities. Rural Economy and Science-Technology, 28(03): 46-48.

Wang, H. B. (2016). Sociological Analysis of Consumption Alienation on WeChat. Jiangxi Social Sciences, 36(11), pp. 219.

Wang, H., & Chu, Y. (2014). Discussion on WeChat Functions from an Interpersonal Perspective. Journal of Modern Information, 34(2), 85.

Wang, H., & Kuan, C. W. (2016). Study on the "Sharing" on WeChat Moment. Journal of Chongqing University of Posts and Telecommunications (Social Science Edition), 28(3), 76–77.

Wang, J. Y., Liang, S. T., Wu, W. Y. (2018). Research on the Industrial Integrated Development Among Primary, Secondary and Tertiary Industries in Rural China. Jiangsu Commercial Forum, 2018(8), 92-94+103.

Wang, Jian (2009). The Construction of Main Functional Zones and the Ecological Compensation System, Beijing, China: The National Administration School Press, 2009.

Wang, Jijun, Wang, Zhengshu, Cheng, Simin, Gu, Wen, Li, Yue, Li, Maosen (2017). The ecological economics of the development of the carbon sink industry in reforestation. Journal of Applied Ecology, 28 (12):1-11.

Wang, L. H., & Shih, Y. C. (2018). WeChat Business-based Analysis of Customer Behaviours and Interests. Journal of Jilin Institute of Chemical Technology, 35(2), 84–92.

Wang, L. J., Kou, G. Z. (2017). Thoughts on Convergence Development of Primary, Secondary and Tertiary Industries. Issues in Agricultural Economy, 2017(6), 82-88.

Wang, L. N., & Lan, C. (2017). Self-expression of Young People on WeChat Moment – A Study Based on Virtual Ethnography. Jinan Journal (Philosophy & Social Science Edition), 39(12), 115–125.

Wang, Mingqing and Li, Yan (2018). Power Unbalance and Coordination in Internal Governance of Chinese Universities. Home Drama. 279(15): 171-173.

Wang, S. Z., Dong, G. L. (2021). Theoretical Perceptions and Practical Directions of Xi Jinping Thought on Ecological Civilization. The Party Building and Ideological Education in Schools, 22, 4-6. DOI:10.19865/j.cnki.xxdj.2021.22.001.

Wang, Shichuan (2017). It is of considerable significance to develop big data in Guizhou. Guizhou Daily, 2017-09-20(004).

Wang, Tianjin (2008). Some Assumptions for Construction of the Carbon Sink Functional Zone in Tibet, Journal of Southwest Nationality University, 203 (7): 137-141.

Wang, Tianjin (2009). Promoting the Construction of Carbon Sink Function Zone and Improving the Income for Farmers and Herdsmen, Journal of Southwest Nationality University, 30 (2): 35-39, 289.

Wang, Tianjin and Tian, Guang (2014). Environmental Anthropology. Yinchuan, Ningxia: Ningxia People's Publishing House.

Wang, Ting (2016). The comparative advantage of Guizhou developing a big data industry. Guizhou University of Finance and Economics, 2016.

Wang, X. D., Zhang, Y., Qian, Y. B. (2020). Gathering an indestructible and powerful force. People's Daily, 2020-09-08(001). DOI:10.28655/n.cnki.nrmrb.2020.008744.

Wang, X. M.(2010) The Consumer Behavior Study of Rural Tourism Based on Segmentation of Lifestyle. Southwest University of Finance and Economics.

Wang, X. Y. (2021). Analysis of Xi Jinping's Important Discourse on Social Mobilization against the Epidemic. Journal of Chongqing University of Science and Technology (Social Sciences Edition), 3, 13-17. DOI:10.19406/j.cnki.cqkjxyxbskb.2021.03.004.

Wang, Yafei and Fan, Jie (2019). National and provincial point-axis Structure analysis based on China's Planning for Functional Zones. Geographical Research, 38 (7): 1651-1663.

Wang, Y. (2008). Shelter and Retreat No Action - Comment on "The Road to Strong Country - China Reform 30 Years". Hainan Today, 51-52.

Wang, Y. (2020). Carrying forward the great anti-epidemic spirit and highlighting the advantages of the socialist system with Chinese Attributes. Teaching and Research, 12, 5-14.

Wang, Y. C. (2014). WeChat Opinion Field: Formation, Features and Opinion Efficacy', Journal of Intelligence, 33(7), 149.

Wang, Y. K. (2008). There is no way out of stagnation and regression--Review of "The Road to Power--China's Reform in 30 Years." Hainan Today Magazine, 51-52.

Wang, Y. Q. (2021). Research on the Development of Study Tour Products in Nanjing from the Experience Economy Perspective. Economic Research Guide, 2021(19), 58-60.

Wang, Yu (2016). Essential ecological function county main functional zoning plan and development. Guizhou Normal University, 2016.

Wang, Yu (2021). The influence and Enlightenment of the Reform of Higher Education System on the Construction of "double first-class" in Local Colleges and Universities. Jiangsu Higher Education. 240(2): 38-42.

Wang, Z. L., Zhang, G. C. (2018). A Model of Leisure Tourism Ranch Development Based on Experience Economy Theory. Heilongjiang Animal Science and Veterinary Medicine, 2018(14), 43-46.

Waxman, C. Hersh, Rivera, H. Héctor and Linn, Brenna et al., (2016). Development of An Observation Instrument to Measure Flourishing Learning Environments. Journal of Chinese Studies, 1 (3): 1-7. DOI 10.1186/s40853-016-0005-9.

Wei, J. (2018). Xi Jinping's Socialist Economic Thoughts on Socialism with Chinese Attributes for A New Era: Innovative Development of Marxist Political Economy on Socialist Modernization. Reform, 11, 139-146.

Wei, Linggui and Wei, Haiming (2014). Research on Existing Problems and Countermeasures of Guangxi's Participation in Pan-Pearl River Delta Regional Cooperation Policies. Journal of Guangxi Normal University, 35 (6): 87-91.

Wei, Y.J., Gao, J. J., Yi, B.W., Liu, J. Y.(2020) Investigation on the Tourism Status of Reading Students in Universities-Take Langfang as an example. Culture Industry (24),3-5.

Weick K. (1976). Educational organizations as loosely coupled systems. Administrative Science Quarterly. 21, 1-19.

Weil, David N, translated by Jin, Zhinong, Gu, Hejin (2011). Economic Growth, Beijing, China: China Renmin University Press, 2011.

Weng, Meng (2021). Sales Topped 1.6 Million Vehicles, SAIC-GM-Wuling Achieved

Excellent Performance 2020. January 4. https://www.autohome.com.cn/news/202101/1096981.html.

Wrong, Dennis H. (2001). Power. Translated by Lu Zhenlun, Zheng Mingzhe. Beijing: China Social Sciences Press.

WTO.(1997) Sustainable Tourism Development: A Local Tourism Planning Guide. Tourism Education Publishing House.

Wu W. J., S.Q. Zhao, C. Zhu, and J. L. Jiang. (2015). Over three decades, a comparative study of urban expansion in Beijing,

Tianjin, and Shijiazhuang. Landscape and Urban Planning, 134, 93-106.

Wu, Chengjian (2016). Functional segmentation of primary functional areas. Nanjing University, 2016.

Wu, H. Q. (2018). The logical progression in building Xi Jinping's "new economic normal" concept. Theoretical Horizon, 12, 16-22.

Wu, Jihai Editor-in-chief(2002). Xiangxi prefecture: the Overview of Western China: Xiangxi Prefecture. Beijing, China: Ethnic Publishing House.

Wu, L. X.(2018) Research on the development of the Shanxi tourism industry based on promoting tourism consumption. Shanxi University of Finance and Economics.

Wu, W.(2020) An Exploration of Rural Tourism Segmentation by Motivation in China: Taking Yangjiale Mouganshan as a Case. Journal of China Tourism Research,16(3),391-405.

Wu, X.X.(2010) The Development of Rural Tourism Products Based on the Theory of Tourism Involvement and Place Attachment. The South China University of Technology.

Wu, Y. (2019). "The Motherland Must be Unified, and It Must also be Unified" - Written on the 40th Anniversary of "Report Taiwan Compatriots." Tai Sheng, 37(03), 49.

Wu, Y. M. (2019). "China must be reunified, and it will be reunified" - On the 40th anniversary of the publication of Message to Compatriots in Taiwan. Taisheng, 3, 49.

Wu, Yancheng (2009). Xiangxi prefecture's Rural Reform and Open Policy in 30 Years, Changsha, China: Hunan People's Publishing House, 2009.

Xi, J. C.(2003) The Analysis On Consumption Structure and potential of Tourist - A study foreign tourist arrivals tourism consumption. Journal of Guilin Institute of Tourism (02),38-41.

Xia, X.H.(2017) Study on the Interaction between Minority Tourism Motivation, Behavior and Cultural Performance. Guizhou Ethnic Studies 38(04),185-188.

Xia, Z.C.(2012) Empirical Study on Rural Tourism Consumption Intention and Behavior Characteristic: A Sample Survey of Wenzhou. Journal of Zhejiang Industry & Trade Vocational College 12(01),54-60.

Xiangxi Tujia and Miao Nationalities Autonomous Prefecture Bureau of Statistics (2012). Statistics Bulletin of the National Economic and Social Development in Xiangxi Tujia and Miao Nationalities Autonomous Prefecture (2011), Jishou City, China.

Xiangxi Tujia and Miao Nationalities Autonomous Prefecture Statistics Bureau (2021). Statistical Bulletin on Xiangxi National Economic and Social Development 2020.

Jishou, China. March 18.http://tjj.xxz.gov.cn/tjsj_187/tjgg/xxzgb/202103/t20210318_1775846.html.

Xiao, Liangwu, Huang, Zhen, Luo, Lingling (2017). Study on the choice of economic growth pole and the cultivation path of the provincial economy. Economic issues, 2017, (05):117-122.

Xiao, W. D., Du, Z. X. (2019). Integration of Rural Primary, Secondary and Tertiary Industries: Kernel Interpretation of Connotation, Development Status and Future Ideas. Journal of Northwest A&F University (Social Science Edition), 19(6): 120-129.

Xie Z.(2016) Research on the development of ethnic and rural cultural industry under the scope of traditional culture protection. Guizhou University.

Xie, H.(2020) A study on the relationship among value co-creation behavior, perceived experience value and loyalty of rural tourists. Anhui University of Finance & Economics.

Xiong A. H., Zhang, H. (2019). Integration of Primary, Secondary and Tertiary Industries in Rural Areas: Development Model, Analysis of Conditions and Policy Recommendations. Theory Journal, 2019(1), 72-79.

Xu, G. (2019). Carry Forward the Spirit of Daring to Fight and Realize the Great Rejuvenation of the Chinese Nation. Governance, 06(39), 18-19.

Xu, H. (2018). Interview with Kishore Mahbubani, Professor at the School of Public Policy, National University of Singapore - China's success is critical worldwide. China Report, 7, 2.

Xu, S. H., Zhang, Z. (2018). On the triple logic of transforming the main social contradiction of socialism with Chinese Attributes in the new era. Journal of the University of Shanghai For Science and Technology (Social Science), 40(03): 246-252.

Xu, Shiju (2016). Analysis of population distribution in the main functional areas of China. Journal of Tongling College, 2016,15(03):7-10.

Yan, G. (2019). With the Awake and Firm Answer of "Tax" - in the "Unforgettable, Remember the Mission" Theme Education, Vigorously Promoting the Spirit of Xibaibo. Journal of the Party University of Shijiazhuang City Committee of CPC, 21(12), 21-24.

Yan, X. (2019). Written to Write An Updated Age Chapter. People's Liberation Army, Oct. 11, 2021: p.7.

Yan, X. F. (2019). Strive to write a newer and more beautiful chapter of the times. PLA Daily, 2019-10-11(007).DOI:10.28409/n.cnki.njfjb.2019.006107.

Yan, Yilong and Hu, Angang (2012). China's eleven five-year plan implementation review. Journal of Tsinghua University (philosophical, social sciences), 2012, 27(04):35-45+158.

Yang Y. F., Lyu, M., Long, F., Liu, L. M., Zhang, C. H. (2020). Rural Tourism: The Path and Practice of Rural Revitalization. Beijing: China Travel & Tourism Press, 111.

Yang, Fating (2017). The supply side will improve the supply of eco-friendly products. China Environment News, 2017-10-25(005).

Yang, H. (2013). Mao Zedong and Socialism with Chinese Attributes-Commemorating the 120th Anniversary of Mao

Zedong's Birth. Social Sciences in Chinese Higher Education Institutions, 26(06), 10-46+156.

Yang, J. (2021). Adhere to the people as the center and solidly carry out local legislative work in the new era. Shandong NPC Work, 9, 49-50.

Yang, Juncai (2-016). The achievements and significance of environmental protection and industrial development in Tibet. China Tibetology, 2016, (04):128-133.

Yang, S., & Xin, W. (2018). China's Reform and Opening-up will Never Stop. Xinxiang Review, 66(23), 9-10.

Yang, X.(1992) Developing "Rural Tourism" Brooks No Delay. Tourism Tribune (2):38-41.

Yang, X.(2020) Model of ethnography for tourism research in ethnic minority villages in southwest China-comment on A Landscape of Travel. Edible Fungi of China 39(11),284.

Yang, Zhenhua (2021). The mechanism of Social Participation in the Construction of "Double World-Class": Content, Characteristic and Approach. Journal of Yangzhou University (Higher Education Study Edition). Vol. 21(25): 1-8

Yao, P. B.(2019) A Study on the Influencing Factors of Tourist Satisfaction in Rural Tourism Destinations: A Case Study of Henan Province. Henan University.

Ye, J. (2020). The Triple Logic of Generating Xi Jinping's Socialist Economic Thoughts on Socialism with Chinese Attributes for A New Era. Journal of Hubei University of Economics: Humanities and Social Sciences, 17(08):4-7+15.

Yin, C. F., & Hu, W. C. (2018). Ethical Function and Potential Dangers of WeChat Moment from the Ritual View of Communication. Morality and Civilization. Morality and Civilization, (2), 126–132.

Ying, Zi and Wang, Haibo（2021）. What Has Guangdong-Guangxi Cooperation Done This Year? This Interview Is Very Clearly. December 25. https://www.ddgx.cn/show/51819.html.

Young, A. (2000). The razor's edge: Distortions and incremental reform in the people's republic of china. The Quarterly Journal of Economics, 115(4), 1091-1135.

Yu, C.(2016) Research on the influence of Tourist's personality characteristics on the product's preference for rural tourism. Hubei University, 2016.

Yu, Jianjun (2012). The development of China's regional economy during the 12th five-year plan period. Journal of Fujian Normal University (philosophical, social sciences), 2012, (02):33-38.

Yu, X. X. (2017). Research on the Development of Eco-agricultural Tourism Products from the Perspective of Experience Economy. Agricultural Economy, 2017 (12), 25-27.

Yu, Y. W., Zhang J.G., Xu Y.(2007) Study on the characteristics of rural tourism consumption behavior-takes the Huzhou Scenic Spot as an example. Agricultural Economy (08),12-14.

Yuan, Guangkuo (2017). Marketing Guangxi brand to promote Guangxi economy. Guangxi Daily, August 23（002）.

Yuan, Haixia and Zheng, Lu(2021). Tibet Autonomous Region Had Completed Afforestation of Nearly 397,700 Hectares during A Period of the Thirteen Five-Year Plan (2016-2020). Tibet Daily Newspaper, March 4. China Tibet Network. http://www.tibet.cn/cn/ecology/202103/t20210304_6965677.html

Yuan, H. G., Qi, W. M., Liu W. D.(2021) The impact of housing wealth on residents' tourism consumption. Journal of Commercial Economics (05),58-61.

Yuan, L. K., Hao, G. A., Shang, G. Z., Gao, B. J.(2019) Study on village spatial planning in mountainous areas from rural revitalization strategy- a case study of Bulaotai village in Fuping county. Forestry and Ecological Sciences 34(02),228-234.

Yuan, Y.(2020) Research on Rural Tourism Development Model and Planning and Design Strategy of Northern Shaanxi·Haojiaqiao.Xi'an University of Architecture and Technology.

Zang, S. N.(2011) Empirical study on the influence of agricultural tourist motivation and satisfaction on loyalty. Fudan University.

Zeng, S. C., Bian, S. Y. (2019). Policy Diffusion Analysis of "Rural Complex" under the Background of Rural Revitalization——A Study of Several Empirical Cases. Chinese Public Administration, 2019(2), 60-65.

Zhai, Y. X.(2020) Study on Rural Tourism Attraction in Fangzheng County, Heilongjiang Province.Heilongjiang Bayi Reclamation University.

Zhang, Bei (2017). Study on the optimization of the foreign trade industry chain of Liuzhou economy. China Business Theory, 2017, (14):120-122.

Zhang， Bin and Lü, Jiehua (2020). Spatial Effects Analysis for Factor Inputs Driving， Industrial Structure Upgrading and Forestry Economic Growth: A Case Study of Heilongjiang Key State-Owned Forest Region. Scientia Silvae Sinicae，56（6）: 142-151.

Zhang, C. M., Weng, S. X., Bao, J. G.(2020) The changes in the geographical patterns of China's tourism in 1978–2018:Characteristics and underlying factors. Journal of Geographical Sciences 30(03),487-507.

Zhang, D. C. (2019). A Summary of Research on Promoting the Integration of Three Industries in Leisure Agriculture. Chinese Journal of Agricultural Resources and Regional Planning, 8, 226-231.

Zhang, D. X., Dai, L. (2019). Three logical dimensions of Xi Jinping's Socialist Economic Thoughts. Journal of Jiangxi University of Finance and Economics, 3, 3-10.

Zhang, Dexiang (2016). The Historical Changes of Chinese University Governance Since 1949—Reflection on Policy Reform. In China Higher Education Research.29-36.

Zhang, G. H., Bao, W. (2012). Research on the Industrialization of Leisure Agriculture and Its Mode in China. Inquiry Into Economic Issues, 2012(10), 30-37.

Zhang, H. D.(2017) Study on the rural cultural tourism in Qiongjiang county, Tongan. Chongqing Normal University.

Zhang, J. Y. (2021). Making an effective connection between poverty eradication and rural revitalization. New Long March (Party Building Edition), 4, 30-31.

Zhang, Jianjun (2017). In the context of building a moderately prosperous society in all respects, the western rural poverty alleviation idea and mode reinvention. Agricultural Economy Issues, 38(04):67-74+111.

Zhang, L. Q. (2021). The Dilemma of Green Marketing of Eco-agriculture from the Experience Economy and Coping Strategies Perspective. Agricultural Economics, 2021(7), 24-25.

Zhang, M., Zhang, G. G., Liu H. Y.(2021) Analysis of the impact of tourism development on the urban-rural income gap: evidence from 248 prefecture-level cities in China. Asia Pacific Journal of Tourism Research 26(6),614-625.

Zhang, X. C., Li, Y.(2019) Analysis on the Tourist Consumption Behavior of Yuanjiacun Tourism Destination in Shaanxi Province. Liaoning Agricultural Sciences (06),36-39.

Zhang, X. M.(2008) The Study of The Rural Tourist Consumer Behavior. Zhejiang Gongshang University.

Zhang, X. P.(2020) Study on the Optimization and Upgrading of Rural Tourism Industry in Longnan under the Background of Rural Revitalization Strategy. Journal of Heilongjiang Vocational Institute of Ecological Engineering 33(05),26-27+143.

Zhang, X., Yang Y. Z, An, H. Y.(2020)Study on Rural Tourism Development of Huangyangchuan Peony Base in Gulang County. Tourism Overview,(22),151- 153.

Zhang, X., Yang, G. H., Zhu, Xia., Qin, C.(2015) A Research of tourist Motivation and Development Strategies to Hmong Original Ecological Cultural Villages: A Case Study in the Xijiang Hmong Village of Guizhou Province. Guizhou Ethnic Studies 36(04),144-147.

Zhang, Y. (2021). Adhering to the leadership of party building and strengthening integrated innovation to build a new pattern of green and high-quality development in the Yellow River Basin. Rural Work Newsletter, 16, 33-35.

Zhang, Y. F. (2021). Xi Jinping's "people-centered" rule of law concept and the dual orientation of the law-based state. ECUPL Journal, 24(06):116-129.

Zhang, Y. G. (2021). Original Contribution of Xi Jinping's Socialist Economic Thoughts on Socialism with Chinese Attributes for A New Era. The Northern Forum, 1, 64-71.

Zhang, Y. G., Chen, X, Yu, R. Z., Yu, X.Y.(2021) The influence of tourists' self-image congruence on rural recreational behavior intention: Theory construction and model extension. Tourism Tribune 36(04),70-82.

Zhang, Y. G., Yu, X. Y. (2020) Influencing factors and path analysis of rural tourism based on tourists' living space changes: A fuzzy set qualitative comparative analysis.Journal of Natural Resources 35(07),1633-1646.

Zhang, Y., & Kong, X. (2021). On the World Responsibility of the Communist Party of China. Party Building Research, 29(08), 46-48.

Zhao, C. H. (2009). Study on Rural Tourism and Its Promotion of the Country Industry Structure Optimizing. Wuhan University of Technology.

Zhao, Rong and Zhang, Ruihong (2017). An Exploratory Study on the Establishment of Shared Governance System: The Case of A University Statute. Fudan Education Forum.15(1): 39-46.

Zhao, Yang and Yang, Sibo (2017). Empirical Analysis of the Influence of Guangxi – ASEAN Trade on Guangxi Economic Growth—— Under "the Belts and Roads" Initiatives. Modern Business Trade Industry, 38 (26): 45-46.

Zheng, Y. (2021). The Chinese Model Expands the Way for Developing Countries to Modernize. Special Zone Economy, 39(07), 9-10.

Zhou, B., Huang, X. M., Ren, Z. L. (2018). Research on Targeted Poverty Alleviation in Tourism Industry in Ethnic Areas - A Case Study of Shenyang County, Chongqing. Journal of South-Central University for Nationalities (Humanities and Social Sciences), 38(01): 85-89.

Zhou, Changshan (2017). To explore the method and significance of forestry management. Private science and technology, 2017, (08):221.

Zhou, W., Feng, W. T. (2019). The Value of Xi Jinping's Socialist Economic Thoughts on Socialism with Chinese Attributes for A New Era and Its Contribution to Economic Theory. Financial Minds, 4(06):37-56+141-142.

Zhou, X. L.(2020) Research on Rural Tourism Development in Qingshan Village, Laoshan District, Qingdao City from the View of Rural Areas. Qingdao University.

Zhu, Huying and Wang, Huiqin (2020). Industrial Integration Between Agriculture and Cultural Tourism in Xiangxi Tujia and Miao Autonomous Prefecture. Hunan Agricultural Sciences,1, 97-102, 107.

Zhu, W. J.(2018) The Influence Factor of Rural Tourist Consumption Behavior Research. Fujian Agriculture and Forestry University.

Zhu, Y.H.(2018) Study on the Development of Xiang Li Culture Tourism in Jinshandian Town, Daye Country. The Henan University of Technology.

Zhu, Z. K., Ma, W. L., Leng, C. X.(2021) ICT Adoption, Individual Income and Psychological Health of Rural Farmers in China. Applied Research in Quality of Life 3.https://doi.org/10.1007/s11482-020-09879-2.

Zhu, Z. X., Liu, J. Q. (2021). Study and Implement Xi Jinping's Thought on the Rule of Law and Promote the Integrated Construction of the Criminal Rule of Law - Review of the First Seminar on The Constitution and the Construction of the Rule of Law in Criminal Enforcement. Tianjin Legal Science, 37(01):73-80.

Zhu, Zhaohui (2016). The High-level Depth Focuses on the Strategic Significance of Xiangxi. China National Newspaper, February 5, 2016:05.Zong, J. Y. (2017). The Theory and Practice of Integrated Development of Primary, Secondary and Tertiary Industries in Rural Areas. Beijing: China Agricultural Press, 27.

Zou, T. Q. (2001). Tourism Development and Planning. Guangzhou: Guangdong Tourism Publishing House, Yu, Y. H. (2011). Research on the Zunyi's Rural Tourism Based on Experience Economy. Journal of Anhui Agricultural Sciences, 39(08): 4853-4854+4874.

Zou, W., Han, J. (2021). Planning to set the tone and move forward in unison. People's Daily, 2021-12-12(001).

Afterword

The current monograph introduces the theoretical thoughts outlining Xi Jinping's socialism with Chinese characteristics. The statements and facts contained in the book illustrate that under Xi Jinping's leadership, China has entered a new era with remarkable accomplishments in modernization. With the strong leadership of the Communist Party of China cored by Xi Jinping, the modernization road with Chinese attributes for China is getting broader and broader.

Under the leadership of CPC, the Chinese people have realized the great rejuvenation of their nation and made the advancement of human civilization. Different countries will choose different modernization paths due to their different primary national conditions, history and culture. Other countries will choose different modernization paths due to their different primary national conditions, history and culture.

The project has received strong support from the leadership of Huaihua College. Dr. Shu Xiaohui, Mr. Li Yangkuo, and Dr. Tian Guang are responsible for compiling the book manuscript. Dr. Shu is a professor at the College of Business of Huaihua University. He is a "121" project talent, a leading disciplinarian of Hunan Province, a young backbone teacher of Hunan Province, a visiting scholar of Andrews King University (2013.7-8) and Bemidji State University (2017.8-2018.8) in the United States. He has presided over one research project funded by the National Social Science Foundation and three research projects funded by the government of Hunan Province. He has published two monographs, more than 60 journal papers and obtained one computer software copyright.

Mr. Li is a faculty member at the College of Business, University of Huaihua. He graduated from Jishou University with a master's degree. His research interests include economic statistics and finance. He has conducted empirical research projects in economic statistics and finance and has published dozens of research papers in academic journals.

Dr. Tian is a globally selected senior professor of business administration at Huaihua University. He earned his Ph. D. in Economic Anthropology from York University, Canada, in 1995 and used to work as a professor at colleges in Canada and the US. His primary research interest is Economic Anthropology, Regional Development, and Cross-Cultural Administration. He has published over one hundred academic articles in peer-reviewed referral journals and authored 25 books published in English and Chinese.

Index

D

E

F

G

H

I

K

L

M

N

O

P

R

S

T

U

V

W

X

Y

Z

Made in United States
Orlando, FL
04 November 2026

90200099R00164